economics
MYTH, METHOD, OR MADNESS?

Selected Readings

Compiled and Edited by

Robert E. Hicks
Walter J. Klages
Frederick A. Raffa

McCutchan Publishing Corporation
2526 Grove Street
Berkeley, California 94704

Library of Congress Catalog Card Number: 73-178122
ISBN: 0-8211-0721-6

Manufactured in the United States of America

PREFACE

This collection of articles, essays, and abstracts has been selected to accomplish the specific purpose of stimulating interest in first year economic courses. Beginning economics students traditionally find themselves confronted by seemingly elaborate theoretical explanations of economic activity. As is often the case, attempts to relate theory to practice fall somewhat short, resulting in student frustration and cries for course relevancy.

Virtually every textbook, particularly popular ones, deals rather extensively with theory. Those which do digress to practical application find that this can be accomplished only at the expense of theoretical essentials. As an alternative, many teachers have used complementary books of readings, designed to achieve course relevancy. Unfortunately, the majority of such readings are articles written by economists, for economists, and very rarely aimed at the layman.

This anthology has been carefully selected for the lower level undergraduate student who is not necessarily an economics major. The range of topics encompasses the ordinary, daily, real world subjects covered in the news media, discussed and demonstrated about by today's youth, and legislated by Congress. "Now Generation" concerns are prescribed in a short, contemporary, nontheoretical, and easy-to-understand form.

CONTENTS

CONTENTS

CONTENTS

I.

ECONOMIC METHODOLOGY

Students of economics usually begin their association with the subject by means of a definition. Standard definitions tend to approximate the following:

Economics is the science which describes, measures, and analyzes the production, distribution, and consumption of wealth.

Such a definition spells out not only the nature of the discipline, but something about the method of investigation. Economics methodology, over time, has transcended a wide range of sophistication. From the Classical Greece-Middle Ages period when economics was part of the much larger concerns of politics and religion, through the normative prescriptions of the Mercantilists and early classical economists, economics has emerged as a comprehensive, dynamic, positive, scientific discipline.

Economic investigation places primary emphasis upon what is, rather than what should be. In determining what is, economics makes use of the scientific method of investigation. Economic methodology, like all the social sciences, differs from the natural sciences due to a very interesting, yet unpredictable creature—man.

1

ECONOMIC METHODOLOGY

The scope and method of a man-related methodology obviously must make some concession to regularity of occurrence, yet must still maintain agreement in general. Generalization must be possible if a discipline is to be scientific.

The process by which economics makes this trade-off and the specific scientific nature of the investigation is seen in the two articles which follow— the classic treatment by Alfred Marshall, and the somewhat broader contemporary version by Brown and Elliot.

SCOPE AND METHOD
OF ECONOMIC ANALYSIS

Alan A. Brown and John E. Elliot

THE SCOPE OF ECONOMICS

Although what we know as "reality" is a seamless whole, our approaches to the study of it are traditionally divided into parts or disciplines, such as economics, history, literature, and physics. This intellectual division of labor has proved generally beneficial, although at times it has been marred by gaps in our knowledge and failures in communication between different fields of study. At the same time, it is fruitless and even positively misleading to separate one discipline, such as economics, from another, where there may be no counterpart in reality. In its evolution and development as a discipline, the scope and boundaries of economics have not remained perfectly fixed.

Economics is an "open" system, in the sense that the number of variables that could potentially affect the behavior of the "economy" is indefinite. When economists place limits upon their studies by focusing upon selected variables and relationships, they typically assume *ceteris paribus* conditions—that is, conditions where one thing is allowed to change while "other things remain equal." As an intellectual device, this procedure contributes order and system to thinking about complex problems; however, economists are usually not in a position to "close" their systems of analysis by laboratory methods, nor to generalize easily from observation ("for all practical purposes"). Attempts to identify the scope and boundaries of economics are thus unavoidably arbitrary, and factors "outside" economics (such as politics, psychology, or technology) may have a profound effect upon the behavior of the economic system. Moreover, different economists may quite legitimately have different, but powerfully held, views as to the scope of the discipline.

From *Perspectives in Economics* edited by A. Brown and E. Neuberger, pp. 1-13. Copyright 1968 by McGraw-Hill Book Company. Used with permission of McGraw-Hill Book Company.

Economics and Its Neighbors

Because its boundaries are indefinite, economics encroaches on other disciplines and strikes pacts with them. This reciprocal behavior is illustrated by the growth of such hybrid titles as economic history, economic statistics, mathematical economics, economic psychology, economic sociology, economic anthropology, and, of course, political economy. During much of the nineteenth century, the term "political economy" was practically synonymous with what is now called economics, supplemented by social and political philosophy. Today, in fact, the older term is coming back into vogue, but with a twist, to mean issues and concepts pertaining to the interdependencies of politics and economics, as, for example, in the theory of collective choice, the determination of government economic policy, decisionmaking in large corporations, and so forth.

Economics both receives from and contributes to other fields of study in a mutually beneficial way. From mathematics, statistics, and history, for example, it receives methodological insights and empirical information to test its hypotheses. From psychology, sociology, politics, law, and technology it takes basic assumptions (about which more later) upon which to build economic theories. To other disciplines, economics contributes a logic for rational choice and comparison of alternatives, a healthy respect for reality and actual patterns of human behavior, a theory of exchange, an ethic of efficiency and economizing, and, perhaps above all, a useful distinction between "possibility functions" and "preference functions"—that is, between identification of alternatives and selection of the best alternative.

Scope by Definition?

Economics has been defined variously as the study of (1) household management (Aristotle); (2) wealth (Adam Smith); (3) material welfare (Alfred Marshall); (4) avarice or self-interest (John Stuart Mill); (5) anything that can be brought within "the universal measuring rod of money" (A. C. Pigou); (6) markets, prices, and market exchange (Gustav Cassel); (7) the allocation of (given) scarce resources among competing (given) ends or uses (Lionel Robbins); and (8) the logic of rational human action (Ludwig von Mises).

These eight definitions represent two major points of view. Definitions (1) through (6) look at life as divided into parts, and identify economics as one of these parts; the last two definitions look at economics as an approach to or an interpretation of life.

In the past half-century, there has been a trend in the literature away from economics as a "part of life" and toward economics as an "interpretation of life." The major criticism of the first point of view is that it limits economic studies in unnecessary or misleading ways. Why, for example, should economists restrict themselves to the study of wealth or the material dimensions of human welfare? Economics is a social science, and as such is presumably

4

concerned with relations among men, not merely relations among things. And what about services? Similarly, why should economics be restricted to the study of individual self-interest, money, or market exchange? What about community interests, barter, or central planning?

Economics defined as an interpretation of life has had a better reception; evidence of this may be found by consulting the first chapter of nearly any text on introductory economics. Economics defined as the allocation of scarce resources among alternative uses, or as the logic of rational purposive action, is more satisfying than economics defined as, say, material welfare. Yet, if we apply interpretation-of-life definitions too broadly, we encounter topics customarily regarded as beyond the scope of economics. If economics is literally the study of choice and resource allocation, then, as the early twentieth-century English economist and Unitarian minister Philip Wicksteed observed, questions such as the following fall within the province of the discipline: How high a cliff would you dive off to save your grandmother, drowning in the icy waters below? How short would you cut family prayers in order to speed a visiting relative to the railroad station?

A Pragmatic Solution: Economics Is What Economists Do

A second trend in recent years has been to refrain from formal definitions in favor of informal descriptions of the major issues that have concerned economists. It is summed up in Jacob Viner's reputed definition, "Economics is what economists do." This approach is not very satisfying; if economics is "what economists do," then what is it that economists do? But it does reflect practical wisdom. First, any definition is arbitrary. Second, economics is not a "word to be defined," but a set of issues to be explored. Third, most definitions are only lightly concealed value judgments as to what an author thinks his professional colleagues *should* do.

A reasonably accurate list of the issues studied in contemporary economics would include the following: (1) the allocation of scarce resources, (2) the distribution of income, (3) the rate of economic growth, and (4) the overall levels of (and shortrun stability in) income, employment, and prices.

Macro and Micro

An alternative way of describing what it is that economists "do" is to divide the subject into *macroeconomics* and *microeconomics*. Macroeconomics aggregates individuals and commodities for an entire economy (regional, national, or international) or for major subdivisions (total consumption, investment, or government spending) of the economy as a whole. Microeconomics studies individual units of economic decision, such as households, business firms, and resource suppliers (landlords, capitalists, workers), their interrelationships, and the behavior of particular aggregates (such as the market for

5

coffee). By emphasizing individual units, microeconomics tends to focus upon relative prices or exchange relations (such as the price of tea relative to the price of coffee), and the allocation of resources and distribution of income, given their overall levels. By contrast, macroeconomics, by emphasizing the economy as a whole, tends to regard relative prices as given and focuses upon overall income, employment, and price levels, depressions and inflations, unemployment versus full employment, and the rate of economic growth.

Over the years, emphasis has shifted between the two major branches of the discipline. From Adam Smith in 1776 to Karl Marx in the mid-nineteenth century, economics was concerned with *both* macro- and microeconomic issues, making no clear or rigorous distinction between them. In the latter part of the nineteenth century, the Austrian, marginalist, and neoclassical economists (for example, Stanley Jevons, Carl Menger, Alfred Marshall, Leon Walras) shifted the attention of the discipline to relative prices and the microeconomic relations of supply and demand for particular commodities and services. In the depressed decade of the 1930s, the English economist John Maynard Keynes and others shifted emphasis back to such macroeconomic issues as national income, unemployment, and depression. In recent years, economists have increasingly emphasized the *interdependencies* between microeconomics and macroeconomics. This is especially evident in the study of economic policy and international and comparative economics, as succeeding chapters of this book show.

In sum, each body of economic analysis has an important contribution to make to solving real-life problems. The central insight of macroeconomics is its view of the economic system as a whole, while that of microeconomics is its view of the mutual interdependencies of the different units of the economic system. The major strength of each is also its major weakness. Manipulation of macroeconomic variables glosses over microeconomic problems of individual choice and behavior, while exclusive emphasis upon microeconomic interrelationships may blind the student of economics to the "fallacy of composition," that is, assuming that what is true for a part of the system is true for the system as a whole.

THE METHODS OF ECONOMICS

Economics as Ethic, Art, and Science

At various times in its historical evolution, economics has been an ethic, an art, and a science. For St. Thomas Aquinas and other medieval churchmen, for example, economics was essentially a branch of applied theology, an ethic of good conduct in this life as a member of an ideal Christian commonwealth in preparation for salvation in a life to come. For mercantilist writers in the sixteenth through eighteenth centuries, economics was essentially an art of advising rulers about means of augmenting the wealth and power of nations. In recent centuries, and particularly in the last quarter-century, economics, while retaining and even expanding and enriching its artistic and ethical dimensions, has become an increasingly sophisticated and exacting scientific discipline.

Like science in general, economics is an ordered body of knowledge, developed in terms of methods and procedures known to, and generally understood and accepted by, a group of specialists (economists in our case) for the purposes of the description, explanation, and prediction of reality. More particularly, economics is a social science; it studies the behavior of men in society as members of groups or as participants in the activities of the market-place. Most particularly, economics is a *generalizing* social science, characterized by the advancement of theories that would describe, explain, or predict the unifying properties of economic experience. In addition, economic theories may help in the formulation of economic policies to achieve individual and social goals, and thus serve as a means of social control. In sum, economic theory contributes importantly to the practical task of helping solve human problems.

The Structure of Economic Theory

The theoretical study of economic problems proceeds by three major steps: (1) specifying assumptions or underlying axioms, (2) formulating hypotheses or theories from the assumptions, and (3) testing the validity of the hypotheses or theories.

Assumptions. In the broadest sense, assumptions are those dimensions of a science which are taken as "given," in the sense that they are beyond the scope of the discipline, or of a specific problem, to explain. In short, they are taken as axiomatic and are used as underlying premises upon which other ideas (hypotheses) are built. Clearly, assumptions lie at the frontiers of a scientific discipline, for any change in them, given conventions for the formulation of hypotheses, may result in different hypotheses.

Most assumptions in economics may be classified as resource-technological, institutional, or psychological-motivational. (1) Assumptions regarding resources and technology specify relationships between resource inputs and outputs, and thus the resulting impact upon productivity (output per unit input, on the average or at the margin) under a given state of technology. (2) Institutional assumptions come in a large variety of forms, such as capitalism versus socialism; competition versus monopoly; the existence versus the non-existence of a commercial banking system with power to create money in the form of demand deposits or checking accounts. (3) Psychological-motivational assumptions usually specify the goals that economic units are assumed to pursue, the principle that guides their conduct in such pursuit, and the relation between psychological variables, such as "utility" or satisfaction, and the magnitude of inputs and outputs. For example, the economic "theory of the household" generally assumes a desire to maximize utility under conditions where the relative marginal utility of two commodities varies inversely with

7

the relative quantities consumed. The economic "theory of the firm" generally assumes a desire to maximize profits, or the difference between expected sales revenues and expected costs.

Questions frequently arise about the realism of assumptions. Assumptions can be unrealistic in the sense of being freed from factual details so as to focus upon unifying properties; this can be a useful device. Assumptions may also be unrealistic in the sense of introducing "pure" or "perfect" cases (pure or perfect in competition, pure or perfect monopoly, perfect elasticity of demand, perfect flexibility of resources). These kinds of assumptions are simplifying and incomplete (because the world is more complex), but often analytically useful as end-points. Or an assumption may be unrealistic in the sense of being patently false. This is unfortunate because hypotheses consistent with and logically derived from false assumptions will also be false.

The proof of the pudding is in the eating. It is often tempting to reject economic theories out of hand for being oversimple or unrealistic. But if such assumptions yield explanatory hypotheses or predictions about the behavior of economic variables which correspond as closely to the real world as more complicated and more realistic assumptions, then more power to them!

Hypotheses. Hypotheses or theoretical generalizations (the terms being for all practical purposes synonymous in economics)* provide a method for the systematic description, explanation, and prediction of economic variables. An economic variable is anything of interest to students of economics which is subject to variation. One set of such variables might include such items as income, output, investment, consumption, and saving—variables measured as *flows* or rates of change over time. A second set might include wealth, capital stock, stock of consumer durable goods, and savings—variables measured as *stocks* existing at a moment in time. A third set of variables might include ratios *between* stocks and/or flows. A price, for example, is a ratio between a flow of expenditures and a quantity of output or resource input purchased or sold. Velocity, to give a second example, transforms a stock into a flow, as in the equation $MV = E$ (money times velocity of circulation or rate of turnover equals expenditures).

A hypothetical generalization regarding relations between economic variables has three central features: a dependent variable, an independent variable, and a *ceteris paribus* condition. The dependent variable is the one whose changes the hypothesis seeks to explain or predict. The independent variable is the one whose changes yield changes in the dependent variable. The *ceteris*

---

*It is fashionable in some disciplines other than economics to distinguish among hypotheses, theories, and laws, in terms of their (ascending) degree of explanatory or predictive value. In other words, a hypothesis is merely "hypothetical"; a theory is one step better, but for all that just a theory; but a law, watch out! Economists are generally content to say that *all* theoretical generalizations, whatever their names, are hypothetical *if . . . then* constructions, with varying degrees of explanatory or predictive value.

8

paribus condition holds constant all factors other than the selected independent variable which could plausibly affect the dependent variable.

Equations 1 and 2 give examples of hypotheses, one for microeconomics and one for macroeconomics:

$$1. \quad D_1 = f(P_1)$$

$$2. \quad C = f(Y_d)$$

Equation 1 states that the demand for commodity 1 (D_1) by one or more consumers is some function f of—that is, depends upon—the price of commodity 1 (P_1). Equation 2 states that the aggregate or overall level of consumption in the national economy C is some function of the level of disposable national output or income Y_d (income actually available for disposition by households between consumption and saving after taxes, depreciation, undistributed corporate profits, and other items are added to, or subtracted from, the total gross national product). Typically, the form of the postulated relation between the independent and the dependent variable is also specified. For example, Equation 1 is typically accompanied by the proposition that D_1 varies *inversely* with P_1, rising (falling) as P_1 falls (rises); Equation 2, by the proposition that consumption varies *directly* with income, rising (falling) as income rises (falls). Either of these propositions may be derived *deductively*, as generalizations from underlying assumptions, or *inductively*, from particular experiences in various markets or countries. A general mathematical formulation of the hypothesis, as thus defined, describes the *direction* of change in the dependent variable caused by a change in an independent variable. An econometric model would hypothesize the expected *magnitude* of change as well, by specifying the value of the functional relation. For example, $C = 0.9Y_d$ says that consumption is 90 percent of disposable national income.

Equations 1 and 2 assume implicitly that "other things" remain equal. Some other things (such as Tibetan goat milk production) may remain equal, for all practical purposes, with changes in Y_d and P_1. Others (such as technology, social institutions, the stock of known natural resources) may remain relatively stable over short periods of time. Still others may vary in "countervailing" ways—for example, P_2 may decrease and P_3 may increase, leaving the overall price level roughly stable. Basically, however, the *ceteris paribus* method is a useful, indeed indispensable, analytical device. It enables one, in the conduct of intellectual experiments, to focus attention on specified functional relations in a simplified, rigorous, and precise way.

Changes in underlying *ceteris paribus* conditions may be made an integral part of a system of hypotheses by shifting the position of the functional relations themselves. For example, an increase in income would normally cause an increase in the quantity of commodity 1 demanded at every price in Equation 1; an increase in the general propensity to save (say, because of pessimistic expectations by households) would be accompanied by a decrease in consumption at all levels of income in Equation 2. In sum, the functional

9

relationship itself may alter because of changes in factors other than the one selected for major emphasis as the independent variable.

Testing Hypotheses. Because economics can be regarded as both a theoretical *and* an empirical discipline, tests for empirical validity should supplement those for logical consistency. A good theory, then, yields good explanations or predictions of reality.

We shall mention here three common problems associated with empirical testing: appropriateness, correspondence, and practicality.

The problem of *appropriateness* is one of selecting the field of observation appropriate to testing a theory. For example, a generalization about an economic system "as a whole" should be tested against data for an entire economic system, not merely for some industry or market within it. Allied to this is the need to state clearly any special conditions that restrict the theory, and thus its real-world counterpart. For example, the hypothesis that an increase in the supply of money will cause inflation under full-employment conditions with a given labor force and given technology is not invalidated by a noninflationary increase in the money supply *if* the economy is initially at less than full employment or *if* technology improves.

The problem of *correspondence* is one of determining the degree of "closeness of fit" between the theory (or its associated predictions) and reality, once observations about reality have been identified. Naturally, the closer the fit the greater the confidence in the theory. But theories differ in scope and complexity, and determining how close is close may be arbitrary. The problem of correspondence is compounded by the fact that an economic theory ("classical theory," "Keynesian theory") is often a set of interdependent hypotheses, some significantly more valid than others. In addition, correlation between two variables, say, does not in itself demonstrate the direction of causation. The fact that income and consumption rise and fall together may demonstrate that income determines consumption. But in the absence of further reasoning and evidence, it may also demonstrate that consumption determines income. Lastly, because science is open-ended, today's good theory may be replaced by a better one tomorrow.

Practicality has a number of facets. The one that needs emphasis here is suggested by the popular expression, "That's a good theory, but it doesn't work out in practice." In one sense this is a tautological statement. If practice means explanatory or predictive value, then a theory is only good if it *does* work out in practice; if it does not, it cannot be called a good theory. In another sense, however, the statement may express the homely truth that a theory whose logical and empirical credentials are in order may not be put to practical use by policy- or decisionmakers. This may be because of the policymakers' failure to understand the theory or the economists' failure to communicate it. Often, it stems from the fact that economic policymaking is essentially an artistic rather than a scientific enterprise, drawing implicitly (if not explicitly) upon economic theory and intuitively and artistically upon a blend of many noneconomic factors and ideas.

THE POLICY IMPLICATIONS OF ECONOMICS

In closing this introductory section, we may gain perspective on economic theory by relating it to broader issues of normative economics, economic systems, and economic policy.

Normative versus Positive Economics

Economic science, or *positive economics,* proceeds from assumptions to explanatory or predictive hypotheses to the testing of hypotheses (and thereby, in a loop, to the revision of assumptions and hypotheses). The purpose of this procedure is to make positive statements about *what is.* By contrast, the purpose of *normative economics* is to make and support, by reasoning and evidence, value judgments regarding *what ought to be.*

Normative economics, like positive economics, advances in three major steps: (1) specifying assumptions, underlying axioms, and conditions; (2) formulating desired objectives from the assumptions or conditions; and (3) testing the objectives in terms of their consequences or impact. Two striking differences can be noticed, however. First, the assumptions of positive economics are *descriptive* (for example, that consumers do in fact desire to maximize utility), while those of normative economics are *prescriptive* (for example, that consumers ought to get what they are willing and able to pay for). Second, if positive scientific theories do not correspond to reality, then so much the worse for them; they should be revised to provide better explanations or predictions of what in fact exists. If reality does not correspond to normative prescriptions, however, so much the worse for reality; it should be revised to correspond more closely to our value judgments of what ought to exist!

As social scientists, economists wish to minimize *bias* in their inquiries—that is, to avoid value judgments that interfere with scientific objectivity. At the same time, it is important to emphasize that the relation between human values and scientific enterprise in economics need not be biased, and indeed, that values may contribute to science and science to the better understanding of values. These potentially constructive interdependencies between normative and positive economics exist at three major levels of inquiry: prescientific, scientific, and postscientific. At the prescientific level, value judgments may profoundly affect the choice both of problems for investigation and of scientific criteria. At the scientific level, value judgments themselves exist as empirical phenomena, and as such are subject to scientific investigation. At the postscientific level, value judgments affect both the objectives of economic policies and the means of reaching them.

Prior to Adam Smith, the famous founding-father-figure of the discipline—and who could be more fundamental than Adam and more common than Smith?—economics was essentially a normative subject. From the late

11

eighteenth century until well into the mid-nineteenth centuries, economics was a blend of positive and normative elements. The nineteenth-century model of the atomistically and efficiently functioning competitive price or market system, for example, was both an explanation of the economic world and a normative rationale of an ideal economic system. With increasing sophistication as a social science in the late nineteenth and early decades of the twentieth century, emphasis began to be placed upon the testable character of scientific propositions as contrasted with value judgments. Recently, economists, especially those concerned with economic policy, have recognized interdependencies between positive and normative issues, and the need to deal more explicitly with value judgments and social goals. Perhaps the essence of bias in normative economics lies not in accommodating social values and judgments in economic theory, but in insulating them from the test of experience and excluding them from critical appraisal.

Economic Systems

Economics emerged as a social scientific discipline simultaneously with the emergence and development of competitive market capitalism as an economic system. As a result, economics was (and to a significant degree still is) the analysis of the social processes of competitive markets in a capitalist economy. Even Marxian economics, popularly associated with socialist and communist movements and ideas, was primarily an analysis and critique of industrializing capitalism.

The correlation of the emergence and development of economics with that of the market system is probably no historic accident. Tradition and command, the premarket methods for coordinating decisions to resolve societies' economic problems, are (at least in the context of economic underdevelopment) singularly unexciting from the standpoint of economic analysis. But the market system poses an intellectual puzzle. How can a society's economic problems be resolved in a systematic way when the power to make economic decisions is dispersed atomistically among millions of individual independent firms and households, whose freedoms are unconstrained by tradition or command? The answer given by classical nineteenth-century economic thought was that inherent in the decision processes of individual firms and households seeking their own economic gain through market exchange is a social process —the competitive market system—which automatically and spontaneously coordinates decisions and resolves society's economic problems in a systematic way.

One of the important facts about capitalism as an economic system, yet at the same time a reality that is difficult, especially for Americans, to subject to dispassionate study, is that it, like other forms or systems of economic organization, is historically transient. It emerged, after several centuries of transition, out of a precapitalist past in Western society. It surged to dominance with the industrialization of England; spread throughout most of the Western world in the nineteenth century; and then, through a variety of devices, penetrated and expanded economic and political control over large areas of the economically underdeveloped world. By 1913, at the peak of its grandeur, it was in virtually unchallenged control of the world economy. A study of comparative economic systems was, for all practical purposes, an examination of capitalism, with perhaps some tangential attention to socialism as a theoretical, vaguely formulated, and utopian-sounding alternative.

In the decades following World War I, this situation was to change dramatically. Capitalism's position of dominance was challenged repeatedly and, in many instances, successfully. New forms of economic organization appeared in rapid and bewildering succession in Italy, Germany, and Russia between the first and second world wars. In the post-World War II period, increasing numbers of underdeveloped countries emerged from a colonial past into political independence with a desire to embark upon rapid industrialization and economic growth and a hostility toward classic, nineteenth-century capitalism as the appropriate route to that objective. Within the former capitalist countries themselves, "capitalism" (as it was continued to be called) was changing, partly through its own internal dynamics, and partly through political and other forms of collective pressure, such as the growth of labor organizations. Capitalism was modified and reformed. By the mid-twentieth century, one thing was clear: The era of absolute capitalist dominance in the world economy had disappeared, and had been replaced with a confusing array of competing economic systems.

The study of comparative economic systems is more of an approach to than a separate part of economics, just as economics in recent decades has itself increasingly been regarded as an approach to rather than a separate part of life. The unifying theme of comparative economic systems is the use of methods of comparative analysis. Because these methods may be applied to the study of topics in *any* subfield within economics (for example, systems of taxation or labor unions in different countries) or to economics as a whole (for example, theories of socialism or the overall performance of selected national economies), comparative economic systems cannot be separated from the general principles of economics or from any of its branches.

Economic Policy

The emergence of new forms of economic systems and modification of old ones in the twentieth century have heightened the interest of economists in the issues of economic policy and brought economics into a closer relationship to applied problems of public affairs. In all contemporary economic systems—"Stalinist" and contemporary communist countries, emergent underdeveloped nations, modified capitalist economies of Western Europe and the United States—collective control over economic decisions plays a substantially greater role than in old-style, nineteenth-century capitalism. Collective control, whether exercised by labor unions, private or public corporations, central

13

banks, governments, or regulatory commissions, involves the formulation and execution of "policies" designed to affect selected economic variables and thereby to eliminate or at least reduce the gap between an actual and a desired state of affairs.

A schematic display of the major processes of economic policy is provided in Figure 1. Reading from left to right, the coordination of economic theories with factual data yields models of economic analysis for the purpose of making decisions. The coordination of objectives with economic models yields policies designed to attain objectives. The formulation of objective-oriented policies, combined with techniques of control and thereby execution, constitutes a plan. The interaction of plans and events, many of which are beyond the control of any plan, yields experience. In the light of experience, successes or failures are evaluated and plans are revised (as illustrated by the lines leading back from experience to other parts of the diagram).

Three key points emerge from this synopsis. First, economic policy is a dynamic and continuing process involving the constant interaction of thought and action, with periodic revision or reformulation in the light of experience. Second, the dimensions of economic policy are far broader than any single "policy" itself, and involve theoretical analysis, factual investigation and measurement, model-building and applications, goals and objectives, plans, the development and application of methods and techniques of social control, and the interpretation of events often beyond the prediction and control of policymakers. Third, economic theory is an important, at times indispensable, contributor to the solution of policy problems. Theories provide an analytical

Figure 1. The Process of Economic Policy

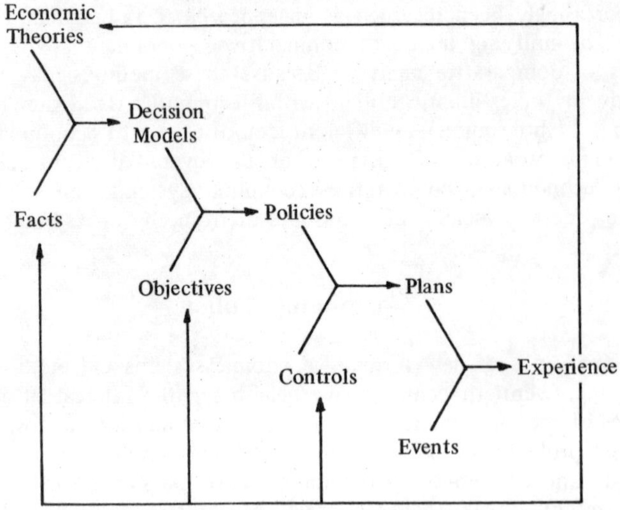

Adapted from Richard Stone, "Models of the National Economy for Planning Purposes," in *Mathematics in the Social Sciences and Other Essays* (Cambridge, Mass.: M.I.T. Press, 1966), p. 69. Used with permission.

14

basis for interpreting facts and identifying, comparing, and evaluating alternative ways of attaining objectives. At the same time, it should be emphasized that there is much more to economic policy than economic theory. The subtle interblending of theory, facts, goals, controls, plans, and events often makes economic policy as much an art as a science.

ECONOMIC GENERALIZATIONS
OR LAWS

Alfred Marshall

Political economy or economics is a study of mankind in the ordinary business of life; it examines that part of individual and social action which is most closely connected with the attainment and with the use of the material requisites of wellbeing.

Thus it is on the one side a study of wealth; and on the other, and more important side, a part of the study of man. For man's character has been moulded by his everyday work, and the material resources which he thereby procures, more than by any other influence unless it be that of his religious ideals; and the two great forming agencies of the world's history have been the religious and the economic. Here and there the ardour of the military or the artistic spirit has been for a while predominant: but religious and economic influences have nowhere been displaced from the front rank even for a time; and they have nearly always been more important than all others put together. Religious motives are more intense than economic, but their direct action seldom extends over so large a part of life. For the business by which a person earns his livelihood generally fills his thoughts during by far the greater part of those hours in which his mind is at its best; during them his character is being formed by the way in which he uses his faculties in his work, by the thoughts and the feelings which it suggests, and by his relations to his associates in work, his employers or his employees. . . .

The advantage which economics has over other branches of social science appears then to arise from the fact that its special field of work gives rather larger opportunities for exact methods than any other branch. It concerns itself chiefly with those desires, aspirations and other affections of human nature, the outward manifestations of which appear as incentives to action in such a form that the force or quantity of the incentives can be estimated and

Reprinted with permission of The Macmillan Company from *Principles of Economics* by Alfred Marshall, pp. 1-2, 15, 31-33, 36-37. Copyright 1948 by The Macmillan Company.

measured with some approach to accuracy; and which therefore are in some degree amenable to treatment by scientific machinery. An opening is made for the methods and the tests of science as soon as the force of a person's motives—*not* the motives themselves—can be approximately measured by the sum of money, which he will just give up in order to secure a desired satisfaction; or again by the sum which is just required to induce him to undergo a certain fatigue.

It is essential to note that the economist does not claim to measure any affection of the mind in itself, or directly; but only indirectly through its effect. No one can compare and measure accurately against one another even his own mental states at different times; and no one can measure the mental states of another at all except indirectly and conjecturally by their effects. . . .

It is the business of economics, as of almost every other science, to collect facts, to arrange and interpret them, and to draw inferences from them. "Observation and description, definition and classification are the preparatory activities. But what we desire to reach thereby is a knowledge of the interdependence of economic phenomena. . . . Induction and deduction are both needed for scientific thought as the right and left foot are both needed for walking." The methods required for this twofold work are not peculiar to economics; they are the common property of all sciences. . . .

Let us then consider more closely the nature of economic laws, and their limitations. Every cause has a tendency to produce some definite result if nothing occurs to hinder it. Thus gravitation tends to make things fall to the ground: but when a balloon is full of gas lighter than air, the pressure of the air will make it rise in spite of the tendency of gravitation to make it fall. The law of gravitation states how any two things attract one another; how they tend to move towards one another, and will move towards one another if nothing interferes to prevent them. The law of gravitation is therefore a statement of tendencies.

It is a very exact statement—so exact that mathematicians can calculate a Nautical Almanac, which will show the moments at which each satellite of Jupiter will hide itself behind Jupiter. They make this calculation for many years beforehand; and navigators take it to sea, and use it in finding out where they are. Now there are no economic tendencies which act as steadily and can be measured as exactly as gravitation can: and consequently there are no laws of economics which can be compared for precision with the law of gravitation.

But let us look at a science less exact than astronomy. The science of the tides explains how the tide rises and falls twice a day under the action of the sun and the moon: how there are strong tides at new and full moon, and weak tides at the moon's first and third quarter; and how the tide running up into a closed channel, like that of the Severn, will be very high; and so on. Thus, having studied the lie of the land and the water all round the British isles, people can calculate beforehand when the tide will *probably* be at its highest on any day at London Bridge or at Gloucester; and how high it will be there. They have to use the word *probably*, which the astronomers do not need to use when talking about the eclipses of Jupiter's satellites. For, though many forces act upon Jupiter and his satellites, each one of them acts in a definite manner which can be predicted beforehand: but no one knows enough about the weather to be able to say beforehand how it will act. A heavy downpour of rain in the upper Thames valley, or a strong northeast wind in the German Ocean, may make the tides at London Bridge differ a good deal from what had been expected.

The laws of economics are to be compared with the laws of the tides, rather than with the simple and exact law of gravitation. For the actions of men are so various and uncertain, that the best statement of tendencies, which we can make in a science of human conduct, must needs be inexact and faulty. This might be urged as a reason against making any statements at all on the subject; but that would be almost to abandon life. Life is human conduct, and the thoughts and emotions that grow up around it. By the fundamental impulses of our nature we all—high and low, learned and un-learned—are in our several degrees constantly striving to understand the courses of human action, and to shape them for our purposes, whether selfish or unselfish, whether noble or ignoble. And since we *must* form to ourselves some notions of the tendencies of human action, our choice is between form-ing those notions carelessly and forming them carefully. The harder the task, the greater the need for steady patient inquiry; for turning to account the experience, that has been reaped by the more advanced physical sciences; and for framing as best we can well thought-out estimates, or provisional laws, of the tendencies of human action. . . .

Economic laws, or statements of economic tendencies, are those social laws which relate to branches of conduct in which the strength of the motives chiefly concerned can be measured by a money price.

There is thus no hard and sharp line of division between those social laws which are, and those which are not, to be regarded also as economic laws. For there is a continuous gradation from social laws concerned almost exclusively with motives that can be measured by price, to social laws in which such motives have little place; and which are therefore generally as much less pre-cise and exact than economic laws, as those are than the laws of the more exact physical sciences. . . .

It is sometimes said that the laws of economics are "hypothetical." Of course, like every other science, it undertakes to study the effects which will be produced by certain causes, not absolutely, but subject to the condition that *other things are equal,* and that the causes are able to work out their effects undisturbed. Almost every scientific doctrine, when carefully and formally stated, will be found to contain some proviso to the effect that other things are equal: the action of the causes in question is supposed to be isolated; certain effects are attributed to them, but only *on the hypothesis* that no cause is permitted to enter except those distinctly allowed for. It is true however that the condition that time must be allowed for causes to produce their effects is a source of great difficulty in economics. For mean-while the material on which they work, and perhaps even the causes

18

themselves, may have changed; and the tendencies which are being described will not have a sufficiently "long run" in which to work themselves out fully. . . .

Though economic analysis and general reasoning are of wide application, yet every age and every country has its own problems; and every change in social conditions is likely to require a new development of economic doctrines.

II.

ECONOMIC
RELEVANCE
AND
SOCIAL CHOICE

This section contains a collection of readings helpful in conquering the Niagara of economic jargon that frequently bewilders beginning students. Too often students become lost in a sea of semantics unless some vehicle is provided to convert abstract economic theory into "real world" situations. No pretense is made that the following articles are all inclusive of macroeconomic theory, only that they help to comprehend the nature, operation, and significance of economic theory and to bridge the gap between abstract economic theory and reality.

The criteria used to select these readings were: first, all of them relate to macroeconomic theory; second, each reading relates to at least one contemporary economic problem; and third, the student does not have to be an economist to understand each selection. The first essay provides an insight of economic activity not included in our measurement of the GNP. Subsequent articles provide the student with an operational application of various sectors of the economy, relate some of the more prominent and persistent problem areas of our society, and broach the area of economic policy. Finally, for the student who, after studying perfect economic theory and observing a "real world" of different dimensions, becomes disenchanted with or distrusts theory and asks "why study theory if it doesn't work in the real world?," a selection is included to assist the student in understanding how we can, or why we don't, make the economy operate more perfectly.

A.

Harmony in Aggregate Economics?

WHAT GNP DOESN'T TELL US

A. A. Berle, Jr.

It is nice to know that at current estimate the Gross National Product of the United States in 1968 will be above 850 billions of dollars. It would be still nicer to know if the United States will be better or worse off as a result. If better, in what respects? If worse, could not some of this production and effort be steered into providing more useful "goods and services"?

Unfortunately, whether the work was sham or useful, the goods noxious, evanescent, or of permanent value will have no place in the record. Individuals, corporations, or government want, buy, and pay for stuff and work—so it is "product." The labor of the Boston Symphony Orchestra is "product" along with that of the band in a honky-tonk. The compensated services of a quack fortune teller are "product" just as much as the work of developing Salk vaccine. Restyling automobiles or ice chests by adding tail fins or pink

From *Saturday Review,* August 31, 1968, pp. 10-12. Copyright 1968 Saturday Review, Inc.

handles adds to "product" just as much as money paid for slum clearance or medical care. They are all "goods" or "services"—the only test is whether someone wanted them badly enough to pay the shot.

This blanket tabulation raises specific complaints against economists and their uncritical aggregated figures and their acceptance of production as "progress." The economists bridle, "We," they reply, "are economists, not priests. Economics deals with satisfaction of human wants by things or services. The want is sufficiently evidenced by the fact that human beings, individually or collectively, paid for them. It is not for us to pass on what people ought to have wanted—that question is for St. Peter. A famous statistic in *America's Needs and Resources*—published by the Twentieth Century Fund in 1955—was that Americans in 1950 paid $8.1 billion for liquor and $10.5 billion for education. Maybe they ought to have cut out liquor and paid for more education instead—but they didn't, and value judgments are not our job. Get yourself a philosopher for that. We will go on recording what did happen."

What they are saying—and as far as it goes, they are quite right—is that nobody has given economics a mandate to set up a social-value system for the country. Fair enough—but one wonders. Closer thinking suggests that even on their own plane economists could perhaps contribute a little to the subject, although, as will presently appear, we must get ourselves some philosophy, too. One branch of social indicating may not be as far removed from cold economics as it would appear. Another branch is more difficult, though even it may yield to analysis.

Any audit of social result, any system of social indicators, requires solving two sets of problems. First, with all this Gross National Product reflecting payment to satisfy wants, did America get what it paid for? In getting it, did it not also bring into being a flock of unrecorded but offsetting frustrations it did not want? Essentially, this is economic critique. Second—and far more difficult—can a set of values be put forward, roughly expressing the essentials most Americans would agree their society ought to be, and be doing, against which the actual record of what it was and did can be checked? This second critique, as economists rightly contend, is basically philosophical.

As for the economic critique, let us take the existing economic record at face. Work was done, things were created, and both were paid for. The total price paid this year will be around $850 billion. But, unrecorded, not included, and rarely mentioned are some companion results. Undisposed-of junk piles, garbage, waste, air and water pollution come into being. God help us, we can see that all over the country. Unremedied decay of parts of the vast property we call "the United States" is evident in and around most American cities. No one paid for this rot and waste—they are not "product." Factually, these and other undesirable results are clear deductions from or offset items to the alleged Gross National Product we like so well.

The total of these may be called "disproduct." It will be a hard figure to calculate in dollar figures. Recorded as "product" is the amount Americans spent for television sets, stations, and broadcasts. Unrecorded is their

24

companion disproductive effect in the form of violence, vandalism, and crime. Proudly reported as "product" are sums spent for medical care, public health, and disease prevention; unheralded is the counter-item, the "disproduct" of loss and misery as remediable malnutrition and preventable disease ravage poverty areas. Besides our annual calculation of "gross" national product, it is time we had some idea of Gross National Disproduct. Deducting it, we could know what the true, instead of the illusory, annual "net national product" might be. (Economists use "Net National Product" to mean Gross National Product less consumption of capital—but it is not a true picture.)

There is a difference, it will be noted, between "disproduct" and "cost." Everything made or manufactured, every service rendered by human beings, involves using up materials, if only the food and living necessities of labor. These are "costs." They need not enter into this calculation. Conventional statistics already set up a figure for "capital consumption," and we deduct this from "Gross National Product." That is not what we have in mind here. We are trying to discover whether creation of "Gross National Product" does not also involve frustration of wants as well as their satisfaction. Pollution of air and water are obvious illustrations but there are "disproducts" more difficult to discern, let alone measure.

Scientists are increasing our knowledge of these right along. For example, cigarettes (to which I am addicted) satisfy a widespread want. They also, we are learning, engender a great deal of cancer. Now it is true that at some later time the service rendered in attempting to care for cancer (generated by cigarettes manufactured five years ago) will show up as "product"; so the work of attempted cure or caretaking will later appear as a positive product item. But that item will not be known until later. What we do know without benefit of figures is that against this year's output of tobacco products whose cash value is recorded we have also brought more cancer into being—an unrecorded "disproduct." We know at the end of any year how many more automobiles have been manufactured. We also know that each new car on the road means added injury and accident overall. Carry this process through our whole product list, and the aggregate of "disproduct" items set against the aggregate of production will tell us an immense amount about our progress toward (or retrogression from) social welfare.

Once we learn to calculate disproduct along with product and discover a true "net," as well as a "gross," we shall have our first great "social" indicator. We shall know what the country accomplished.

It could be surprising and disillusioning. It might disclose that while satisfying human wants as indicated by the "gross" figure, in the process we had also violated, blocked, or frustrated many of these same wants and, worse, had done a great deal we did not want to do. Carrying the calculation further, we would probably find (among other things) that while satisfying immediate wants from today's productivity, we had been generating future wants (not to say needs) to repair the damage, waste, and degeneration set up by current production.

Some of today's "gross" product carries with it a mortgage—it sets up brutal defensive requirements that must be met by tomorrow's work and things. Some forms of productivity may prove to generate more decay, damage, or waste annually than their total amount, while neglect of some production may annually place a usurious claim on future years. Failure to maintain cities at acceptable standards is a case in point: it sets up huge but unrecorded claims on the manpower and product of coming decades. It is entirely possible to score annual increases of Gross National Product as we presently figure it—and yet, after reckoning "disproduct," be little better off at the end of any year than at its beginning.

Calculation of "disproduct" is admittedly difficult. If seriously tackled, I think it at least partially possible. At first it would be far indeed from exact. All the same, "disproduct" is a plain fact of life—look out of your window and you can see some. Crude calculation of the probable amounts needed to offset many items of "disproduct" is not insoluble; technicians in some lines have fairly concrete ideas along these lines already. Actuaries compute the "disproduct" resulting from automobile accidents, and your car insurance bill is calculated accordingly. Carry the process through and a crude though probably incomplete item could be developed. Using it, one could judge whether, materially at least, the country had moved forward or backward.

In this first bracket of critique, economists are not required to make value judgments of what is "good or bad." They, with the advice of the technical men in the various sectors, could merely be asked to tackle calculation of "disproduct" as well as of "product."

The second branch of the problem is harder. It raises the question of whether a good deal of Gross National Product should not be steered by social or political action toward creating a more satisfactory civilization. That, of course, requires some elementary assumptions as to what a satisfactory civilization ought to be and do. Can any such assumptions be made?

Constructing enough of a value system to use as critique of a Gross National Product indeed does seem not beyond common-sense possibility. The job does, without question, require setting out some values on which there is sufficient agreement to engage social opinion and, one hopes, social action. Production steered toward realizing these values can be described as "good." Production frustrating or tearing them down can be stigmatized as "bad." Let us try drawing up a list, tentative in the extreme. I think there would probably be considerable agreement that it is "good"; but if not, make a dinner table game of drawing a better one:

1. People are better alive than dead.
2. People are better healthy than sick.
3. People are better off literate than illiterate.
4. People are better off adequately than inadequately housed.
5. People are better off in beautiful than in ugly cities and towns.
6. People are better off if they have opportunity for enjoyment—music, literature, drama, and the arts.

7. Education above the elementary level should be as nearly universal as possible through secondary schools, and higher education as widely diffused as practicable.

8. Development of science and the arts should continue or possibly be expanded.

9. Minimum resources for living should be available to all.

10. Leisure and access to green country should be a human experience available to everyone.

Anyone can add to or change this list if he likes, my point is that at least a minimum set of values can be agreed on. We have done more here than draw up a list of pleasant objectives. We have set up criteria. By applying our list to the actual and recorded output of our Gross National Product, we begin to discern that some of these values are perhaps adequately pursued, some inadequately, some not served at all. Even now, the Gross National Product figure is broken down into many lines. It would have to be split up further or differently for purposes of criticism. The elementary value-system we have projected (or some better edition of it) could provide the basis for critique. It could permit discovery of whether the recorded outturn of our vast hubbub of activity, after subtracting "disproduct" from "product," tended toward producing social results more or less in accord with the objectives implied by our values. If Governor Nelson Rockefeller is right in believing that in a decade the Gross National Product of the United States will be a trillion and a half dollars, it should be possible to steer increasing amounts of it toward realization of this or any similar list of values, and the objectives it suggests.

I am aware that no American value-system can be real except as it expresses a common divisor of the thinking of 200 million Americans. Only totalitarian police state dictatorships, denying their citizens choice of life and action, can lay down complete and all-inclusive value-systems, force their populations and their production into that mold, and audit the results in terms of their success in doing so. Free societies cannot. They must content themselves with common denomination of basic value judgments on which most of their people have substantial consensus—leaving them free to do as they please in other respects. When a free society attempts to impose value judgments going beyond consensus—as they did when the Prohibition Amendment was adopted in 1919—it fails. Yet because there is a wide measure of consensus on values, America does move along, does generate its enormous Gross National Product (and let us hope solid Net National Product) precisely because there is substantial agreement on what its people really want.

Also there is probably a high factor of agreement on priorities—that is, on what they want most. There are doubtful areas, of course. I will not risk a guess whether priority would be given to military preparedness over education were a Gallup Poll taken—more expenditures for defense and less for aid to education. But I am clear that both in values and in priorities a large enough measure of agreement does exist so that if we put our minds to it a critique of our outturn performance expressed in Gross National Product can be had.

ECONOMIC RELEVANCE AND SOCIAL CHOICE

And we ought not to be stopped or baffled or bogged down because philosophers cannot agree on the nature of the "good," or because scientists cannot predict with certainty the social effects of value judgments carried into action. Wrong guesses about values show up in experience, as happened in the Prohibition experiment. In light of experience, they can be corrected. With even rudimentary social indicators, the current cascade of emotional and sterile invective might be converted into rational dialogue. Constructive use of social-economic forces and even of currents of philosophical thinking might become possible.

I realize, of course, that up to now it has been assumed that social indicators, based on an expressed value-system, could not be achieved. Well, only a generation ago scholars assumed nothing could be done to alleviate the impact of assumedly blind economic forces, let alone guide them. We know better today; rudimentary capacity to control and steer these forces already exists; the so-called New Economics increasingly guides their use. Similar thinking and similar tools can provide material on which social policy can be based. Combined with the economic tools currently being forged, social objectives might be brought out of dreamland into range of practical achievement.

Discussion and debate would inevitably result from comparison of actual operations with desired results. More intense and perhaps more fruitful controversy would be engendered in areas where there were items not appearing in our tentative list of values for lack of sufficient consensus. Protagonists would insist they be included; opponents would object. This could be healthy. It would be ballasted by realization that, were consensus achieved, constructive action could be possible. Any caterwaul that American society is "sick" could be qualified by emerging factual knowledge showing that either the accusation was untrue or, if true, that measures for cure could be taken. The debate might disadvantage some people; for one thing, it might reduce the torrent of boring despair-literature presently drowning the reading public. Possibly even contrasting currents of new Puritanism might emerge perhaps providing a not unpleasant contrast, if not relief.

Knowing where American civilization is going is the first essential to saving it (if it is to be saved) or changing it (if it is to be altered).

TOO MANY TRIVIA?

Henry C. Wallich

In addition to free advice about growth, the nation has received helpful suggestions of another sort, in a rather opposite vein. It has been argued that we have all the production we need and to spare, but that too much of our growth has gone into private consumption, too little into public. We are said to be wasting our substance on trivia while allowing urgent public needs to go uncared for. This view does not complain of inadequate growth. But it sees us riding in tail-finned, oversized automobiles through cities that are becoming slums, finds our children sitting glued to the latest TV models but lacking schools where they can learn to read properly, and generally charges us with putting private profligacy ahead of public provision.

The general doctrine that in the United States public needs tend to be underfinanced in relation to private I first heard many years ago from my old teacher Alvin Hansen. It has always seemed to me to possess a measure of appeal. Throughout this book, I have been at pains to argue that with rising wealth and industrialized living, the need for public services advances, and probably faster than living standards. In part this reflects simply the familiar fact that the demand for services tends to expand faster than the demand for goods. In part, the social conditions of modern life are also accountable for the growing need for governmental services. Private business is learning to meet many of these new needs—for instance in the field of insurance. It is not inconceivable that some day we shall become rich enough to be able to indulge increasingly a preference for privately supplied services. But at present, and as far ahead as one can see, the trend seems the other way. I would footnote this reference to my earlier passages by observing that to recognize a rising trend in the need for public services and to claim that at present we have too little of them are two different things. The more than doubling of

From pp. 165-171, *The Cost of Freedom* by Henry C. Wallich. Copyright © 1960 by Henry C. Wallich. By permission of Harper & Row, Publishers, Inc.

federal and also of state and local expenditures [between 1950 and 1960] should drive home that distinction.

The thesis that public services are neglected and private consumption inflated with trivia has found its most eloquent interpretation in *The Affluent Society* by John Kenneth Galbraith. . . . Galbraith argues that this imbalance is nourished by advertising, which creates artificial wants. He sees it further accentuated by an obsession with production, which keeps us from realizing that our problems are not those of want but of affluence. The imbalance is epitomized by our supposed tendency to limit public expenditures to what is strictly essential, while we apply no such criterion to private expenditures.

One may reasonably argue that Galbraith exaggerates the distorting influence of advertising. That would not alter the basic assumption on which his thesis rests—the assumption that there are better wants and worse wants. Scientific detachment notwithstanding, I find it extraordinarily difficult to disagree with this proposition. To rate an attendance at the opera and a visit to an (inexpensive) nightclub as equivalents, because the market puts a similar price on them, goes against my grain. So does the equation of a dollar's worth of education and a dollar's worth of chromium on an automobile. And a plausible case could probably be made, on the basis of the evolution of the species, that opera and education do represent more advanced forms of consumption.

But what consequences, if any, should be drawn from such judgment? Does it yield a basis for trying to discourage the growth of the less "good" expenditures? In a free society, we obviously want to move with the utmost circumspection. It is worth remembering that even Thorstein Veblen, who went to some extreme in deriding the "leisure class" and its "conspicuous consumption," did not take an altogether negative view of all conspicuous waste. In *The Theory of the Leisure Class* he said,

No class of society, not even the most abjectly poor, foregoes all customary conspicuous consumption. . . . There is no class and no country that has yielded so abjectly before the pressure of physical want as to deny themselves all gratification of this higher or spiritual need.

For a fair appraisal of the case against trivia, we would also want to know the approximate size of the bill that is being incurred for various frills and frivolities. Gadgets in cars and homes have drawn the special ire of the critics. It is interesting to note, therefore, that expenditures for all kinds of durable consumer goods, including automobiles, run about 14 percent of personal consumption. The greater part of this, presumably, goes for the essential parts of fairly essential equipment. What is left for ornaments and gadgets does not loom impressively large.

Whatever our private feelings about the gadgetry in our life, we probably do well not to stress them too hard. It is only too easy for some members of a community to work themselves into a fit of righteousness and to feel tempted to help the rest regulate their existence. In an extreme form, and not very long ago, this happened in the United States with the introduction of prohibition. Some of us may lean toward special taxation of luxuries, but surely no one wants sumptuary legislation banishing from our show windows and homes the offending contrivances. A new puritanism directed against wasteful consumption, however understandable, would make no great contribution to an economy that requires incentive goods to activate competition and free markets. Neither would it be compatible with the freedom that we value.

It is the positive side of the case—the asserted need for more public service —that must chiefly concern us. One can listen with some sympathy to the case and to the account of the biases in our economy that work against public and for private spending. The pressure of $10 billions worth of advertising is a bias of that sort. The natural reluctance of taxpayers to vote taxes the benefits of which will be shared by others is a second. A third is the somewhat vague nature of many public benefits—education, welfare, and health, for instance. They are of a kind that the taxpayer himself might tend to neglect a little were he to purchase them in the marketplace. Then there is the peculiar relationship of state and local authorities to the federal government, which restrains public expenditures by leaving most of the socially useful expenditures to the former while giving the more productive tax sources to the latter. And finally, there is the American tradition which in the interests of freedom puts a special premium on private activity over public.

But what we are in some danger of overlooking are the biases on the other side—the pressures that work for greater public spending. If advertising promotes sales to individuals, those who supply the public authorities are not without means of their own to promote their wares. If some taxpayers object to taxes that will benefit others besides themselves, there are others who vote for expenditures expecting that they will benefit where they have not contributed. Politicians in general have not been averse to voting funds for well-supported worthy causes. Vocal minorities that know what they want often can outmaneuver inarticulate majorities that don't know how to stand up for their own interests. Finally, our tax system itself has a built-in bias to encourage spending, because it collects relatively small amounts per head from taxpayers in the lower brackets, while those in the upper brackets pay a good deal. If the benefits that individuals in different brackets derive from public services are not too disparate, taxpayers in the lower brackets obviously are getting theirs at a bargain. Since they constitute a majority, they are in a position to increase the number of these bargains.

As between the forces that inhibit and those that advance public expenditures, no one can say for sure where the balance lies. But on the evidence that 30 years ago taxes of all kinds added up to less than 10 percent of the Gross National Product, whereas today they account for well over 25 percent, we have no reason to suspect that the expansive forces lack vigor—even allowing one-third of the present load for major national security.

Meanwhile, those who would like to see public services taking a still larger share must bear in mind two facts, one economic, the other political. The economic fact is that the free provision of public services paid for by taxation

31

is a very inefficient way of catering to consumer needs. I am not referring to popular suspicions about the efficiency of public administration, but to the manner in which costs and benefits are adjusted to each other, or fail to be adjusted. In private dealings, the consumer purchases the exact amount of the exact product he wants, and so gets the most for his money. The taxpayer voting for certain public services has no means of securing such nice adjustment. He may find himself getting less, or more, or something other than he wanted. He has no incentive, moreover, to economize in the use of many of the services offered—usually they come to him free of charge. Our methods of making public decisions and apportioning public services leave much to be desired as compared with the neat job done by the free market.

The political problem that confronts advocates of larger public expenditures is of a different order. We return here to the point stressed earlier in this section—the tendency of our society to produce a balance of interests that impedes ready shifts among private and public resources. This applies also, of course, to budgetary expenditures. Barring some outward disturbance that shakes the balance of interests, such as a military emergency, the balance of expenditures in the budget will also tend to remain stable. If there are to be budget cuts, they are likely to cut all around. If the purse strings are to be relaxed, they are likely to be relaxed not just in one direction, but in all. That is the result of a balance which makes all interests share burdens and benefits in accordance with their bargaining strength.

The consequences, when larger expenditures are proposed, tend to be those we have often observed. The proponents of new expenditures rarely demand that all forms of public spending be enlarged. They have some particular purposes in mind. But the prevailing balance of interests works against such favors for any one group, extended to the exclusion of all the rest. If one form of expenditure is expanded, political pressures develop for giving everybody else something he wants.

The "balance of interests" effect need not, of course, be taken in its most literal sense. Obviously the proportions among different public expenditures always are shifting in some degree. Some expenditures are subject to factors that cannot be controlled, such as fluctuating interest rates or crop yields. Some have a built-in momentum, as does Social Security. And as public opinion and political constellations shift, so does the balance among public functions. Marginal improvements in particular public programs are never out of reach. Major increases, however, are not likely to occur unless accompanied by major shifts in the balance of interests. With that balance intact, the politics of the case incline toward, not "first come, first served," but "come one, come all."

This imposes a heavy surcharge upon expenditures that intrinsically may have much to recommend them. It alters the practical attractiveness of such proposals. To spend public money for a good program is one thing. To have to loosen up on half a dozen unrelated programs as a condition of expanding one is quite another.

A political surcharge of this kind can make the implicit cost of desirable programs very high. Some may argue that this cost will have to be faced. Nevertheless, it should give pause even to those who feel strongly about their proposals. In a free country, no group can expect to change the balance of interests save as they succeed in swinging some of its components to their side. Once more we must note that freedom has its price. . . .

FIRST STEPS IN BANKING

Punch

Q. What are banks for?

A. To make money.

Q. For the customers?

A. For the banks.

Q. Why doesn't bank advertising mention this?

A. It would not be in good taste. But it is mentioned by implication in references to Reserves of £249,000,000 or thereabouts. That is the money they have made.

Q. Out of the customers?

A. I suppose so.

Q. They also mention Assets of £500,000,000 or thereabouts. Have they made that too?

A. Not exactly. That is the money they use to make money.

Q. I see. And they keep it in a safe somewhere?

A. Not at all. They lend it to customers.

Q. Then they haven't got it?

A. No.

Q. Then how is it Assets?

A. They maintain that it would be if they got it back.

Q. But they must have *some* money in a safe somewhere?

A. Yes, usually £500,000,000 or thereabouts. This is called Liabilities.

Q. But if they've got it, how can they be liable for it?

A. Because it isn't theirs.

Q. Then why do they have it?

A. It has been lent to them by customers.

Q. You mean customers lend banks money?

A. In effect. They put money into their accounts, so it is really lent to the banks.

From *Punch*, April 3, 1957, pp. 440-441. © *Punch*, 1957.

Q. And what do the banks do with it?
A. Lend it to other customers.
Q. But you said that money they lent to other people was Assets?
A. Yes.
Q. Then Assets and Liabilities must be the same thing?
A. You can't really say that.
Q. But you've just said it. If I put £100 into my account the bank is liable to have to pay it back, so it's Liabilities. But they go and lend it to someone else, and he is liable to have to pay it back, so it's Assets. It's the same £100, isn't it?
A. Yes. But——
Q. Then it cancels out. It means, doesn't it, that banks haven't really any money at all?
A. Theoretically——
Q. Never mind theoretically. And if they haven't any money where do they get their Reserves of £249,000,000 or thereabouts?
A. I told you. That is the money they have made.
Q. How?
A. Well, when they lend your £100 to someone they charge him interest.
Q. How much?
A. It depends on the Bank Rate. Say five and a half percent. That's their profit.
Q. Why isn't it my profit? Isn't it my money?
A. It's the theory of banking practice that—— **1705588**
Q. When I lend them my £100 why don't I charge *them* interest?
A. You do.
Q. You don't say. How much?
A. It depends on the Bank Rate. Say half a percent.
Q. Grasping of me, rather?
A. But that's only if you're not going to draw the money out again.
Q. But of course I'm going to draw it out again. If I hadn't wanted to draw it out again I could have buried it in the garden, couldn't I?
A. They wouldn't like you to draw it out again.
Q. Why not? If I keep it there you say it's a Liability. Wouldn't they be glad if I reduced their Liabilities by removing it?
A. No. Because if you remove it they can't lend it to anyone else.
Q. But if I wanted to remove it they'd have to let me?
A. Certainly.
Q. But suppose they've already lent it to another customer?
A. Then they'll let you have someone else's money.
Q. But suppose he wants his too—and they've let me have it?
A. You're being purposely obtuse.
Q. I think I'm being acute. What if everyone wanted their money at once?
A. It's the theory of banking practice that they never would.
Q. So what banks bank on is not having to meet their commitments?
A. I wouldn't say that.

35

Q. Naturally. Well, if there's nothing else you think you can tell me . . . ?
A. Quite so. Now you can go off and open a banking account.
Q. Just one last question.
A. Of course.
Q. Wouldn't I do better to go off and open a bank?

THE FABLE OF THE CAT

George E. Cruikshank

The meeting in Mouseville was uncommonly well attended. Every seat in the hall was taken. In the crowd were a sizable number of mice who were alarmed by recent events. Others at the meeting were quite calm, not at all concerned. And the rest—the vast majority—seemed bewildered. They simply wanted to be told what *really* was happening in their community.

The chairman, a no-nonsense type, quickly set forth the reason for the meeting. An old problem, it seemed had returned to make life difficult for Mouseville and its inhabitants. After nine years of peace and quiet a cat was reported to be moving into the neighborhood.

When the squeaks of dismay had died down, the chairman hastened to explain that reports of a cat were no more than that. No positive identification had yet been made. And there was considerable difference of opinion among knowledgeable members of the community as to whether such a cat even existed.

"I say there is too much loose talk about a cat," spoke up one member of the group who, owing to his position, could exert a powerful influence over the entire community.

"I heartily agree," was the comment uttered by another respected leader, who ranged high in the councils of government. He went on to say: "Even if something were to threaten us for two consecutive quarters I still would not jump to the conclusion that it was a cat, necessarily." An even more reassuring statement was made by a mouse who the audience knew held learned degrees in political economy—even though his statements sometimes lacked a sense of total commitment to proper English usage. With his cigar stabbing the air for emphasis, he stated: "There ain't gonna be no cat!" The flat prediction brought a chorus of approval and much pawclapping from a small group of

From *Morgan Guaranty Survey,* March 1970. Reprinted by permission.

mice who concerned themselves with Mouseville's political process. Their leader spoke out: "It is abolutely unacceptable to have a cat—especially in an election year."

SQUEAKERS OF GLOOM

Despite such attempts to allay the community's fears, not all the members seemed convinced. Some of the mice suspected that there might be a cat in the neighborhood. There *was* a certain smell in the air. Others were certain of it. The latter group, one by one, stood up to speak out against complacency.

From a builder of snug three- and four-bedroom nests: "I know a cat when I see one. This is a huge cat that is threatening my very life."

The gunslinging manager of the Trap-Free Growth Fund complained: "There is no doubt of it. It's a cat in bear's clothing."

Said the plump proprietor of Honest Sam's Auto Emporium, concerned about slumping sales of the new compact Rodent: "Consumers are not buying. They're worried about the cat."

There was no doubt in the mind of a workmouse, recently let go from his job: "To me it's a whole family of cats—a real disaster."

The tide of concern in the meeting clearly was rising. There seemed no end to those who were jumping to their feet to warn of impending danger. Even those mice who were merely visiting Mouseville felt constrained to speak up. One of these, a variety of Friedmouse hailing from the midwest, said: "We are bound to have a ferocious cat because the cheese supply has been flat for nine months."

A big-city mousebanker, worried about sinking prestige, creditcard backlash, and depreciated bond accounts, added: "Maybe we can now hope that our lords and masters will parcel out a slightly bigger ration of cheese. An extra sliver a day could keep the cat away."

A short, gnome-like mouse—obviously a foreign visitor—applauded that comment and advised: "You U.S. mice must do something about the cat. Every time you get a cat we have a lion in Europe." That comment led the mouse seated nearby, sad of face with whiskers that drooped forlornly, to warn in lugubrious tones: "The cat is the least of our worries. Pollution is going to kill us all."

Up to that point in the meeting the issue had been rather cleancut. Some thought that there was no cat to worry about; others thought to the contrary. Then things began to get fuzzy.

One mouse insisted that what he had seen was a tiny kitten, not a cat. He called it a "mini-cat"—and drew some delighted squeaks from the audience for his originality. Another member of the community, an industry economouse cautious by nature although not always really careful, allowed that he had detected something but that he needed more time to decide what it was he had seen. "Maybe if I had a little longer to analyze the reports I have been getting I could be more certain," he added, a bit lamely.

HARMONY IN AGGREGATE ECONOMICS?

By this time the audience was getting restive. A meeting called to eliminate confusion was merely adding to it.

"Words, words, figures, figures," cried one mouse, his tail twitching with impatience. "I hear descriptions, none of which is on the same base, that vary from a small furry animal, of unspecified origin, to a huge alley cat that will turn out to be worse than anything we have had to face since the Great Cat of the early 1930s. Is there a cat or isn't there?" The comment brought a chorus of agreement, much stamping of feet and lashing of tails. The meeting was threatening to get out of hand.

DEFINING A FELINE

Then the chairman displayed his storied wisdom. *The Institute,* staffed by economice with formidable powers of analysis, would decide whether there was a cat or not. Who would dispute the findings of *The Institute?* After all, was it not *The Institute* that had always made the determination? It could be counted on to make a calm, scholarly, dispassionate judgment, going in great depth into the size of the cat, when it arrived, and how long it had been around.

It was a masterstroke. The audience was delighted. Now they would know whether they should worry about a cat or go on munching their cheese free of worry.

Alas, one mouse was not quite satisfied. He raised his paw for attention—a timid gesture, almost as if he hoped the chairman would not notice. But the chairman did notice. The question came tumbling out: "When can we expect to get the news—whether there is a cat or not?"

The chairman had hoped no one would ask. But now the query had been made. He replied, as briskly as possible: "The last time *The Institute* was called upon to make a judgment about a cat was in 1960-61. It took the better part of a year to decide that there had been a cat. But, as a matter of general practice, *The Institute* does not announce that there is a cat until the cat has left the neighborhood."

As the chairman had feared, his reply led inevitably to further comments and queries. "That's a long time to wait to find out about the cat," shouted one mouse. Another asked: "What shall we do in the meantime?"

The chairman huffed and puffed but no answer came to mind. To his immense relief he saw the venerable elder of the community slowly rise from his chair and beckon for attention. The chairman was happy to oblige. All eyes shifted to the slightly stooped figure with white whiskers. He spoke:

"Fellow citizens, do not be excessively concerned about the various descriptions of the cat that you have been hearing. The mini-cat, the two-quarter cat, and so on. You can get caught in semantic quicksand.

"If there is a cat it will not be long now before we will all know. Any cat worthy of the name will not stay hidden indefinitely, I promise you. Meantime, do not panic and take rash action over a cat that may or may not materialize."

39

The quiet, measured tones of the oldtimer calmed the assembled mice. They liked his pragmatic approach—of crossing *that* bridge when they came to it. Besides, it put off to another day the dreary and difficult business of deciding what to do about a cat, if in fact there was one.

The mice filed out of the hall. The chairman silently congratulated himself on his adroit handling of the meeting. But in truth it must be said that the amount of bewilderment in Mouseville had not been reduced by as much as a cat's whisker.

ECONOMICS, ECONOMIC DEVELOPMENT, AND ECONOMIC ANTHROPOLOGY

George Dalton

Little else is requisite to carry a state to the highest degree of opulence from the lowest barbarism, but peace, easy taxes and a tolerable administration of justice.

Adam Smith

There is a deep-seated yearning in social science to discover one general approach, one general law valid for all time and all climes. But these primitive attitudes must be outgrown.

Alexander Gerschenkron

I should like to address the question, "Is economic theory culture-bound?" in two contexts: as the question relates to the economist's field, economic development, and as it relates to the anthropologist's field, economic anthropology.

In the last 10 years several prominent economists have questioned the relevance of conventional economics (for example, price, aggregate income, and growth theory) for dealing with the processes and problems of economic development. This is an old theme stated in a new context. Similar examples are the German *methodenstreit* debate; von Mises and von Hayek versus Taylor, Lange, and Lerner on planning without market prices under socialism; and the marginalist controversy after World War II. In all of these, the same question was debated: the extent of realism, relevance, and adequacy of formal economics in dealing with real-world processes and problems of importance.

In order to answer the question as it relates to economic development, one must first answer two other questions: What are those special characteristics

From *Journal of Economic Issues,* June 1968, pp. 172-186. Reprinted by permission.

of the structure and performance of underdeveloped countries which lead some economists to question the relevance of economics? What are those special characteristics of conventional economics which seem to these economists to be misleading or irrelevant in the context of underdevelopment? We turn first to the special characteristics of underdeveloped countries.

1. The basic fact of the underdeveloped world is the existence of some 100 underdeveloped nation-states, principally in Africa, Asia, Latin America, and the Middle East. The economic, political, and social differences among them are much greater than are the differences among the few developed capitalist nations of Western Europe and North America for which economic theory was invented. The fact of extreme diversity within the underdeveloped world—that it includes Liberia as well as India and Mexico—means that nothing like a single analytical model of underdevelopment is feasible: the structures, processes, and problems are too different.

2. Half or more of these countries are developing their polities and societies as well as their economies. They are in the process of structural transformation politically and culturally as well as economically and technologically. They are combining their Industrial Revolutions with their French Revolutions and their nation-building Mercantilist periods. They are creating nationwide political and social institutions as well as national systems of banking, taxation, and transportation.

One reflection of this simultaneity of structural change is that all the other social sciences now have interests in Asia, Africa, and Latin America which are counterparts to the interests of economists. What economists call development, political scientists call "modernization," sociologists, "role differentiation," and anthroplogists, "culture change." These accompanying political and social changes make economic-development processes even more complicated. Indeed, from a Western economist's viewpoint, a sort of non-Euclidean universe is sometimes created: If building roads and radio transmitters, in order to connect hitherto isolated regions in African countries, is thought to provide valuable integrating devices for increasing the political interaction among ethnically different citizens of what is now one nation and for spreading the usage of English or French, then cost-benefit analysts must guess at the worth of these amorphous political and linguistic benefits of roads and radios.

3. These countries are not only underdeveloped, they are also overexposed. By this I mean two things: They are pursuing development deliberately, consciously, and quickly; and they are following policies which, except for Japan and Soviet Russia, are outside the experience of the already developed nations. The United States and Britain developed less consciously, less as a matter of deliberate national effort, less as an urgent responsibility of governmental initiative. One consequence of current development as an effort of conscious purpose is that the economic policy of governments is pressing. Whatever one means by the economics of development, it is not a field or pure theory but an applied field. Neither Marshall nor Keynes invented economic theory with civil servants waiting in the next room to put it into

practice. A second consequence of this overexposure—the pressing public need to formulate development policy in the quick pursuit of higher income—is the creation of impossible expectations and therefore inevitable disappointments. Satisfaction or disappointment with development progress is a fraction, the numerator being realized results, the denominator, expectations. Rarely in the underdeveloped world does the fraction approach one.

There are other reasons, moreover, for built-in disappointment with realized results. Not only is development policy conscious, deliberate, and pressing; too often, as Wolfgang Stolper reminds us, it is made on the basis of fragmentary data. In primary producing countries, it should be remembered, economic policy is very much less autonomous than it is in developed economies. Underdeveloped countries are dependent upon external prices and financial aid to an unusual extent.

4. Finally, the least-developed one-third or more of the underdeveloped countries have what I shall call micro-development problems of a sort which are unfamiliar to Western economists but which in part are familiar to Western agricultural economists and rural sociologists: problems of how to transform subsistence agriculture and how to create more persons of entrepreneurial initiative.

To sum up: The reality of underdevelopment—the set of real-world circumstances to which economists address their theory—entails the following: wide diversity because of the large number of countries included; social, cultural, political, and economic complexity because of the simultaneous changes toward modernization being experienced; and the pressing need to make policy decisions within constraints set by inadequate information and exaggerated expectations.

We turn now to the second set of components which bear on our problem, those characteristics of economics which make some economists argue that conventional economics is irrelevant or downright misleading for the analysis of the processes and problems of development. Here I need only summarize what has been so clearly spelled out by Myrdal, Seers, Hagen, and others. It is useful, I think, to put these characteristics of economics into three sets that are by no means mutually exclusive.

1. Many economic concepts, such as the multiplier, and much economic analysis, such as the Keynesian theory of aggregate income determination, were contrived in response to the special problems (for example, chronic unemployment) of already industrialized, already developed, nationally integrated, large-scale market economies; underdeveloped countries have other problems for which neither the concepts nor the analysis is relevant.

2. Many economic concepts, such as the accelerator, and much economic analysis, such as growth theory, are interesting, useful, applicable—indeed, even operational—because of the special structure of already industrialized, already developed, nationally integrated, large-scale market economies; underdeveloped economies have different structures, and neither the concepts nor the analysis is relevant.

3. The leading ideas of economics, such as equilibrium analysis, and the inherited policy preferences of economists, such as laissez faire, reflect the special ethic of Anglo-America—a sort of Marshallian mentality—and the special political, social, and even religious institutions and traditions of Anglo-America. Africans, Asians, and Latin Americans have markedly different histories, social structures, and political experiences and therefore find the leading ideas and policy preferences of conventional economics uncongenial.

Among the development economists, two utterly different things are meant by "applying economic theory." It means a general method of approach used to identify problems, to measure sectoral relationships, and to put important questions to an economy. Here, the economist as diagnostician of structure and measurer of performance is useful in all underdeveloped countries. The second meaning is quite narrow: it is that the micro- and macro-market processes which economists analyze in developed economies somehow have functional equivalents in underdeveloped economies, and so the analyses and the policy conclusions drawn from them somehow can be directly "applied" in underdeveloped economies. This second meaning of "applying economic theory" is the one that rightly has been criticized.

One of the sad ironies of underdevelopment is that the less developed economically a country is, the less able it is to apply economic analysis and policy because of its social and political structures. Those countries needing economic improvement the most are the least capable of making effective use of both economic analysis and economic aid.

The interesting question is not: "Is economics relevant or irrelevant for underdeveloped countries?" This is not a good question because there is so much economics and so many underdeveloped countries. A better question is: "For which underdeveloped countries is what portion of economics directly relevant; and how must economics, where it is not relevant, be supplemented with socioeconomic analysis, and of what sort?"

The work of Irma Adelman and Cynthia Taft Morris serves as a point of departure. They have shown that a large set of underdeveloped countries can be divided into three groups, low, intermediate, and high, and that such a separation into subsets is analytically useful because the socioeconomic structures and the socioeconomic problems of development for each subset are markedly different.

At the lowest level of development are countries which are principally but not exclusively in sub-Saharan Africa and are overwhelmingly agricultural, having large subsistence sectors, a few primary commodities for export, little social capital, and few market institutions. In economic terms, these are not yet national economies, but rather congeries of primitive and peasant villages hardly linked at all to the national society, polity, or economy. Direct taxation and banking do not reach the bulk of the village communities, and markets transact considerably less than half of what is produced. There is no national integration culturally or politically; rather, there is ethnic and linguistic diversity. (The small West African country, Liberia, is in the middle of this lowest group. It is a "dual" economy and an "enclave" economy. Foreign

44

firms producing iron ore and rubber for export account for most of the commodities produced for sale.)

To this least developed subset of countries, whose economies, polities, and societies are least like those of developed nations, we can put the question: "How relevant is conventional economics to analyze their processes and problems?" The answer, I think, is that economics is necessary but not sufficient and that only a relatively small portion of that large set of concepts, theories, and measurements which we call economics is applicable.

The most directly applied economics in such countries is statistical measurement to establish quantitatively the nature of each one's structure and performance. The first job of the economist in such countries is to create or improve national income accounts and other hard-data series—to establish the factual base necessary to avoid costly mistakes.

The second job of the economist is that which former Secretary of Defense McNamara is reputed to have accomplished so successfully in the underdeveloped Pentagon: to establish cost-benefit criteria for making policy decisions. Here the economist is very much at home, whether he is at the Pentagon or in agricultural Nigeria. Economics is a gigantic machine to compare costs with benefits.

In the subset of least developed countries, there are other important jobs of analysis for economists to do, but these jobs are socioeconomic analyses, which require the economist (alone, or in collaboration with other social scientists) to analyze and make policy within the special institutional constraints of each country: how to transform subsistence agriculture, how to increase agricultural productivity, what kind of educational system to establish and with what priority of budgetary outlay.

If someone should tell me that conventional economics was not designed to answer such questions, I would agree; but I would also reply that neither does conventional sociology, anthropology, political science, or psychology answer such questions. And I would argue further that economists—from Marx and Veblen to Lewis and Hagen—have been notably more successful in doing socioeconomic analysis than the other social scientists have been in crossing over into socioeconomic analysis from their special subjects.

To sum up: For that subset of underdeveloped economies which is least developed, only a narrow range of economics is directly applicable, and the most formidable problems encountered are socioeconomic and purely political and social problems entailed in creating modern nationwide institutions.

Economic theory is culture-bound in the sense that its main lines of analysis relate to the special structures and problems of large-scale, industrialized, developed capitalist economies. Economic development, as done by economists, and economic anthropology, as done by anthropologists, are recent fields of specialization whose subject matter is a hundred or more national economies, on the one hand, and hundreds (if not thousands) of small-scale village economies, on the other, in Africa, Asia, Latin America, Oceania, and the Middle East. A large proportion of both sets of economies have economic and sociopolitical structures and problems markedly different from those of the already-developed economies. Except for the most advanced subset of the underdeveloped national economies, institutional processes and problems of a sort unfamiliar to economic analysis are pervasive, and they make necessary socioeconomic analyses of a novel sort. A number of economists—Myrdal, Lewis, Hagen, Adelman and Morris, and Polanyi—have already made important contributions to the socioeconomic analysis of underdeveloped national and village economies.

There is a methodological lesson to be learned from these literatures of contention in economic development and economic anthropology. The fact that intelligent men can disagree—and disagree rather heatedly—over long periods of time almost certainly means there are ingrained semantic difficulties underlying their disagreement. They are attaching different meanings to the same words. In both disciplines, the crucial words are "applying economic theory." The anthropologists think they are applying economic theory when they use the vocabulary of price theory to describe whatever transactions they observe in primitive economies. Instead of saying that a Trobriand Islander gives yams to his sister's husband partly to fulfill an obligation to his closest female relative and partly in recognition of her rights to land he is using, they say the Trobriander is "maximizing prestige." This is to use the terminology of economics as a fig-leaf to cover their theoretical nakedness.

The development economists who are critical of conventional economics are really saying that many underdeveloped countries have social and political processes and problems which impede economic development and have economic structures of a sort for which aggregative concepts like "gross investment" are not operational. They are right. However, the conclusion should be not to discard economics, but to learn about social and political processes, and to disaggregate.

UNEMPLOYMENT: LACK OF DEMAND, STRUCTURAL, OR TECHNOLOGICAL?

Walter W. Heller

Mr. Chairman and members of the committee, we are pleased to have an opportunity to participate in these hearings on employment and manpower. The employment problem is not only of the greatest importance to the country and at the center of government economic policy, but is of particular interest to an agency operating, as the council does, under the mandate of the Employment Act of 1946.

Recent discussions may have generated an impression of greater disagreement among the nation's economists about the origins and solutions of the employment problem than actually exists. For in fact, the great majority of those who have studied the matter carefully would agree with the administration's view that our excessive unemployment today cannot be traced to a single cause nor eliminated by a single cure. Rather, it has a mixture of causes which must be dealt with by a mixture—an amalgam—of cures.

One problem, and a central one, is that total expenditures in the economy —total demand for goods and services—are not sufficient to generate an adequate total number of jobs. We can, for convenience, call this kind of unemployment "demand-shortage" unemployment. In our view, demand-shortage unemployment can and must be attacked by vigorous policies— principally tax reduction—to raise the total demand for goods and services.

Another problem is that the characteristics of our available workers—their locations, skills, education, training, race, sex, age, and so on—do not fully match the characteristics employers are seeking in filling the jobs that are available (or that would be available at full employment). In a dynamic, changing economy there is always some of this mismatching, and we call the unemployment that results from it "frictional." But when the pockets of such

From the statement of Walter W. Heller, Chairman, accompanied by Gardiner Ackley and John P. Lewis, members of the Council of Economic Advisers, before the Subcommittee on Employment and Manpower of the Senate Committee on Labor and Public Welfare, October 28, 1963.

unemployment become large and stubborn—especially when they impose chronic burdens on particular disadvantaged groups and regions—we speak of the unemployment problem as "structural."

This type of unemployment is also a serious problem, which requires major policy actions to overcome its corrosive effects. Structural problems are not new. And the available evidence does not show that the proportion of our total unemployment problem that we label "structural" has increased significantly, nor that its character has materially changed. But this in no way diminishes the need for attacking these structural problems with vigorous policies—principally education, training and retraining, and special regional programs—to match the supply of labor skills more closely to the changing demand for labor skills.

Along with demand-shortage and structural unemployment, one also hears a great deal about the problem of "technological unemployment"—of men being put out of work by machines and, more particularly, by the process which has come to be called "automation." This is, indeed, a serious and continuing problem. But two points should be emphasized at the outset.

First, "technological unemployment" is not a third form of unemployment, separate from the other two. Rather, it expresses itself through these other forms. Technological change causes obsolescence of skills and therefore produces some of the mismatching between available workers and jobs that we call "structural" unemployment. Moreover, by raising output per worker, technological change is one of the principal sources of growth in our *potential* total output or GNP—which, if not matched by corresponding growth in *actual* GNP, opens a gap in demand and thereby causes demand-shortage unemployment.

Second, those who maintain that the economy now faces a problem of "technological unemployment" that is somehow new, and more formidable than in the past, implicitly assert that the rate of technological change has recently speeded up. Unless this is the case, the problem is not new—it has always been with us and has not proved to be a longrun problem for the economy as a whole. The continuing process of rapid technological change, which has constituted the very core of the American economy's strength and progressiveness for at least 150 years, has always put particular workers and businesses out of jobs and required particular adjustments that have been difficult and sometimes painful. It poses a new general problem for the economy only if technological change becomes so rapid that the demand adjustments and labor market adjustments it requires cannot be accomplished by the economic processes of the past. . . .

These, then—demand-shortage elements, structural elements, and a possible aggravation of both by accelerated technological change—are the principal ingredients of the unemployment problem your Committee is examining. It would be unwise and imprudent to ignore any of these ingredients either in diagnosing the problem or in prescribing remedies.

The primary attack on high unemployment must be through fiscal measures to speed the growth of total demand and thereby to create new job opportunities. But this need not—indeed, must not—impede a simultaneous attack on our stubborn structural problems. The two approaches are not merely complementary; they are mutually reinforcing. On the one hand, training and other programs to facilitate labor mobility can ease and speed the process by which demand-stimulated increases in output are translated into increases in employment. On the other, since structural maladjustments tend to flourish in slack markets, a vigorous expansion in demand helps cut structural problems down to size. . . .

UNEMPLOYMENT AND TAX REDUCTION

The American economy has been plagued with persistently excessive unemployment for six years. The unemployment rate has been five percent or more for 71 consecutive months. Since 1957, it has averaged six percent. Even in the face of annual advances of about $30 billion in GNP (annual rate), unemployment has not been diminishing. Thus, although GNP rose from $556.8 billion in the third quarter of 1962 to $588.5 billion in the third quarter of 1963, the unemployment rate remained the same in both quarters. And even with a prospective increase of $100 billion in the GNP rate from early 1961 to early 1964 (a rise of 20 percent in current dollars and about 15 percent in constant dollars), the unemployment rate will have come down only about one and one-half percentage points in that three-year period.

The persistence of this high level of unemployment is sometimes cited as evidence of structural difficulties which will blunt the effect of the proposed $11 billion tax cut now being considered by the Senate Finance Committee and make it difficult to reach the interim full-employment goal of four-percent unemployment, let alone our ultimate goals beyond the four-percent level. The structural problem will be examined in some detail later in this statement. But here, several points should be noted to indicate why the road to four-percent unemployment is clearly open to demand-powered measures.

1. The pre-1957 postwar performance of the U.S. economy gives ample evidence of its ability to achieve four percent and even lower levels of unemployment without excessive strain.

2. The availability of 1.1 million excess unemployed workers (even by the modest four-percent criterion and not counting the labor force dropouts resulting from slack job opportunities) and of substantial excess capacity (even after large gains, the average operating rate in manufacturing is running at only 87 percent of capacity) demonstrates that we are still suffering from a serious shortage of consumer investment and demand.

3. There are virtually no signs of economic tension, of the barriers that would divert the force of demand stimulus away from higher output, more jobs, and higher incomes into higher prices—there are no visible bottlenecks in the economy, wage rate increases have been the most moderate in the postwar period, and the record of price stability in recent years has been outstanding.

In reference to the first point, the unemployment rates in the first postwar decade deserve a further word. In the period of vigorous business activity in 1947 and 1948, unemployment averaged 3.8 percent of the labor force. After the recession of 1949 and the recovery of 1950, the rate was relatively stable from early 1951 to late 1953, averaging 3.1 percent. Since that time, the rate has drifted upward. In the period of stable unemployment from mid-1955 to late 1957, unemployment averaged 4.3 percent, an increase of more than one-third above the 1951-53 period. In the first half of 1960, unemployment averaged 5.3 percent, nearly one-fourth above the 1955-57 level. Following the recession and recovery of 1960-61, the rate fluctuated within a narrow range averaging 5.6 percent in 1962 and 1963 to date, a little higher than early 1960. Looking at the 1947-57 period, the average unemployment rate was below four percent in each of the following years: 1947, 1948, 1951, 1952, and 1953, and below four and one-half percent in 1955, 1956, and 1957.

When one looks behind these figures to get a grasp of the economic conditions that produced them, the most notable difference between the pre-1957 and post-1957 periods is found in the strength of market demand. In the first postwar decade, markets were strong. Backlogs of consumer demand had to be worked off. The demands of the Korean conflict had to be met. Outmoded plants and equipment had to be replaced or modernized, and capacity had to be enlarged. Deficiencies in housing, office facilities, and public works had to be made up.

But 1957 marked a watershed. In the ensuing period, demand has slackened at a time when our labor force growth has been accelerating in response to the postwar jump in the birth rate. Business-fixed investment dropped off from 10-11 percent of the GNP to only nine percent—indeed, the level of such investment in 1962 barely struggled back to its level in 1956, while GNP was rising by nearly one-fifth (both in constant prices).

Thus, the clearest and most striking change since 1957 is the weakening of demand. So the clearest and most urgent need today is to remove the over-burden of taxation which is retarding the growth in demand to full employment levels. Income tax rates enacted to finance war and fight inflation—though reduced in 1954—are still so high that they would yield a large surplus of revenues over expenditures if we were at full employment today. They are, in short, repressing demand and incentives in an economy operating well short of its capacity.

To avoid misunderstanding, it is important to stress that any employment program would be unbalanced and incomplete without determined measures (a) to upgrade and adapt the skills and education of the labor force to the more exacting demands of our advancing technology and (b) to facilitate the flow of workers from job to job, industry to industry, and place to place. Nevertheless, our principal reliance for a return to the four-percent-or-better levels of unemployment we took for granted in the early postwar period must be on measures to boost demand for the products of American industry and agriculture.

The amount of the increase in total demand which would be necessary to reduce unemployment to the four-percent interim-target level can be approximated in several ways. We have made direct estimates of the relationship between unemployment rates and output levels; and we have independently estimated the potential GNP that the economy could produce at four-percent unemployment. Both of these approaches yield consistent estimates of the output and demand requirements associated with four-percent unemployment at a given time. Except for small differences reflecting cyclical variations in productivity and erratic fluctuations in labor force participation rates, these estimates of potential output (in constant prices) are very closely approximated by a three and one-half percent trend line passing through actual GNP in mid-1955. The several methods of computing potential GNP were reviewed in some detail in our *Annual Reports* both for 1962 and 1963, and are analyzed more fully in a recent paper by one of the council's consultants. Although estimates of this kind cannot be precise—and efforts to improve and update them as new data come in must continue—the careful crosschecking by different methods provides confidence in their general order of magnitude.

These estimates show that the gap between actual GNP and the potential GNP at four-percent unemployment has been substantial in every year since 1957. In both 1962 and 1963, it has approximated $30 billion.

Our analysis thus suggests that total demands for goods and services would have had to average some $30 billion higher than it was in each of these past two years for unemployment to average four percent. The basic purpose of the tax cut is to close that $30 billion gap—and to realize the benefits to employment, growth, and our international competitive position that will flow from this advance.

To be sure, by the time the full effects of the proposed two-stage tax cut will be reflected in demand and output, the economy's potential will have grown considerably, and total demand growth will therefore have to be considerably more than $30 billion. But when the tax cut lifts the expanding level of private demand in the United States economy by the extra $30 billion (in terms of 1963 GNP and price levels) that can confidently be expected, it will have achieved its basic purpose. Had this increase been effective during the past six years, it would have eliminated our persistent slack and allowed our unemployment rate to average four percent.

The process by which an $11.1 billion tax cut can add as much as $30 billion to total demand has been frequently described and needs only to be summarized briefly here.

If the new proposed personal income tax rates were in full effect today, disposable after-tax incomes of consumers would be approximately $8.8 billion higher than they are, at present levels of pretax incomes. In addition, if the lower corporate tax rates were now in effect, after-tax profits would be about $2.3 billion higher. Based on past dividend practice, one can assume that corporate dividends received by individuals (after deducting personal income taxes on such dividends) would then be more than $1 billion higher, giving a total increment of consumer aftertax incomes—at present levels of production—of about $10 billion.

Since consumer spending on current output has remained close to 93 percent of disposable income in each of the past dozen years, one can safely project that consumer spending would rise by about 93 percent of the rise in disposable incomes, or by over $9 billion.

But this is far from the end of the matter. The higher production of consumer goods to meet this extra spending would mean extra employment, higher payrolls, higher profits, and higher farm and professional service incomes. This added purchasing power would generate still further increases in spending and incomes in an endless, but rapidly diminishing chain. The initial rise of $9 billion, plus this extra consumption spending and extra output of consumer goods, would add over $18 billion to our annual GNP—not just once, but year-in and year-out, since this is a permanent, not a one-shot, tax cut. We can summarize this continuing process by saying that a "multiplier" of approximately two has been applied to the direct increment of consumption spending.

But that is not the end of the matter either. For the higher volume of sales, the higher productivity associated with fuller use of existing capacity, and the lower tax rates on corporate profits also provided by the tax bill would increase aftertax profits, and especially the rate of expected aftertax profit on investment in new facilities. Adding to this the financial incentives embodied in last year's tax changes, which are yet to have their full effect, one can expect a substantial induced rise in business plant and equipment spending, and a rise in the rate of inventory investment. Further, higher consumer incomes will stimulate extra residential construction; and the higher revenues that state and local governments will receive under existing tax rates will prompt a rise in their investments in schools, roads, and urban facilities. The exact amount of each of these increases is hard to estimate with precision. But it is reasonable to estimate their sum as in the range of $5 to $7 billion. This extra spending would also be subject to a multiplier of 2 as incomes rose and consumer spending increased. Thus there would be a further expansion of $10 to $14 billion in GNP to add to the $18 billion or so from the consumption factor alone. The total addition to GNP would match rather closely the estimated $30 billion gap.

THE PERSISTENT PROBLEMS OF STRUCTURAL UNEMPLOYMENT

The tax cut would thus increase demand to levels consistent with a four-percent rate of unemployment. It would ease our most pressing unemployment problems. But no one can assume that our worries about unemployment would then be over. Some of its most distressing and inequitable aspects would remain.

To be sure, tax reduction will create new jobs in every community across the nation and expand employment in every industry. The overwhelming majority of American families will benefit directly from the income tax cuts that will accrue to 50 million taxpaying individuals and 600,000 taxpaying corporations. Their direct rise in aftertax income will soon be translated, through the marketplace, into stronger markets for all kinds of goods and services and a quickening of the business pulse in all communities. With average working hours already at a high level, this added demand and activity will in large part be translated, in turn, into additional jobs, and income for the unemployed. Thus, the nontaxpaying minority will, in a very real sense, be the greatest beneficiaries of the tax program.

Experience . . . clearly shows (1) that the unemployment rate will decline for every major category of workers and (2) that the sharpest declines will occur where the incidence of unemployment is the highest: among teenagers, the Negroes, the less-skilled, the blue-collar groups generally.

But even so, the unemployment rates of many groups will still be intolerably high. Back in 1957, for instance, when the average unemployment rate was just over four percent for the whole economy, the rates were much higher for many disadvantaged groups and regions—e.g., 10.8 percent for teenagers, 8.0 percent for nonwhites, 9.4 percent for unskilled manual workers, and 11.5 percent for workers in Wilkes-Barre, Hazleton, Pennsylvania.

These *high specific unemployment rates, which persist even when the general rate falls to an acceptable level,* are the essence of the problem of structural unemployment. Even a fully successful tax cut cannot solve problems like these by itself. They require a more direct attack.

To reduce the abnormally high and stubborn unemployment rate for Negroes requires a major improvement in their education and training and an attack on racial discrimination. To reduce the persistent high rate for the unskilled and the uneducated groups demands measures to help them acquire skills and knowledge. To reduce excessive unemployment associated with declining industries and technological advance requires retraining and relocation. To reduce high unemployment in distressed areas of Pennsylvania, Michigan, Minnesota, and elsewhere calls for special measures to rebuild the economic base of those communities and assist their workers.

Both the Administration and the Congress have recognized that these measures must be taken concurrently with measures to expand aggregate demand. Coal miners in Harlan County are structurally unemployed *now,* and so are Negro and Puerto Rican youths in New York City. Yet, programs to reduce structural unemployment will run into severe limits *in the absence of an adequate growth of demand,* i.e., in the absence of rapid expansion of total job opportunities. Such expansion is needed to assure that retrained and upgraded workers, for example, *will* find jobs at the end of the training period and *will not* do so at the expense of job opportunities for other unemployed workers. As structural programs create new and upgraded skills, they will in some cases fit the participants for jobs that had previously gone begging. But for the most part, the needed jobs must be created by expansion of total demand.

Quite apart from the human significance of structural unemployment, it also has great economic importance. For only as we reduce structural and frictional unemployment can we achieve the higher levels of total output which would be associated with unemployment rates below our four-percent interim target. The council emphasized this point in its 1963 *Annual Report* (p. 42), as follows:

Success in a combined policy of strengthening demand and adopting manpower supplies to evolving needs would enable us to achieve an interim objective of 4-percent unemployment and permit us to push beyond it in a setting of reasonable price stability. Bottlenecks in skilled labor, middle-level manpower, and professional personnel [now] tend to become acute as unemployment approaches 4 percent. The result is to retard growth and generate wage-price pressures at particular points in the economy. As we widen or break these bottlenecks by intensified and flexible educational, training, and re-training efforts, our employment sights will steadily rise.

Every worker needlessly unemployed represents a human cost which offends the sensibilities of a civilized society. But each worker needlessly unemployed also represents a waste of potential goods and services, which even an affluent society can ill afford. More intensive measures to attack structural unemployment are necessary to reduce the unemployment rate not merely to four percent, but beyond. . . .

B.

Problems and Policies

WHY A RISING FEDERAL DEBT IS NO CAUSE FOR ALARM

David B. McCalmont

... Editorials and public speeches frequently express the widely felt alarm regarding increases in the federal debt: "We are hopelessly burdening our grandchildren"—"A larger debt requires larger interest payments, and these will require higher tax rates"—"We've got to begin paying back sometime. We're only postponing the day of reckoning"—"If the national debt continues to rise, our nation will go bankrupt."

A large majority of economists and an increasing number of business and political leaders are finding such arguments unconvincing for reasons that will be set forth here. The weight and importance of any debt, it will be argued, depend upon its size in relation to the debtor's income and assets. A $100,000 debt, which would indeed be burdensome to a man with only $150,000 worth of assets and an income of $6,000 a year, would be of little importance to a man with assets of $15,000,000 and an income of $600,000.

From *Business Horizons,* Fall 1964, pp. 65-71. Copyright 1964 by the Foundation for the School of Business, at Indiana University. Reprinted by permission.

Similarly, the debt of a nation should be judged not by its absolute size but by its size relative to national income and wealth.

Debt always has two sides. If indebtedness increases, someone becomes the owner of a new claim against the debtor. To this owner, the new debt constitutes "wealth," and the interest paid on the debt is "income."

GROWTH OF THE PRIVATE DEBT

We take these things for granted when considering the debt incurred by nongovernmental corporations and by individuals. When we notice that the outstanding indebtedness of Columbia Gas System, Inc. has increased more than 50 percent since 1956, we are not fearful for the safety of that enterprise, because we know that its assets and income have also increased. Similarly, we need not be alarmed when we notice that total private debt in the United States rose by $672 billion between 1945 and 1963—an increase of 435 percent—and that by December 1963 this debt had reached the unprecedented high of $826 billion (see Figure 1).

At first this seems a staggering debt for American business firms and consumers to bear. Yet little concern is expressed. Now and again some mild worry has been voiced regarding the growth of credit buying by consumers. However, consumer credit amounted in December 1963 to only $70 billion. The rest of the $826 billion of private debt was business debt.[1]

Figure 1. Gross Private Debt, 1930-1963 (end of calendar year)

[1] Even if one includes as consumer debt all the mortgages on homes, consumer debt was only a third of the $826 billion total.

Americans have not been alarmed by this enormous increase in private debt because they have been wise enough to realize that, even though it is huge, it is nevertheless smaller in proportion to total assets and incomes than in 1930 (see Figure 2).

GROWTH OF THE FEDERAL DEBT

A look at the growth of private debt in the United State provides a more realistic perspective from which to view the growth and level of the federal debt.[2] In 1930 the federal debt was a mere $16 billion; even by 1940 it was still only $51 billion. The war effort against Hitler raised it to $279 billion, but since the end of World War II it has risen only $31 billion, or 11 percent. During this same period, private debt, as we have seen, rose by 435 percent.

Growing private debts, it is often argued, are backed by the growing income-producing abilities and market values of the debtors' business assets, while federal debt is said to have no comparable "backing." This objection that comparisons between private debt and governmental debt are beside the point underestimates the power of the federal income tax. With this tax, the government can, if need be, reach all income and all income-producing

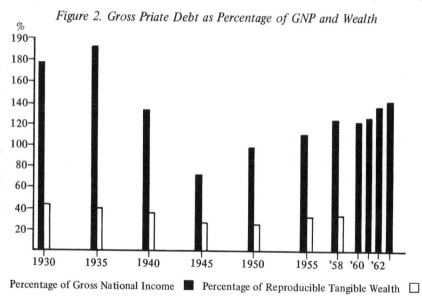

Figure 2. Gross Priate Debt as Percentage of GNP and Wealth

Percentage of Gross National Income ■   Percentage of Reproducible Tangible Wealth ☐

---

[2] There are several different concepts of federal debt. We will deal with the gross concept called the "public debt" because this is the one that figures most prominently in the news. The public debt excludes the unguaranteed debt of federal agencies like the Federal National Mortgage Association but includes the U.S. securities owned by federal agencies and trust funds.

property in the country. Thus all such income and property is, in a very real sense, backing for the public debt.

National Income and Wealth

Relating the federal debt to the gross national income (GNP) and to total wealth is, therefore, both realistic and legitimate.[3] Figure 3 shows each year's debt as percentages of both GNP and the tangible wealth with which it was associated. The percentage of GNP in 1963 was less than half as large as in 1945. In relation to income, in other words, the federal debt in 1963 was less than half as important as it was in 1945, because national income had grown about 170 percent during this period while the federal debt had grown about 11 percent.

Similarly, the nation's wealth grew so rapidly after 1945 that in 1958 (the most recent year for which such information is available) the federal debt was less than half as important, relative to national wealth, as it was in 1945. Yet in 1945 the United States showed no sign of being in danger of collapse because of the burden of its debt. Today far less danger exists.

In judging the significance of future increases in the federal debt, we must not compare it with present levels of GNP and wealth, for neither of these will remain frozen at its present level. Estimates of the expected rate of growth in GNP range from three percent to five percent per year. Assuming a four percent rate, GNP can be expected to grow at least $24 billion a year in

Figure 3. Federal Debt as Percentage of GNP and Wealth, 1930-1963

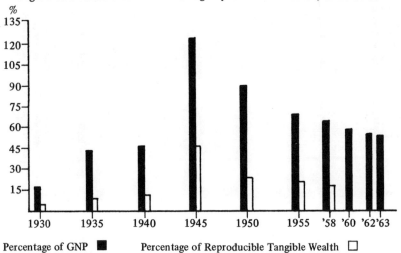

Percentage of GNP ■   Percentage of Reproducible Tangible Wealth □

---

[3] In national income accounting, "gross national product" (GNP) and "gross national income" are identical. We will therefore use the terms interchangeably.

the immediate future and to increase even more in later years as the four percent rate is applied to a larger and larger base. With income growth of this magnitude, the federal debt could be permitted to grow $12 billion a year (about four percent of the present $310 billion debt) without becoming a larger percentage of GNP.

. . .INFLATION AND THE DEBT

Wartime analogies inevitably raise the issue of the connection between the national debt and inflation. Because increases in the price level during the war and the immediate postwar period occurred simultaneously with increases in the federal debt, people are prone to reason that any increase in the debt is inflationary. The cause of the wartime and postwar inflationary pressure, however, was not the high level of the federal debt nor the fact that it was increasing, but only that the increase was too rapid in relation to the 1940-45 productive capacity. Deficits incurred to fight World War II were too large in relation to the slack then existing in the economy; the federal government ran deficits totaling $218 billion, an average deficit of $43 billion a year, at a time when GNP was rising from only $101 billion a year to $214 billion. The average annual deficit amounted to almost 24 percent of the average GNP during that five-year period. Small wonder that total demand exceeded total capacity and that prices moved upward! Considering that GNP for the first quarter of 1964 was $609 billion, a comparable deficit at the present time would be about $145 billion a year.

Most economists would agree that a federal deficit of $145 billion in fiscal 1965 would be inflationary. But it by no means follows that a deficit of $25 billion a year (and the resulting increase in GNP) would substantially disturb the price level. As for the mere $2.7 billion deficit proposed by the Administration for fiscal 1965 in the national income accounts budget, any upward effect it might have upon the price level may well be negligible.

This conclusion is reached because there is still much slack in the American economy today [1965]. The number of persons totally unemployed has been running in excess of five percent of the civilian labor force. In addition, some 2,000,000 workers who desire full-time jobs but can obtain only part-time work have been losing productive time roughly equivalent to 670,000 fully unemployed persons. Altogether this amounts to unemployment of roughly 5.9 percent of the labor force.

In most industries production is still at a level substantially below that at which unit costs might be expected to rise. The consumer price index, which some economists believe contains a built-in upward bias, has nevertheless risen a total of only 3.8 percent in the past three years (April 1961 to April 1964), while the wholesale price index has remained unchanged. In such an economic climate substantial general price increases are not greatly to be feared.

But what about periods when plants are running more nearly at capacity and when the unemployment rate is below two percent of the labor force? At such times the federal government would not desire to stimulate the economy and would therefore (barring war) not be adding to its debt. So the issue would be academic.

INTEREST PAYMENTS

After worries about inflation have been put aside, the problem of interest payments comes next. If the public debt grows, we are told, more tax money must be raised to pay interest, thus requiring higher tax rates.

In the first place, there is no ironclad necessity that all the money to pay interest on the federal debt be obtained by taxation. If the government has decided that a deficit is desirable for the stimulation of the economy, it could achieve that deficit simply by making some or all of its interest payments with borrowed money. If it did so, there would be less need of revenue from federal taxes, not more.

Yet even if taxes remain the only source of interest payments, persons who worry about the burden of the debt forget that unchanged tax rates can and do bring in increasing revenues in measure as the national income increases. To judge the significance of larger annual interest payments on a larger federal debt, therefore, such payments must be compared with the national income with which they are associated.

Figure 4 shows that the computed annual interest payments on the public debt as of mid-1964 were a smaller percentage of the nation's gross income (1.8 percent) than they were in 1946 (2.5 percent), and also that, from 1955 to 1964, interest payments remained about the same percentage of the growing GNP. Actually, the amount paid out as interest would have become smaller in relation to GNP if the level of interest rates, on private as well as on public obligations, had not risen drastically after 1954. . . .

Figure 4. Interest on the Federal Debt as Percentage of GNP, 1920-1964

Even if interest payments were to become an amount equal to a larger percentage of GNP than they are now, there would be no increased "burden" on the economy as a whole. Americans own 95 percent of all federal securities. Accordingly, nearly all of the $7.5 billion in interest payments in 1963 was merely transferred to the personal and corporate incomes of American recipients. The larger these annual interest payments become, the greater will be this contribution to the financial well-being of the American families and businesses that receive them. Neither we nor our grandchildren, therefore, have anything to fear from the "burden" of growing interest charges on a growing federal debt.

ABOUT THOSE GRANDCHILDREN

Those who deplore the national debt worry unceasingly about the evil effect that they believe its enlargement will have on our grandchildren. Let us pause to examine the conditions of life of these unfortunate grandchildren who are to be so grievously burdened by our alleged "fiscal profligacy." Whether these unhappy grandchildren will be living 10, 20, or 40 years from now is not very clear; 20 years would be a reasonable compromise.

Thanks to the medical research paid for and executed mostly by previous generations, our grandchildren of 1984 will receive far superior medical service, will suffer less pain, and will have a longer life expectancy than the present generation. Technological advance and capital accumulation, also paid for and executed mostly by their predecessors, will enable them to enjoy a level of living that will make the present level look very modest by comparison.

Consider the improvement over the last 20 years in the average American's aftertax income, even after full allowance is made for the increase in the price level. In 1943, per capita income after taxes (converted to dollars of 1963 purchasing power) was only $1,704. In 1963 (in dollars of the same purchasing power) it was about $2,127, an increase of 25 percent.

Between 1964 and 1984 technological progress is not likely to slow down; indeed, it may well accelerate. Even if it merely holds its own with past performance, our grandchildren living in 1984 will have real aftertax personal incomes of about $2,800 per year per capita. In the year 1962 the median multiperson family income was about $6,750. In 1984 it is likely to be at least $8,600, measured in dollars of the same purchasing power, and it might well be as high as $12,000. These are the people on whose behalf the parents and grandparents of today are being asked to exercise "fiscal restraint" and to economize by doing without enough education, enough housing, and enough jobs!

Apart from all this, the argument that enlarging the federal debt will burden our grandchildren is based upon two false assumptions: (1) that the grandchildren will have to repay the debt, and (2) that their payments will have to be made to someone other than themselves. Neither assumption is valid.

As we have already seen, the private sector of our economy never pays off all its debt. Individual firms do pay off individual obligations. However, except at time of severest depression, new borrowing always exceeds repayments made on the old. Decade by decade, private debt *in toto* has continued to rise. Decade by decade it will continue to rise. Our grandchildren will not have to "pay it off" because it will never be "paid off."

There is no more reason why the governmental sector, as a whole, should pay off its debt. Individual government bond issues can and will be retired, but new borrowing will always exceed these repayments. This procedure is normal and proper for governmental units as well as for business firms in a growing economy.

However, assuming for the sake of argument that the federal debt were to be paid off 20 years from now, to whom would the repayments be made? Inasmuch as only five percent of our national debt is owed to foreigners, practically all of the repayments would be received by our grandchildren. Grandchildren would pay; grandchildren would receive. In the case of individual grandchildren, the amounts paid and received might not balance, but for grandchildren as a group there would be no loss of income or wealth—unless higher tax rates were needed to accomplish the repayment and unless these rates impaired taxpayers' incentive to produce, thus diminishing the amount of human energy and risk capital devoted to production.

All of this, however, is academic because the debt can and will continue to grow and never need be paid off. Accordingly, we shall not involve ourselves here with the much debated issue of whether higher tax rates dull or sharpen the incentive to produce.

So far as the well-being of our grandchildren is concerned, then, the advocates of federal deficits have the stronger case. The level of living enjoyed by our descendants will depend upon their own productivity. This in turn will depend in no small measure upon the quantity and quality of the capital equipment—the roads, harbors, houses, and manufacturing plants—that we build and pass on to them and upon the amount of education and health service that we provide for them in their childhood. If this inheritance of capital goods, education, and health can be enlarged by incurring a larger federal debt, then a debt increase is a positive benefit to our grandchildren.

CAN A NATION GO BANKRUPT?

But neither we nor our grandchildren can be benefited, it is said, because the nation will go bankrupt. When a private debtor becomes bankrupt, a court frees it from any obligation to make any future payments to the creditors. A sovereign nation needs no discharge in bankruptcy in this sense, for no one can sue a sovereign state without its consent. What people mean when they talk about "national bankruptcy" is that they fear the federal government will be obliged to default on its debts.

No basis for such a fear exists with respect to the United States. When the U.S. Treasury markets a new issue of federal securities in order to raise money to pay off maturing issues, the question is always: "What rate of interest must the Treasury offer in order that the market will absorb the issues?" never: "*Will* the market absorb the issue?" Remember that the federal debt does not mature all in one lump. As of October 31, 1963, for example, only $135 billion was subject to redemption at the demand of the public within one year's time.

The public possesses so much confidence in the worth of federal obligations that they are bought even though their yields are lower than those of private securities. This is because buyers take rational account of the fact that the taxing power and the power to control the banking system are more dependable guarantees of repayment than are the sales revenues of private firms.

ADVANTAGE OF A LARGER DEBT

Few critics of a growing federal debt stop to consider that federal securities play an extremely useful role in our economy quite apart from anything that the government may do with the borrowed money. If there were no federal debt, we could not feel wealthy and secure because of our possession of treasury securities or because of the possession of such securities by our insurance companies or savings and loan associations. If the federal debt did not grow in tune with the growth of the nation, both private and institutional investors would have to venture their funds to a greater and greater degree upon the purchase of private indebtedness.

If our banks, insurance companies, and savings and loan associations were obliged to substitute private securities for federal, they would become either less safe as repositories of our savings or else greater risks to federal insuring agencies. On the other hand, if our financial institutions felt it necessary to compensate for the decreased safety of their investment holdings by becoming more conservative in their choice of private borrowers and by decreasing the percentage of loans in their total assets, they would be obliged to withdraw financial support from many a new and promising innovation or enterprise that otherwise would have become a reality. Viewed in this light, a growing federal debt is a positive benefit.

The federal debt, we must conclude, poses no menace to the American people. Viewed against the background of rapidly increasing national income and wealth, the debt is moderate in size and has been shrinking, relatively, ever since 1945. But whatever its size, it shows on both sides of the nation's balance sheet of assets and liabilities, so that its net burden is negligible. Our constantly growing income-tax base makes possible the payment of ever larger amounts of interest out of taxes, if so desired, without the need of increased tax rates and without the emergence of the transfer effects feared by some observers.

Clearly, worries regarding the growth of the national debt should no longer deter our government from incurring whatever future deficits may be required to cause the national income and output to grow at a rate consonant with the full potential of the American economy.

THE GERMAN NIGHTMARE

Donald B. Woodward and Marc A. Rose

The war put a severe strain on the German economy, but the depreciation of the mark was not beyond recovery; after the armistice, the mark was quoted at about 12 cents.

Then came the peace negotiations. When the full weight of the terms imposed under the Treaty of Versailles became apparent, the Germans felt their situation hopeless—and so did financiers in other countries. The new government's financial difficulties kept increasing. The nation's debt was heavy, and much of it was not funded.

MONETIZING THE DEBT

It was necessary to resort to the expedient of printing marks, mere fiat money, to pay the government's expenses. By early 1920, the mark was worth about one cent, gold. The decline was checked at that point, and there was even some improvement; but late in 1921, the mark began to sink again in terms of foreign exchange. Reparations had been fixed at 132,000,000,000 gold marks, or some $33,000,000,000. More and more, Germany was completely discouraged at the outlook; financial recovery looked impossible, and the occupation of the Ruhr in January, 1923, seemed to show that the harder the Germans tried to beat their way upward the more the demands that would be made upon them.

The Treasury proceeded to issue bills to the Reichsbank at an accelerating rate, discounting them for paper money. The printing presses ran more and more rapidly; pieces of currency were issued in denominations of millions of marks. Prices, of course, kept rising, which steadily increased the government's expenses and made it necessary to print more money. The spiral was started; nothing, it seemed, could break it. Under the conditions, there was little incentive to try.

The banks, which had participated very little at the outset, began to discount bills at the Reichsbank and to increase their loans and deposits. Ultimately, the municipalities began to issue money, also the railroads, and many other institutions. Metal coins previously used for small change disappeared into hoarding or were converted into paper, the bullion content being worth vastly more than the stamped value of the coins.

Before the war, the total money in circulation in Germany had averaged about 6,000,000,000 marks. At the end of 1923, the authorized circulation was 518,000,000,000,000,000,000—518 billions of billions. No estimate ever has been attempted of the amount of other currencies in circulation. Conditions were utterly chaotic.

In November 1923, the situation was taken in hand. A new currency unit, the rentenmark, was established, its value put at 1,000,000,000,000—a million million—of the marks it was to supersede. The new rentenmark was fixed at parity with the prewar mark—that is, at 23 cents. Incidentally, it was pure fiat money, but its value was successfully controlled in terms of gold.

The Dawes plan was made effective in 1924, fixing Germany's obligations to the outside world at a point more nearly within reason. With that encouragement, the reichsmark was established on a gold basis, also at 23 cents.

THE CONSEQUENCES OF HYPERINFLATION

That was the end of inflation. Behind this bare story of the course of events are a million human comedies and tragedies. No one ever will record even a small part of them. But some of the most fantastic and absurd incidents are remembered.

As this one: the total German mortgage debt before the war was about 40,000,000,000 marks. At the peak of the inflation, 40,000,000,000 marks were worth less than a cent. All the mortgages in Germany could have been paid off for one cent, American. A box of matches sold for more than 6,000,000,000 marks, which it will be remembered was the total amount of money in circulation in Germany in prewar years.

Things happened as in a fever-ridden dream. Prices changed by the hour. Before the summit was reached, a ham sandwich was quoted at 14,000 marks one day and 24,000 marks the next. An article in a retail store priced at 5,000,000,000 marks in the morning had increased to 12,000,000,000 by afternoon. A sheet of writing paper cost 120 marks—$30 dollars at prewar exchange—while yet the inflation was young. Interest rates rose to 900 percent, and even then lenders at times were not protected, because by the time they were paid—even tenfold—the sum they received was worth less than the sum they lent.

What this meant in terms of human hardship can easily be imagined. Savings patiently built up by a lifetime of thrift might buy as much as a package of cigarettes. Life insurance policies matured—and the proceeds would not buy a handkerchief. It might be cheaper to light a cigar with a bond than to buy a match. The thrifty were penalized; the only wise folk were the spendthrifts. The nation became a spendthrift one, of course; everyone who received money rushed madly to convert it into goods. Things would be worth more tomorrow, perhaps this very afternoon. Money would be worth less. Debts were wiped out; farm mortgages were paid off with a sack of potatoes.

Translated into economic jargon, the creditor class was ruined; debtors were freed. People who had lived on investments were paupers.

The government tried to protect its citizens but could not do much. Prices of necessities were fixed from time to time to assure people of food and a roof over their heads, but fixing prices at a reasonable level one day did not solve the problem the next. Wages were moved up frequently—in the early stages, every month, then every 10 days, but they always lagged behind the cost of living. The principle of fixing wages on a sliding scale geared to the cost of living was adopted, but it never was very popular with labor, because most workingmen did not understand its complexities, and those who did protested that the scale was inadequate. Labor troubles were widespread.

While great classes were being pauperized, other skillful manipulators were becoming fabulously wealthy. The speculators' method was to borrow money, buy goods or real estate or factories, then pay off the debt in worthless money. Then they could either keep the tangibles or sell them and repeat the operation.

Business of course boomed, for everyone was buying goods. A great boom developed in the stock market, from the scramble to buy shares in tangible properties.

Toward the close of the era, many localities began to quote prices in foreign currencies, usually dollars. Various institutions issued scrip redeemable in goods—rye, barley, coal, wood, and even kilowatt hours.

It was impossible, obviously, to plan ahead in terms of paper money. Construction and similar industries languished.

After monetary stabilization, there was a brief depression, but business did not for long stay inordinately dull, since there had been an accumulation of demands for goods and services that could not be supplied during the inflation —demands for new homes and improved factories, for example. So recovery progressed with reasonable rapidity.

But profound changes had been made in the social structure. There were new rich and new poor. The middleclass, by and large, suffered most. The very poor had had little to lose; many of the wealthy had known how to protect themselves. Businesses emerged with most of their debts wiped out.

THE CONCEPT OF THE FULL EMPLOYMENT BUDGET SURPLUS

Council of Economic Advisers

... The federal budget has influenced economic activity in recent years in two ways: through the workings of the built-in stabilizers, and through discretionary changes in the budget program. It is not easy to separate these two influences. In order to do so, it is necessary, first, to view federal fiscal transactions in the same accounting framework used to describe the whole economy. The *national income accounts budget* is a way of measuring and classifying federal transactions which accords with the national income and product accounts for the economy. Second, it is convenient to have a numerical measure of the expansionary or restrictive impact of a budget program on the economy. The *full employment surplus* is such a measure. This section discusses these two somewhat unfamiliar but highly useful tools and then applies them in an analysis of recent and prospective budget policies.

THE NATIONAL INCOME ACCOUNTS BUDGET

The effects of federal receipts and expenditures on the income stream are most accurately represented when the budget is viewed in the framework of the national income accounts. These accounts present a consistent record and classification of the major flows of output and income for the entire economy, including the transactions of the federal government. There are three major differences between the federal budget as it is conventionally presented (the so-called "administrative budget") and the accounts of the federal sector as they appear in the national income. The major differences between these two budgets, and between both of them and the consolidated cash budget, are schematically summarized in Figure 1. There are other, less significant

From *Annual Report of the Council of Economic Advisers,* January 1962, pp. 77-81.

Figure 1. Major Differences Among Three Concepts of the Federal Budget

Item	Budget Concept		
	Administrative	Consolidated Cash	National Income Accounts
Timing of receipts	Collections	Collections	Accruals
Treatment of net loans and other credit transactions	Included	Included	Excluded
Treatment of trust fund transactions	Excluded	Included	Included

Source: Council of Economic Advisers.

differences among the budgets, such as the treatment of intragovernmental transactions.

First, the national income accounts budget, like the consolidated cash budget, includes the transactions of the trust funds, which amount currently to about $25 billion per year and have a significant impact on the economy. Highway grants-in-aid, unemployment compensation payments, and social security benefits are examples of trust fund transactions. Because the traditional budget—or administrative budget—is primarily an instrument of management and control of those federal activities which operate through regular congressional appropriations, it excludes the trust funds, which have their own legal sources of revenue.

Second, transactions between government and business are, so far as possible, recorded in the national income accounts budget when liabilities are incurred rather than when cash changes hands. This adjustment in timing affects both government purchases and taxes, shifting them to the point in time at which they are likely to have their principal impact on private spending decisions. The choice of an accrual, rather than a cash, basis for timing is particularly important for the highly volatile corporate income tax. Since these taxes are normally paid more than six months after the liabilities are incurred, payments of corporate income taxes, as recorded in the administrative budget, run substantially below accruals in a period of rising economic activity. For fiscal year 1962, this difference is estimated at about $3 billion.

Finally, unlike the administrative budget, the national income accounts budget omits government transactions in financial assets and already existing assets. The largest omission is the volume of loans extended by the federal government. This volume is estimated at $4 billion net of repayments in fiscal year 1962. While these loans have important effects on economic activity, they are properly viewed as an aspect, not of fiscal policy, but of monetary and credit policy. Borrowers from the federal government, like borrowers from private financial institutions, acquire cash by incurring debts. They add thereby to their liquidity, but not directly to their incomes.

68

THE FULL EMPLOYMENT SURPLUS

The magnitude of the surplus or deficit in the budget depends both on the budget program and on the state of the economy. The budget program fixes both tax rates and expenditure programs. The revenues actually yielded by most taxes, and the actual expenditures under certain programs like unemployment compensation, vary automatically with economic activity. To interpret the economic significance of a given budget it is, therefore, essential to distinguish the *automatic* changes in revenues and expenditures from the *discretionary* changes which occur when the government varies tax rates or changes expenditure programs. The discussion that follows runs in terms of the national income accounts budget.

In Figure 2 this twofold aspect of fiscal policy is portrayed for the fiscal years 1960 and 1962. Since tax revenues and some expenditures depend on

Figure 2. Effect of Level of Economic Activity on Federal Surplus or Deficit

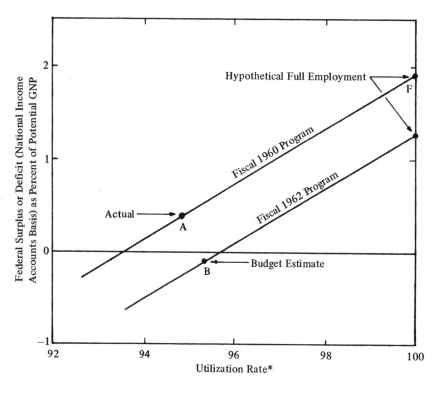

*Actual GNP as percent of potential GNP.
Source: Council of Economic Advisers.

the level of economic activity, there is a whole range of possible surpluses and deficits associated with a given budget program. The particular surplus or deficit in fact realized will depend on the level of economic activity. On the horizontal scale, Figure 2 shows the ratio of actual GNP to the economy's potential, labeled the "utilization rate." On the vertical scale, the chart shows the federal budget surplus or deficit as a percentage of potential GNP.

The line labeled "Fiscal 1960 program" represents a calculation of the budget surplus or deficit which would have occurred at various levels of economic activity, given the federal expenditure programs and the tax rates of that year. For the reasons explained earlier, the same budget program may yield a high surplus at full employment and a low surplus or a deficit at low levels of economic activity. The actual budget position in fiscal year 1960, a surplus of $2.2 billion or 0.4 percent of potential GNP, is shown at point A; this accompanied a level of GNP five percent below potential. Had full employment been achieved that year, however, the same basic budget program would have yielded a surplus of about $10 billion, or nearly two percent of Gross National Product (point F in the Chart.) The line labeled "1962 program" similarly shows the relationship between economic activity and the surplus or deficit, for the budget program of 1962; the expected deficit is shown at point B, and the full employment surplus at point G.

It is the height of the line in Figure 2 which reflects the basic budget program; the actual surplus or deficit depends on both the height of the program line and the level of economic activity. In other words, discretionary fiscal policy, by changing the level of government expenditures or tax rates, shifts the whole program line up or down. The automatic stabilizing effects of a given budget program are reflected in the chart by movements along a given line, accompanying changes in economic activity. One convenient method of comparing alternative budget programs, which separates automatic from discretionary changes in surplus and deficits, is to calculate the surplus or deficit of each alternative program at a fixed level of economic activity. As a convention, this calculation is made on the assumption of full employment. In Figure 2, the points F and G mark the full employment surplus in the budget programs of fiscal years 1960 and 1962, respectively. The statement, "the fiscal 1960 budget had a larger full employment surplus, as a fraction of potential GNP, than the 1962 budget" is a convenient shorthand summary of the fact that the 1962 budget line was below the 1960 line, yielding smaller surpluses or larger deficits at any comparable level of activity.

The full employment surplus rises through time if tax rates and expenditure programs remain unchanged. Because potential GNP grows, the volume of tax revenues yielded by a fully employed economy rises, when tax rates remain unchanged. Full employment revenues under existing tax laws are growing by about $6 billion a year. With unchanged discretionary expenditures, a budget line drawn on Figure 2 would shift upward each year by about one percent of potential GNP.

The full employment surplus is a measure of the restrictive or expansionary impact of a budget program on overall demand. Generally speaking, one budget program is more expansionary than another if it has a smaller full employment surplus. One budget program might have the smaller full employment surplus because it embodies greater federal purchases of goods and services, in relation to potential GNP. By the same token, it leaves a smaller share of full employment output for private purchase. This means that full employment is easier to maintain under the budget program with the smaller surplus, because less private demand is required. It also means that inflation is more difficult to avoid, because there are fewer goods and services to meet private demand should it prove strong. Alternatively, one budget program might have a smaller full employment surplus than a second because it involves either lower tax rates or larger transfer payment programs. In that event, private aftertax incomes are larger at full employment for the first budget program than for the second. As a result, private demand would be stronger under the first program.

If the full employment surplus is too large, relative to the strength of private demand, economic activity falls short of potential. Correspondingly, the budget surplus actually realized falls short of the full employment surplus; indeed, a deficit may occur. If the full employment surplus is too small, total demand exceeds the capacity of economy and causes inflation.

But whether a given full employment surplus is too large or too small depends on other government policies, as well as on economic circumstances affecting the general strength of private demand. If the full employment surplus is too large, more expansionary monetary credit policies may strengthen private demand sufficiently to permit full employment to be realized. Changes in tax structure, stimulating demand while leaving the yield of the tax system unchanged, might have the same effect. Similarly, restrictive changes in other government policies can offset the expansionary influence of a low full employment surplus. . . .

PETITION FROM THE MANUFAC-TURERS OF CANDLES, WAX-LIGHTS, LAMPS, CHANDELIERS, REFLECTORS, SNUFFERS, EXTINGUISHERS; AND FROM THE PRODUCERS OF TALLOW, OIL, RESIN, ALCOHOL, AND GENERALLY OF EVERYTHING USED FOR LIGHTS

Frederic Bastiat

To the Honorable the Members of the Chamber of Deputies:

"Gentlemen,—You are in the right way: You reject abstract theories; abundance, cheapness concerns you little. You are entirely occupied with the interest of the producer, whom you are anxious to free from foreign competition. In a word, you wish to secure the *national market* to *national labor.*

"We come now to offer you an admirable opportunity for the application of your—what shall we say? your theory? No, nothing is more deceiving than theory;—your doctrine? your system? your principle? But you do not like doctrines; you hold systems in horror; and, as for principles, you declare that there are no such things in political economy. We shall say then, your practice; your practice without theory, and without principle.

"We are subjected to the intolerable competition of a foreign rival, who enjoys, it would seem, such superior facilities for the production of light, that he is enabled to *inundate* our *national market* at so exceedingly reduced a price, that, the moment he makes his appearance, he draws off all custom from us; and thus an important branch of French industry, with all its innumerable ramifications, is suddenly reduced to a state of complete stagnation. This rival, who is no other than the sun, carries on so bitter a war against us, that we have every reason to believe that he has been excited to this course by our prefidious neighbor England. (Good diplomacy this, for the present time!) In this belief we are confirmed by the fact that in all his transactions with this proud island, he is much more moderate and careful than with us.

"Our petition is that it would please your honorable body to pass a law whereby shall be directed the shutting up of all windows, dormers, skylights,

From *Sophisms of Protection* (New York: G. P. Putnam & Sons, 1874), pp. 88-95.

shutters, curtains, vasistas, *oeil-de-boeufs,* in a word, all openings, holes, chinks, and fissures through which the light of the sun is used to penetrate into our dwellings, to the prejudice of the profitable manufactures which we flatter ourselves we have been enabled to bestow upon the country; which country cannot, therefore, without ingratitude, leave us now to struggle unprotected through so unequal a contest.

"We pray your honorable body not to mistake our petition for a satire, nor to repulse us without at least hearing the reasons which we have to advance in its favor.

"And first, if, by shutting out as much as possible all access to natural light, you thus create the necessity for artificial light, is there in France an industrial pursuit which will not, through some connection with this important object, be benefited by it?

"If more tallow be consumed, there will arise a necessity for an increase of cattle and sheep. Thus artificial meadows must be in greater demand; and meat, wool, leather, and above all, manure, this basis of agricultural riches, must become more abundant.

"If more oil be consumed, it will cause an increase in the cultivation of the poppy, the olive tree, and the colza.* These plants, luxuriant and exhausting to the soil, will come in good time to profit by the increased fertility which the raising of cattle will have communicated to our fields.

"Our heaths will become covered with resinous trees. Numerous swarms of bees will gather upon our mountains the perfumed treasures, which are now cast upon the winds, useless as the blossoms from which they emanate. There is, in short, no branch of agriculture which would not be greatly developed by the granting of our petition.

"Navigation would equally profit. Thousands of vessels would soon be employed in the whale fisheries, and thence would arise a new navy capable of sustaining the honor of France and of responding to the patriotic sentiments of the undersigned petitioners, candle-merchants, &c.

"But what words can express the magnificence which *Paris* will then exhibit! Cast an eye upon the future and behold the gildings, the bronzes, the magnificent crystal chandeliers, lamps, lusters, and candelabras, which will glitter in the spacious stores, compared to which the splendor of the present day will appear little and insignificant.

"There is none, not even the poor manufacturer of resin in the midst of his pine forests, nor the miserable miner in his dark dwelling, but who would enjoy an increase of salary and of comforts.

"Gentlemen, if you will be pleased to reflect, you cannot fail to be convinced that there is perhaps not one Frenchman, from the opulent stockholder of Anzin down to the poorest vender of matches, who is not interested in the success of our petition.

"We foresee your objections, gentlemen; but there is not one that you can oppose to us which you will not be obliged to gather from the works of the

---

*The colza is a kind of cabbage. Oil is extracted from its seed.

partisans of free trade. We dare challenge you to pronounce one word against our petition, which is not equally opposed to your own practice and the principle which guides your policy.

"Do you tell us, that if we gain by this protection, France will not gain, because the consumer must pay the price of it?

"We answer you:

"You have no longer any right to cite the interest of the consumer. For whenever this has been found to compete with that of the producer, you have invariably sacrificed the first. You have done this to *encourage labor,* to *increase the demand for labor.* The same reason should now induce you to act in the same manner.

"You have yourselves already answered the objection. When you were told: The consumer is interested in the free introduction of iron, coal, corn, wheat, cloths, &c., your answer was: Yes, but the producer is interested in their exclusion. Thus, also, if the consumer is interested in the admission of light, we, the producers, pray for its interdiction.

"You have also said, the producer and the consumer are one. If the manufacturer gains by protection, he will cause the agriculturist to gain also; if agriculture prospers, it opens a market for manufactured goods. Thus we, if you confer upon us the monopoly of furnishing light during the day, will as a first consequence buy large quantities of tallow, coals, oil, resin, wax, alcohol, silver, iron, bronze, [and] crystal for the supply of our business; and then we and our numerous contractors having become rich, our consumption will be great and will become a means of contributing to the comfort and competency of the workers in every branch of national labor.

"Will you say that the light of the sun is a gratuitous gift, and that to repulse gratuitous gifts, is to repulse riches under pretense of encouraging the means of obtaining them?

"Take care,—you carry the deathblow to your own policy. Remember that hitherto you have always repulsed foreign produce, *because* it was an approach to a gratuitous gift, and *the more in proportion* as this approach was more close. You have, in obeying the wishes of other monopolists, acted only from a *half-motive;* to grant our petition there is a much *fuller inducement.* To repulse us, precisely for the reason that our case is a more complete one than any which have preceded it, would be to lay down the following equation: $+ X + = -$; in other words, it would be to accumulate absurdity upon absurdity.

"Labor and Nature concur in different proportions, according to country and climate, in every article of production. The portion of Nature is always gratuitous; that of labor alone regulates the price.

"If a Lisbon orange can be sold at half the price of a Parisian one, it is because a natural and gratuitous heat does for the one, what the other only obtains from an artificial and consequently expensive one.

"When, therefore, we purchase a Portuguese orange, we may say that we obtain it half gratuitously and half by the right of labor; in other words, at *half price* compared to those of Paris.

74

"Now it is precisely on account of this *demi-gratuity* (excuse the word) that you argue in favor of exclusion. How, you say, could national labor sustain the competition of foreign labor, when the first has everything to do, and the last is rid of half the trouble, the sun taking the rest of the business upon himself? If then the *demi-gratuity* can determine you to check competition, on what principle can the *entire gratuity* be alleged as a reason for admitting it? You are no logicians if, refusing the demi-gratuity as hurtful to human labor, you do not *à fortiori,* and with double zeal, reject the full gratuity.

"Again, when my article, as coal, iron, cheese, or cloth, comes to us from foreign countries with less labor than if we produced it ourselves, the difference in price is a *gratuitous gift* conferred upon us; and the gift is more or less considerable, according as the difference is greater or less. It is the quarter, the half, or the three-quarters of the value of the produce, in proportion as the foreign merchant requires the three-quarters, the half, or the quarter of the price. It is as complete as possible when the producer offers, as the sun does with light, the whole in free gift. The question is, and we put it formally, whether you wish for France the benefit of gratuitous consumption, or the supposed advantages of laborious production. Choose, but be consistent. And does it not argue the greatest inconsistency to check as you do the importation of coal, iron, cheese, and goods of foreign manufacture merely because and even in proportion as their price approaches *zero*, while at the same time you freely admit, and without limitation, the light of the sun, whose price is during the whole day at *zero*?"

DON'T WE KNOW ENOUGH
TO MAKE BETTER
PUBLIC POLICIES?

Max Ways

People today can do more because they know more. As science keeps adding to the stock of truths, as educational systems and other communication media step up the distribution of knowledge, the scope of individual and collective action widens everywhere in the world.

But not much else is that clear about the way knowledge and action are related in contemporary life. How much is the quality—as distinguished from the quantity—of what we do improved by the expansion of what we know? Can knowledge ever become so complete that we will enter a Golden Age where all problems will have answers and everything will be done right? Or is modern society in danger of rattling apart because the progress of knowledge is so uneven in its application to the world of action?

Since current public discussion makes no serious efforts to grapple with such questions, opinion veers wildly from extreme optimism to extreme pessimism. From day to day, we expect either too much or too little from this unique kind of civilization that learns so fast and yet blunders so horribly, that achieves so magnificently and yet seems to leave undone more and more of that which ought to be done. Trite, but deeply significant of our confusion, is the remark that, if man can reach the moon, he ought to be able to solve this, that, or the other mundane problem.

Americans are more deeply involved than any other people in the knowledge-action nexus and, therefore, more bewildered and frustrated by the disappointments it seems to generate. Almost every area of American public policy, from international affairs to crime-in-the-streets, is gnawed by popular anxiety arising from the question of why a nation that knows so much does not handle its affairs better. The flow of information that reaches the President, the Congress, and the people concerning the world outside our borders

From *Fortune*, April 1971, pp. 64 ff. Copyright 1971. Reprinted by permission.

must be several thousand times greater—and better—than it was two generations ago. Yet we blunder. All the instruments of foreign policy—weapons, economic aid, channels of communication, institutions of cooperation—have vastly improved, thanks at bottom to what we have recently learned. Yet the international scene that we confront is not less dangerous than it was. At home, data about the U.S. economy multiplies and becomes more precise, while the conceptual apparatus for analyzing it has strengthened even more markedly. Yet we are repeatedly disappointed in our efforts to deal with the interlocked problems of inflation and unemployment. Whole libraries of research are spewed forth annually about the social questions of race, poverty, crime, and urban decay; millions of citizens now know much more than they did about these matters. Yet policy results are, to say the least, unsatisfactory. Without our expanded knowledge we would not be able to foul up the physical environment as we do. Yet when we turn to straightening out the mess, we never seem to know enough.

THREE LEVELS OF DISTRUST

Popular reaction to these frustrations falls into three groups. Most extreme and conspicuous is the one that says, "A nation that knows so much must be very evil to do no better than we are doing." Some in this group try to escape the guilt by turning their backs upon a society characterized by rational inquiry linked to purposive action. Hippie communes, drug taking, the admiration for Oriental passivity and occult lore are obvious examples of this tendency. Many sensitive and enraged young people blame knowledge for corrupting action. The natural sciences are denounced for pandering to gross materialism. The social sciences are even more scathingly indicted as mental fetters forged by an oppressive Establishment to repress the spontaneous joy and harmony of instinctual life. In this attitude there is a yearning for cleansing and drastic action, freed from the pale cast of thought. The word "revolution," never so popular before, is in its current usage sentimental in the most contemptible sense; "revolution" now simply expresses a petulant wish that some thunderclap of social action will clear the air, discharging tensions built up around the guilty belief that we have used our knowledge badly or, alternatively, that our knowledge has debased us.

Less conspicuous but more worrisome is the reaction of the partial dropouts. Many successful men who wear ties, own boats, prefer J. & B. to LSD, and occupy the chairs of corporation executive or professor are riddled with doubt about the validity of their own careers and of the society in which they play leading roles. They want to retard the pace of what they regard as "the rat race." While retaining their respect for knowledge, some of these want to see the rate of society's action (as measured, for instance, by Gross National Product) slowed down until such time as knowledge, catching up, can ensure a higher quality of performance.

77

The vast majority of Americans, however, are neither self-proclaimed revolutionaries nor crypto-dropouts. The members of this third group are puzzled and made insecure by the seemingly shameful discrepency between what we know and the quality of what we do. They come to regard policy makers, including those for whom they voted, as antiheroes, stumbling inadequately from one challenge to another. Experts, too, are distrusted for what appears to be repeated failure to understand events in their fields of special competence. People lose confidence not only in their leaders and teachers but in themselves.

This crisis of confidence, a product of all the accumulated disappointments, is a much graver danger than any particular failure of U.S. society in action. Our worst disease is the idea that this is "a sick society." Faith in democracy in recent years has depended too heavily on the horrible examples presented by rival systems. To concede that some societies are sicker than ours will not instill enough confidence to sustain effective democratic vigor. In short, the knowledge-action mystery now undermines the assumptions on which self-government rests.

WHEN EXPECTATIONS CAN'T BE MET

The trouble extends far beyond politics. In every sector of contemporary life, disappointment is sharpened whenever knowledge falls short of mastering events. Business management is—and must be—more and more loaded with costly expertise. When markets suddenly shrivel, when quality control slips, when R. & D. aborts at some point short of profits, indignant stockholders want to know why all the expensive knowledge did not forestall failure.

Our admiration for the advances of medical science turns into bitter recrimination (and sometimes into lawsuits) when patients die of causes still far beyond the reach of medical skill. Such pressure might be viewed as spurring medicine on toward further discovery and better performance. Its more immediate and potent effect is to create distrust where there should be trust, and to demoralize a profession that knows it cannot meet the expectations of those it serves.

Another example: child care is enlightened by more knowledge than it used to have—with the result that those parents who rear a neurotic child are automatically blamed (and blame themselves) as if the neighborhood library held ready recipes on how neuroses can be infallibly averted. The higher level of expectation leads many parents to approach child rearing with such trepidation—or such soaring goals—that their performance may be worse than it would have been if nothing new about the parent-child relationship had been learned in the last hundred years.

It is right, of course, that standards of what we demand of ourselves and of others and of our society should rise as knowledge rises. But when expectations consistently outdistance performance, we ought to reexamine our notions of how much practical improvement should reasonably be anticipated from the advance of knowledge. Possibly a tendency to expect too much from knowledge produces, in its disappointment, much of the guilt, cynicism, and bitterness that now discolor private and public life in the U.S.

THE HEAVENLY HANGOVER

For more than two centuries Western culture has been conscious of an accelerating enlightenment. For much of that period, and especially in the latter half of the nineteenth century, this advance kindled a boastful optimism that science and education would gradually solve all practical problems. This utopian view of progress-through-knowledge is commonly supposed to have been demolished by the outbreak of World War I.

But perhaps this vision did not die in Flanders. Perhaps it crept home—furtive, maimed, disfigured—and still lives among the half-hidden assumptions through which we perceive the action of our time. Every now and then a voice is heard explicitly repeating the utopian promise in accents not very different from those of 60 years ago. If we listen carefully to one of these utopian statements we may begin to understand how we have been promising ourselves more than we can deliver.

A few months ago Dr. Bentley Glass, in his address as retiring president of the American Association for the Advancement of Science, denied the conventional view that science pursued "endless horizons," in Dr. Vannevar Bush's phrase. On the contrary, Dr. Glass said, the rate of discovery may already be slowing down for the cheerful reason that science is exhausting the unknown. The universe, he argued, is finite or, at least, "the laws of life, based on similarities, are finite in number and comprehensible to us in the main even now." Dr. Glass, a biologist, conceded his science is still far from knowing all about any single species. But the life sciences now have so much knowledge in hand or in prospect that basic understanding of the genetics, structure, and behavior of living things did not seem far away. As he put it, "a total knowledge of all life forms is only about 2×10^6 times the potential knowledge about any one of them." Two million is a large but finite number, and since much of what is learned about one species may be applicable to many others, the life sciences could foresee their own completion to the point where no frontiers lie ahead.

He went a giant step beyond even this ambitious dream. From the expected scientific triumph he inferred a fundamental change in the realm of action. Mankind, he said, would enter "a Golden Age." By this he meant not merely a better age or an age more spacious for choice; he meant a utopia, a condition where problems and progress and history cease.

Probably not many of the distinguished scientists who heard Dr. Glass fully share his expectation. But his audience did not break out laughing nor rise in disagreement. Press reports of his address have provoked no major controversy, an indication that such utopian visions may run underground through the contemporary psyche. Dr. Glass was merely making explicit an optimism

79

about knowledge and life that many people vaguely share—part of the time. When these hopes are thwarted by the course of events, the same people, swinging to pessimism, believe that today's world is headed for hell in a hand basket.

But was the utopian vision worth trusting in the first place? How can science at any point in its progress have a scientific basis for assessing the extent of all that it does not yet know? Don't speculations like those of Dr. Glass smack of a medieval mode of thought, alien to the essential spirit and procedures of modern science? When a medieval mind speculated that creation was finite, it also posited a Creator who was infinite; its idea of a Golden Age rested not on man's total intellectual conquest of the finite, but on his participation through salvation in the Infinite. "Scientific" utopias smuggle the idea of heaven back into a worldly context where it does not fit—where, indeed, it may act as a poisonous stimulant, preparing the hangover of disillusionment and disgust.

There is considerable evidence that the more we learn the more we need to know. Few scientists think they are running out of questions. And it is the common observation of nonscientists that society in action faces more "problems" now than it did 50 years ago. Nobody can be sure, of course, that the generation of new questions and new problems will continue to accelerate forever. On the other hand, nobody can foretell the limits, if any, at which the multiplication of questions and problems must stop.

The awful truth seems to be that as knowledge advances ignorance does not diminish. If contemporary man does not learn to live with this paradox he will come to despise both his knowledge and his practical achievements, which are first made possible by knowledge and which then put him in the position of needing more knowledge than he has. Any new need for knowledge, any field of ignorance of which we are made aware, may prove more difficult to overcome than the vanquished ignorance from whose carcass it grew. In this fundamental and also highly practial sense, the pursuit of knowledge is not a "finite" activity. The hunt flushes the quarry, hitherto unseen, and the quarry sustains the hunter—if he's lucky.

A TOUCH OF THE OLD ADAM

For a generation the U.S. has been struggling to shape national policies toward the linked objectives of growth, full employment, and a stable price level. Again and again, success was confidently proclaimed. As recently as the mid-sixties, management of the national economic framework by Washington was widely deemed to have passed beyond crude repairs into the rarefied realm of "fine-tuning." The late sixties, however, brought another round of disillusionment. Last year saw a high rate of inflation, a high rate of unemployment, and no growth—a combination that had been considered improbable under almost any set of policies.

From repeated flaws in forecasting the impact of policy on economic life should we conclude that economics, the strongest of the social sciences, has learned nothing in these areas where it has concentrated so large a part of its recent effort? Are the laws of this science chimerical? If not, why were they so imperfectly validated in action?

The difficulty lies at the root of economic science—and, by analogy, at the root of any science when it is applied to the world of raw and total phenomena. Science, selecting what looks promising for study, begins its task of discovery by pretending to see less than it does. Much of what has been put aside by a science continues to affect the actual world. Later, science as applied to action may be ambushed by the unselected facts it left behind.

Adam Smith understood quite well that man was not a simple mechanism motivated solely by the desire to maximize his material self-interest. Indeed, Smith's "other book," *The Theory of Moral Sentiments,* deals with many of those human motivations that he systematically excluded from *The Wealth of Nations.* But by proceeding as if economic man, a fictional construct in Smith's head, represented actual flesh-and-blood men, Smith was able to found the science of economics. Without the gross oversimplification on which it is based, economics, bogged down in the complexities of actual human behavior, could hardly have got off the ground.

THE WILD CARDS MULTIPLY

Upon the soft footing of a useful fiction rose a tremendous body of sophisticated economic knowledge whose propositions are very firm—as far as they go. But they do not claim to go as far as many people suppose they do. Even when applied to a primitive society, the science of economics does not begin to cover the range of activities that the layman thinks of as economic life. In that sphere men act on incomplete information and are impelled by complex and obscure motives that economic science, restricted by its basic oversimplifications, never tried to analyze.

Nor does much help come from other sciences. Psychology's attention to business behavior and motives has not been deep or brilliantly fruitful, for psychology, following its own (doubtless valid) patterns of selection and emphasis, has been more interested in the bedroom and the nursery than in the marketplace.

While economic science was advancing, the actual world of economic activity was not standing still, waiting to have its picture taken through an improved lens. Economic science has been an indispensable ingredient in the tremendous changes that have occurred and are still occurring in actual life. But these new situations are more complex than the old. They are harder to analyze and predict by a scientific method that does not deal firmly with most of the psychological factors or the "moral sentiments."

An economic model that pays little heed to human psychology might describe well enough an economy where most people lived on the edge of necessity, where the objects traded were few and familiar, where the patterns of work were fixed, and where most trading was on a cash basis. In that situation, many regularities or "laws" could be considered as "determining" behavior. The responses of the actors were then much easier to predict than in our present economy where producers and consumers have a wider and free range of choice, where purchases can be speeded up or postponed, where the interventions of government drastically affect the market, where investment decisions are made by millions of people, where credit—with its psychological components of confidence and fear—is the pervasive medium of exchange.

There is no real doubt that the propositions of economic science are true and that they are refined and extended every year. The question is whether economics (plus all other knowledge that can be brought to bear on the business scene) improves as fast as the scene itself moves toward greater complexity and undetermined freedom. The control of inflation, for instance, may still in its scientific essence depend on whether the money supply grows faster than productive capacity. But the actual rate of inflation can be affected (at least in the shortrun) by such factors as how much inflation people *expect.* Their expectations, in turn, will depend on mental, emotional, and cultural conditions that are hard to measure and interpret.

Those charged with responsibility for predicting the consequences of government economic policies must make judgments about what Congress will do with the defense budget, about how the rank and file of labor unions will react to higher taxes and to jawboning on exorbitant wage increases, about how much unemployment will be acceptable under changing standards of social justice, about how investors will be affected by tensions in the Middle East or on U.S. campuses. Such judgments, noneconomic and nonscientific, do not fit easily into a model designed to explain ongoing business life primarily by the determined regularities of economic science.

That is why forecasting the level of business activity or assessing the future impact of government policy has not become easier or more successful, despite the advances of economic science. The wild cards multiply even as economists raise their skill in dealing with the determinable elements.

THE TEMPTATION TOWARD SIMPLICITY

This continuing—and perhaps increasing—uncertainty is not always reflected in the way economists and policy makers talk about the future. The listening public wants and expects a high degree of certainty. Forecasts freighted with ifs, buts, and maybes would be disregarded. Leaders are supposed to sound confident.

If a President of the United States gives the impression that he is highly doubtful about whether inflation is under control, his caution may further stimulate the fear of inflation. Such fear itself can have (though it will not necessarily have) an inflationary influence. On the other hand, if a President sticks his neck out and sounds more confident than his knowledge warrants, then many people who believe him may be in for another sickening round of disillusionment.

In recent weeks President Nixon and his economic advisers have adopted a more confident tone about this year's growth, unemployment, and inflation than most private forecasters believe is justified. For the first time, a precise estimate of the Gross National Product—"ten sixty-five and all that"—is bandied about in the public discussion. The point here is not to argue for some higher or lower estimate. The point is to doubt the wisdom of such specious exactitude. If the figure proves far wrong, there will be another spate of talk about stupid government blundering. If the ten sixty-five figure proves right we may see a new round of public overconfidence in Washington's ability to forecast the economy.

Nixon's present economic policies rely heavily on the analysis of Arthur Laffer, a 30-year-old economist on leave from the University of Chicago. Laffer's economic model may not prove superior to others, but it is surely simpler. In estimating where the economy will be a year from now, he uses only four indicators: federal spending, interest rates, stock prices, and the rate of expansion of the money supply. Most people who bet on horse races use more elaborate analytical models than that—and the U.S. economy is considerably more complex and less determinable than a horse race.

A LONG WAY FROM ASSISI

Last December, in a remarkable farewell speech as he left the White House where he had been coping with urban problems, Daniel Patrick Moynihan recalled the warning of the Swiss historian, Jacob Burckhardt, who foresaw that the twentieth century would be the age of "the great simplifiers" and that "the essence of tyranny would be the denial of complexity." Moynihan called the tendency to oversimplify "the single great temptation of our time" and "the great corrupter." He said that "what we need are great complexifiers, men who will not only seek to understand what it is they are about, but who will also dare to share that understanding with those for whom they act." Refusal to admit the genuine intellectual difficulties of policy formation in the contemporary world brings with it "the moralistic style" and the public tendency to lurch "from crisis to crisis with the attention span of a five-year-old."

Moynihan's point can be illustrated in a field where he was directly concerned, the effort to improve the welfare system. The system would not exist if the moral standards of the society had not risen to the point where the majority accepted responsibility for the material subsistence of the poor. Today the system is widely regarded as unsatisfactory. Consensus on this has formed not because the public heart has hardened, but because welfare's cost seems to be out of line with the amount of visible good it is doing for relief recipients.

This last standard is a rather modern development. At the time when St. Francis impulsively gave his fine clothes to a beggar, nobody seems to have been very interested in what happened to the beggar. Was he rehabilitated? Did he open a small business? Or was he to be found the next day, naked again, in an Assisi gutter, having traded the clothes for a flagon of Orvieto? These were not the sorts of questions that engaged the medieval mind. The twentieth century has developed a more ambitious definition of what it means to help somebody. We are used to getting action—and we want better results than the welfare system has been producing. We are bothered by the possibility that the present system may be actually hurting a lot of welfare recipients.

From one point of view, the charitable impulse has become less pure. Spontaneity has been lost along with the warmth generated in the hearts of donors. From another viewpoint, this change represents a strengthening of the moral impulse, which is now more intent on benefits to the donees.

But the impulse of charity, however strong, will not of itself optimize the recipients' benefits. To do that requires knowledge upon which the consequences of assistance can be predicted. We need, for instance, more certain knowledge than we have ready to hand about the causes of poverty, about how different economic incentives and pressures will operate on different groups of people in different parts of the country, about the longrange impact of different forms of assistance on family structure. Lucky St. Francis whose century had not advanced to confrontation with these formidable areas of ignorance!

Moynihan and others, after exploring these uncertainties, proposed a set of basic changes in public-assistance policy. Nobody knows for sure that the new proposal, called the Family Assistance Plan (FAP), will work better than the system we now have. Even if the new plan were put into effect, it might take many years to get a firm evaluation of it—and by then the situation of the poor and the public's standards may both have shifted.

Such, however, is the inescapable context of all policy making in a truly complex and rapidly changing society. Either we accept the framework of acting on the basis of very incomplete knowledge or else we condemn ourselves to retaining unchanged those institutions, like the present welfare system, for which we have lost respect.

In the months during which welfare reform has been bogged down in Congress there has not been much public interest in the intricacies of the plan's possible effects. Instead, the public still gets from the press a plethora of local atrocity stories about the present setup, implying that any fool could design a better welfare program.

A "moralistic style," deplored by Moynihan, continues to dominate the discussion of welfare. Some of the simplifiers are dead certain that present welfare eligibility rules are unduly restrictive because taxpayers are too stingy. Other simplifiers are equally certain that thousands of freeloaders could be thrown off the relief rolls if officials were not culpable wasters of public money.

PROBLEMS AND POLICIES

Delay in this and many other efforts to form better policies is often ascribed to conservatism, simple resistance to change. But there is a new kind of inertia in modern society. Casting about for a higher degree of certainty, public opinion delays its choice among the many uncertain courses offered.

Supersalesmanship and "bold" promises are often needed to overcome the new inertia. President Nixon's 1970 support of FAP was hedged with such commendable caution that some observers called him lukewarm toward it. For instance, he said a year ago, "While I cannot guarantee that the new Family Assistance Program will work, I know that the present welfare program won't work." Now, to break the long stalemate in Congress, he may be tempted toward reckless predictions, going further than the state of information warrants, about how effective the new program will be. If FAP disappoints inflated promises, the result will be further public pessimism and disgust.

"CAITIFF, WE HATE THEE"

Nothing is more demoralizing than the belief that today's high-knowledge society has "forgotten" how to do something that our ancestors did well. The prime exhibit here is crime and punishment, or law enforcement.

Suppose we were sure, which we are not, that the methods used in bygone times had held the incidence of crime far below the present level. Would that tell us much about how to deal with crime in this very different kind of society? We have learned much—but not nearly enough—about what causes criminal behavior. In the light of the new knowledge we assign some responsibility for crime to factors outside the conscience of the criminal. When we say (correctly) that the conditions of society affect the incidence of crime, we undermine to some extent the moral confidence with which former centuries condemned the guilty.

A judge in those days might speak the way he imagined God would sound on Judgment Day. Consider Thomas Carlyle's version of a death sentence expressing universal moral law: "Caitiff, we hate thee ... Not with a diabolic, but with a divine hatred ... As a palpable deserter ... against the whole Universe and its laws ... we ... solemnly expel thee from our community, and will, in the name of God, not with joy and exultation, but with sorrow stern as thy own, hang thee on Wednesday next ..." Such an utterance in an American court today would make the caitiff laugh all the way to the Supreme Court.

The old way of dealing with crime has been superseded, not forgotten. The new way includes a greatly increased respect for the rights of accused persons. It includes ambitious new goals of reforming those convicted. Moreover, it includes a desire to alter social conditions that predispose to crime.

All three changes, praiseworthy in themselves, confront us with new practical difficulties that we don't yet know how to overcome. Now that the courts restrict police methods in obtaining confessions, the task of gathering information that will stand up in court has become harder. The art of detection does not necessarily improve as fast as the burden on it increases.

85

There have been many experiments in the reform of prisoners and much has been learned. But the progress of knowledge applicable to the new goal lags behind the rate at which the remnants of the old methods lose their efficacy. We are now operating with a mixed system that works badly as a penal deterrent to crime and even worse as a reforming therapy.

Correcting the social conditions that foster crime will require tremendous accretions of knowledge that are not yet in sight. Hopes turn toward improving the quality of family life, of schooling, and of other communication media that shape the attitudes of the young. But experts in these fields disagree—passionately. Firm, believable predictions of what behavioral results will follow from given social changes are hard to find.

No simple and immediate solution to our crime problem is in prospect: not in some "forgotten" knowledge of the past; not in the present state of social science. Until we accept that, we won't mobilize the sustained social energy required to make some headway against the complex and longrange problems posed by crime.

THE AGENDA OF DISCOVERY

The technological processes and products that befoul the environment are obviously dependent on secretly acquired knowledge. But when we seek to correct our ecological atrocities, we often find that we lack needed kinds of knowledge—chemical, biological, economic, behavioral.

A fallacious assumption appears at this point: it holds that a society automatically gets the kind of knowledge it really wants and deserves—that if, for example, Americans really cared about one another's health, they would long since have found out how to keep the air and rivers of an industrial society clean. This way of thinking substitutes a simple, easy moralistic judgment for what is in fact a novel and difficult set of knowledge-action challenges. And the insistent imputation of guilt, which is supposed to lead us into environmental repentance, may have the actual effect of sapping the energies required for practical reform.

The belief that modern society can readily order up whatever kind of knowledge it "really wants" is part of the utopian illusion. Not much is known about the process by which science sets its priorities. The main determinants of the agenda of discovery appear to be internal to each science. The felt needs of society, even when expressed in huge public appropriations for research, seem to be secondary, though sometimes important, influences on the course of discovery.

This is the case partly because science is—and should remain—free of direct social control, and partly because science is organized by specialization whereas many knowledge needs of society present themselves as transdisciplinary problems. Many scientists are unwilling to drop their fruitful specialized research and commit their careers to the bewildering complexities of transdisciplinary attack on the new areas of ignorance disclosed by the environmental challenge.

PROBLEMS AND POLICIES

The task is not hopeless. Public policies can be developed to speed up the growth of knowledge relevant to the environment—and this can be done without destroying the freedom and the specialized organization of research. Then, by education, law, technical invention, and business innovation this knowledge can be translated into action. But the process will not be quick. It cannot achieve a complete triumph, a Golden Age. For by the time we have eliminated present environmental evils we will have developed some new ones, either because novel forms of action will produce environmentally undesirable byproducts or because we will have raised—again—our standards of what is acceptable.

INTELLIGENCE BY THE TON

The public-policy area that provokes most anxiety is that of foreign affairs. The knowledge base on which U.S. foreign policies are formed includes the most massive and expert-loaded intelligence service the world has ever seen. It can channel information by the ton to policy makers. The academic community, not much interested before World War II in current information about other countries, now has many centers for the deep study of foreign affairs. American business has a vast new network for processing information from abroad. And the general public, through press and electronic media, is given a detailed and direct (if somewhat oddly stressed) view of the world. All this, however, does not imply any gain in the adequacy of available knowledge for the tasks of policy formation.

Consider what else has changed. A few generations ago the aims of U.S. foreign policy were clear and relatively modest: to be let alone; to protect and foster certain "national interests," conceived in a definite and tangible way (e.g., the Panama Canal); to serve the world as an example of (and sometimes as a preceptor on) the virtues of progressive democracy. In those days the U.S. knew enough to pursue its limited foreign aims with self-respect and a reasonable degree of success.

Our present aims are much more difficult to formulate. They are larger and, in some obscure but real sense, "higher." We have painfully learned the need for a stronger international order; the U.S. has a responsibility for contributing to its construction. In relation to that goal, specific national interests, while still important, are subordinate. But this higher aim, itself the product of evolving knowledge, does not come ready packaged with a kit that tells what we need to know for its practical pursuit.

Meanwhile, the field of action in which foreign policy operates has become much more complex. There are more nations and every one of them "counts" in some situation or other. The aims of these other nations, too, have become more complex and harder to read. In any nation, including the dictatorships, the public opinion that shapes policy is a broader, more heterogeneous, and less predictable element than it used to be. This increased complexity in the world of international affairs is itself a consequence of the spread of knowledge—and at point after point this world confronts the U.S. with a new field of action in which we find ourselves ignorant relative to the requirements.

The sad story of the U.S. in Vietnam can be seen as three failures of knowledge, three miscalculations: (1) Washington miscalculated how much military punishment the Vietcong and Hanoi would take before quitting; (2) it miscalculated how much help Saigon would need before consolidating its own jurisdiction; (3) it miscalculated the level of casualties and cost that U.S. public opinion would tolerate. These three knowledge areas, each difficult, have complex interactions with one another (e.g., Hanoi's will to persist and the U.S. public's will to persist are not fully independent variables).

So the Vietnam war is an unsatisfactory operation—like the anti-inflation policy, the welfare system, law enforcement, and environmental protection. Too many such failures could be fatal to a society. But it doesn't follow that the leaders of a society involved in such mistakes are idiots or moral lepers. U.S. mistakes do not prove that the society is "sick" but rather that life in an age with high levels of knowledge and of action is a hard and hazardous adventure.

MORE HUMBLE AND MORE RESOLUTE

The U.S. can and must do a better job of selecting specific lines of knowledge to be emphasized and specific lines of action on which to concentrate. But no hope lies in retarding the general pace of either knowledge or action, for each makes inescapable new demands on the other. No hope lies in the rancorous moralism, the false certitude, the arrogant simplifications that characterize so much of the current public discussion. The real complexities of our present and future call for a public temper both more humble and more resolute.

This is, of course, a very different vision from Dr. Bentley Glass's Golden Age, based on the definitive triumph of science. Dr. Glass, indeed, perceived a flaw in his own paradise. "Man requires," he said, "a challenge and a quest if he is to avoid boredom. The Golden Age toward which we move will soon look tawdry if we no longer see endless horizons. We must, then, seek a change within man himself. As he acquires more fully the power to control his own genotype and to direct the course of his own evolution, he must produce a Man who can transcend his present nature . . . Perhaps the Golden Age of no progress will be but a passing phase and history may resume."

But even without the prospect of a Golden Stasis, even without waiting for the biological technique that will enable him to alter his genotype, man is more and more deeply involved in responsibility for changing himself, for influencing his own social and moral evolution. This is what the knowledge-action spiral is all about.

As the first Adam discovered, the pursuit of knowledge is a risky enterprise. Curiosity may indeed kill more than the cat. But if, as Dr. Glass well says, "Man requires a challenge and a quest" the supply of those commodities, at least, seems to be indefinitely assured.

III.

BUSINESS
ENTERPRISE AND
THE CONSUMER

The fundamental preoccupation of microeconomic theory encompasses consumer behavior, market demand, price formation, output, and business policy as they relate to the structure of a market economy. A mastery of these economic fundamentals is crucial to the student's insight into the nature and functioning of the economic system, at the same time serving him as a guide for rational decision making.

The focus of the following articles is on the application of microeconomics in a modern market society. The first three articles of the section entitled "The Essence of Private Interest" elaborate on the nature and necessity of the price system, explaining some of the critical functions of a capitalistic economy, and introducing the student to the process of capital formation and roundabout production.

In the subsequent section, the student is introduced to a discussion of the impact of variables other than price on commodity demand, followed by a discussion of one of the most essential concepts in economics, opportunity cost.

The articles in the last section were chosen to familiarize the student with the wide range of socio-economic problems, in which microeconomics as a social science finds its application. The studies selected for this purpose cover topics as diverse as the use of cigarettes as money, the economics of pollution control, and the social passion that rules Ralph Nader.

While this selection of articles is by no means exhaustive of the huge body of economic literature, it should leave the student with a substantially improved understanding of the impact of economic analysis on public policy and private choice. Moreover, virtually all of this material may be assimilated by the student without the instructional assistance of the lecturer.

A.

The Essence
of Private Interests

THE NATURE AND NECESSITY
OF A PRICE SYSTEM

Joseph A. Schumpeter

The reason why it may be useful to insert into our considerations a few remarks on the nature of price, highly theoretical though they may seem on the one hand and trivial though they may seem on the other, is simply that recent discussion on fundamental economic reform has shown that some people take the view, not new, of course, in itself, that prices and especially prices plus profits are nothing but an incident in the life of acquisitive society, that they are an obstacle to the full use of existing productive possibilities, and that they might with advantage be done away with. Prices have been compared to tolls levied for private profit or to barriers which, again for private profit, keep the potential stream of commodities from the masses who need them. The writer believes it to be a mistake to consider such views as beneath discussion and thereby to insure their survival. Among the theoretic

---

From *Economic Reconstruction* by Joseph A. Schumpeter, pp. 170-174. Copyright 1934 by Columbia University Press. Reprinted by permission of the publisher.

tools needed in order to deal with this view are some of the oldest of our science, dating back to the seventeenth century and also some of the most recent ones which have been contributed to our theoretical arsenal only in the last few years. As the problems involved are familiar ground to economists, it will be possible to confine the following remarks to a few points, in fact little more than headings which could be worked out more fully. . . .

In order to show that price is a phenomenon incident to all forms of organization of society and to economic action in general, it is sufficient to look upon it as a coefficient of economic choice. That is to say, by paying a price for any commodity, buyers show a preference for that commodity as compared with other commodities which they could also buy if they wanted to, for the same money. At the point at which they stop buying, the price will exactly measure that preference for every one of them, and this is what is meant by calling price a coefficient of choice.

Now if we take the organization of a centralized socialist state as an example of noncapitalist forms of society, it stands to reason that the central management would have nothing to go by in its decisions on the questions of the what and how of production unless it gave the comrades an opportunity to express their preferences with quantitative precision. This is equivalent to saying that the coefficient of choice of the members of such a society would have to be found out somehow, for instance, by assigning to them a certain number of claims to units of product in general and allowing them to express their preferences for the various commodities by means of those units. If then prices can be considered to be coefficients of choice, then the coefficients of choice of the comrades would be essentially prices. Moreover, in order to choose between the various possible methods of production, it would be necessary for the managers to attribute values to the means of production at their command which it would be possible to deduce from the coefficients of choice expressed by the comrades. These values would be essentially the same thing as the prices of the means of production in a capitalist organization.

The last sentence already shows that the phenomenon of price covers in fact the whole range of economic action. If a man produces whisky rather than bread from his rye, then what he does can be interpreted as bartering bread for whisky, and at the point at which he stops doing this we shall again be able to obtain a quantitative expression of his preferences and again get a coefficient of choice which in all respects is the same thing as price in a market. It is obvious that the choice between these two alternatives is not determined by technical considerations. It should be equally obvious that economic considerations of precisely the same kind enter into the choice of the method of producing either bread or whisky, and that it would be incorrect to say that the decision about the what of production is an economic matter and the rest, namely, the decision about the how of production, a technological matter. For whenever there is more than one way of producing a thing, and methods of production differ as to the relative quantities of the means of production they require, it will be necessary to take account of their relative scarcity, or to put it in another way, to consider how valuable the other products are which could also be produced by the individual units of the means of production which the producer contemplates using for a given purpose. These values of alternative production show themselves in capitalist society in the money price of the means of production and would show themselves in equivalent expressions in any other form of society. This explains why technically backward methods of production may still be the most rational ones provided the more perfect methods would require less of a plentiful factor and more of one which is less plentiful, and why the technically most perfect method of production is so often a failure in economic life. Hence rational production can never rest on exclusively technological considerations, at least not as long as all means of production are not at the command of a society in unlimited quantities. An economic dimension is, therefore, always necessary for the guidance of production, and this economic dimension at all times and under all circumstances finds expression in coefficients of choice which are fundamentally the same thing as prices in capitalist society. Of course, this does not mean that these coefficients would be numerically the same under all circumstances and in all forms of society, but they would always be of the same nature and fulfill the same purpose from which it follows that any attempt to do without them would be devoid of sense. . . .

CAN ANYONE
EXPLAIN CAPITALISM?

R. Joseph Monsen, Jr.

If people on the streets of Moscow and New York were stopped and asked to define capitalism (assuming that anyone on a New York street could be stopped), the Russians, I suspect, would have little trouble in answering such a question, the Americans a great deal. While the description of capitalism given by the Muscovites might sound like something out of Dickens, they would probably be quite unanimous and positive about it. The New Yorkers, however, would be uneasy about even the word "capitalism," and their definitions would be both varied and vague. Without drawing a moral from such an imaginary poll, it is quite clear that in the United States today there are a number of ideas about what this thing called capitalism really is.

Schools in this country are making increasing efforts to explain American capitalism and our economic system within the classrooms. In most plans to develop a program that will explain our economic system to students, however, two crucial factors are overlooked: the bias of those developing such material and the attitude of the teacher toward capitalism. These factors will necessarily color any explanation the student receives. It may be argued that this is true of all education. I would agree. But in the case of capitalism the problem is considerably more involved and controversial than in most. For even if capitalism is defined quite neutrally as a system in which private ownership operates in a market environment for profit making, the critical role of government remains to be interpreted. Yet in the United States today no issue is more hotly debated than the extent to which government should participate in economic affairs. There is little doubt that the role of government as perceived by J. K. Galbraith or by Arthur Schlesinger, Jr., is considerably larger than that accepted by Barry Goldwater, William Buckley, or the National Association of Manufacturers.

From *Saturday Review,* December 14, 1963, pp. 13-15, 26. Copyright 1963 Saturday Review, Inc.

THE ESSENCE OF PRIVATE INTERESTS

This difference of opinion concerning the role of government brings us to the central point of this article: that in the United States today at least five major versions of capitalism can be found. The role of government in these versions is a major characteristic.

These separate versions of capitalism may, in fact, be considered as separate ideologies—ideologies because they present explanations or rationalizations that are used by groups to justify their own positions. Economic ideologies, like religious dogmas, have their "true believers" as well as those adherents who espouse them for more practical ends.

To understand our economy today one must have some idea of what our major ideologies about capitalism are and who espouses them. Congressional debates and public argument in the press on major issues become much easier to follow once the positions of various groups are linked to their ideologies. We frequently hear that we have no economic ideology in this country, or that we have finally reached, as Daniel Bell entitled his book, *The End of Ideology*. Nothing could be further from the truth. Even though Marxian and collectivist ideologies are not significant in the mainstream of American thought today, to argue that we have no other economic ideologies is extremely naive.

THE CLASSICAL IDEOLOGY

Of the ideologies of American capitalism prominently in print today, the oldest is what has been called the classical ideology of capitalism. It is disseminated in the United States largely by the National Association of Manufacturers, the Foundation for Economic Education, the Committee for Constitutional Government, the United States Chamber of Commerce, and the American Enterprise Association, to name only some of the better-known organizations. While at times these groups may vary, through their many publications they present the major interpretation of this most traditional version of the American capitalist ideology. The importance of this ideology in business circles is indicated by a report estimating that out of more than $32,000,000 spent by corporations to influence legislation, some $27,000,000 was in the form of donations for use by the organizations disseminating the classical ideology.

The essence of the classical ideology is its concept of individually owned private property in a decentralized market operated by the forces of supply and demand in the quest for profit. The official stand of the NAM concerning the role of government in the economy is that the solutions to the basic economic problems of what, how, for whom, and at what price goods should be produced must be left to the voluntary adjustments of a free market rather than to the central authority of government. While this view does not demand that there be *no* government regulation, it does argue that because of the effectiveness of competition as a regulatory device, government intervention and regulation of the market are seldom needed. The classical ideology maintains, then, that there is no need for government countercyclical spending. Deficit spending is not only unnecessary but, according to the classical ideology, "irresponsible" on the grounds that it produces inflation, raises the specter of national bankruptcy, and may create recessions by interfering with the natural, competitive market.

This ideology, opposed to deficit spending, is reinforced in the public mind by the analogy between private and public finance; just as individuals risk bankruptcy by deficit spending, so, it is argued, does government. Such ideological statements carry highly emotional and moral overtones. America's traditional Puritan ethic stresses economic independence, thrift, and freedom from debt, all of which buttress the charge that the government is acting "irresponsibly," "profligately," "immorally," if it utilizes deficit spending—no matter what the conditions of the economy. When the classical capitalist ideology applies the Puritan ethic of personal finance to government financial policy in this way, it is apparent that the central idea of deficit spending and Keynesian economics is in direct conflict with it.

The anachronism involved in the classical ideology (as espoused by both Barry Goldwater and Harry S. Byrd) is that for more than a decade both Republican and Democratic administrations have followed the Keynesian idea of using deficit spending to bolster the economy in times of recessions and unemployment. The further notion that deficit spending should also take place in periods of prosperity is a recent elaboration of Keynes's original theory. Deficit spending in nonrecessionary periods is justified today largely as a means of stimulating greater economic growth.

THE MANAGERIAL IDEOLOGY

If the classical ideology had been more flexible in accepting a somewhat greater economic role for government, as well as in allowing the use of deficit spending under certain circumstances, its main rival as a business creed, known increasingly as the managerial ideology, would probably never have developed. The managerial ideology had its birth with the formation of the Committee for Economic Development in 1942. Since that time, this ideology has been vigorously disseminated by the CED and such business magazines as *Fortune*.

Politically the managerial ideology received its greatest patronage during the Eisenhower Administration. For there was, as *Business Week* observed, "a marked similarity between the CED and the new Administration [Eisenhower's] that involved more than the names of men. Both represent the views of a forward-looking businessman, a sort of progressive conservative."

The managerial ideology of capitalism takes its name from the increasing control by professional management of the large corporation. While the managerial ideology is a reaction to the traditional classical creed, there are great similarities between them. The issues in which similarities occur, however, are usually those about which the managerial ideology is silent. The managerial ideology points largely to the basic changes that have occurred

96

within the economy in the past few decades. It attempts to portray the manager of the large corporation as a trustee for the worker, consumer, and owner.

The dispute over the proper function of government not only partially caused the development of the managerial ideology but indeed remains one of the principle differences between it and the classical ideology. The managerialists accept a considerably greater role for government than the traditionalists will approve. The CED has taken the position that government action is essential in attempting to control business fluctuations—even if such a policy includes deficit spending (though here the managerialists talk in terms of balancing the budget over the whole business cycle and not necessarily in every year, as the NAM requires). The editors of *Fortune* expressed the managerial position by saying: "It is now almost universally accepted that . . . in the event of a serious depression government . . . undertakes very large countercyclical spending programs."

The managerial ideology's acceptance of a larger role for government is considerably more realistic today than the classical ideology's on this issue. In this regard, the classical ideology is less descriptive and more normative than the managerial creed, for it must argue that it represents the way things "ought" to be, not necessarily the way they are. The managerial ideology deemphasizes the traditional forces of supply and demand as the determinants of prices and accepts a governmental role deeply involved in business affairs, attempting to face what it feels are the realities of modern capitalism. To a large degree, the managerial ideology of capitalism is successful in that it provides arguments in currently accepted terms.

THE IDEOLOGY OF COUNTERVAILING POWER

Since its election in 1960 the Kennedy Administration has on a number of occasions used a sort of semi-official ideology attributed to the well-known Harvard economist and former Ambassador to India, John Kenneth Galbraith. With the publication in 1952 of his book, *American Capitalism: The Concept of Countervailing Power,* Professor Galbraith set forth the main themes of this ideology. Since then, we have seen the term "countervailing power" spread until today it is hard to find any discussion about American capitalism that does not make some reference to it. In fact, Galbraith is now probably the most widely known economist in this country. While countervailing power cannot be considered as full-blown an ideology as the classical ideology, it has nonetheless become one of the most popular explanations of modern American capitalism.

What is the concept of countervailing power upon which this ideology is based? Most succinctly, it is "the neutralization of one position of power by another." For Galbraith argues that "private economic power begets the countervailing power of those who are subject to it." The development of strong unions, then, in this argument, was inevitable in America to neutralize or balance the power of large companies. While this may not be historically correct, the thesis is that as one group develops in power, others arise to offset its power and prevent their own exploitation. By this reasoning, the strongest unions should develop in those industries where the strongest corporations exist.

The role of government in this interpretation is to assist the development of checks and balances of power. Thus, under this view, the concept of competition as the autonomous regulator of economic activity has been superseded. The potential role of government is, therefore, perhaps greater under the ideology of countervailing power than in any of the other major ideologies of modern American capitalism. In this sense, it may be expected to gain more supporters from among politically liberal citizens than from among conservatives, who are more apt to endorse the classical ideology.

While the countervailing power thesis as an economic theory has been subject to much criticism, as an ideological explanation of modern American capitalism it has become internationally known and suggests the basic flavor of modern American capitalism abroad perhaps more than any other capitalist ideology. Whether countervailing power as an ideology will develop independently or will merely be appended to one of the others, only time will tell. The concept of countervailing power appears, in the last analysis, to be far more adaptable as an ideology for the defense of American capitalism than as an economic theory to explain it; this feature, I might add, it shares with the other major ideologies of capitalism.

THE IDEOLOGY OF PEOPLE'S CAPITALISM

The label "people's capitalism" has become increasingly fashionable as a title for the contemporary American economic system. The United States Information Agency, which at one time made use of the slogan, admitted quite frankly that "this type of terminology is designed as an eye-catcher, as a thought-provoker. The aim is to suggest at the outset that the American system is a far cry from nineteenth-century stereotypes of capitalism."

The central focus of the ideology of people's capitalism is the widening of both equity ownership and decision-making power among the populace. To its supporters, people's capitalism in America today is distinguished more by its emphasis on this system of property diffusion than by its present structure.

The origin of the term "people's capitalism" is alleged to have been developed in 1956 by the American Advertising Council for the USIA, which used the concept abroad. General Electric and Standard Oil of New Jersey have used the phrase in their ads in this country. Business economists such as Marcus Nadler and corporation executives such as Roger Blough of U.S. Steel have publicly used the term often. As Victor Perlo noted in the scholarly *American Economic Review*, "Future editions of economic texts can hardly fail to discuss the theory—or slogan—of people's capitalism."

THE ESSENCE OF PRIVATE INTERESTS

The New York Stock Exchange's president, Keith Funston, has vigorously promoted the thesis that America is becoming a people's capitalism. In an issue of IBM's magazine *Think,* Mr. Funston says "*If stock distribution gets wide enough, it will bring capitalism to the ultimate goals of socialism* [author's italics], the people owning the instruments of production, but without sacrificing the incentive system of capitalism. I'm not predicting this will happen in a specific period of time, but we are heading along the lines of a people's capitalism and a stronger democracy." While the shortrange goal of greater stock or equity distribution is quite understandable as an aim of the New York Stock Exchange, one wonders whether its members would really desire the longrange achievement of "the ultimate goals of socialism."

Such an atmosphere of conviction and debate in statements about people's capitalism is common. Similarly, contradiction among its various expositors is not unusual. It is possible to find advocates of people's capitalism who infer that the role of government should be broad and active to insure a rapid widening in equity ownership within the country; and those, too, who feel that government should not play anything but a limited role within the economy. Besides lack of consensus on the role of government, problems involved in the responsibility of professional management are not solved by the ideology.

The most important challenge to the ideology itself, however, comes from those, such as Perlo, who question whether there has been *any* significant increase, in recent decades, in the relative diffusion of ownership and decision making in the U.S.

Incomplete as the concept may be for a full explanation of modern American capitalism, there is little doubt that the ideology of people's capitalism is widely used as a defense, justification, and explanation of our contemporary economic system both at home and abroad. As such, it is one of the primary American capitalist ideologies.

THE EXPORT IDEOLOGY

A synthesis of the major American capitalist ideologies, as described by USIA, has been called enterprise democracy. This ideology, perhaps best thought of as our "export" ideology, has been developed over several Administrations. In his book *What We Are For,* Arthur Larson, former head of the USIA under President Eisenhower, has given one of the few explanations specifically intended for home use of what our "export" ideology is.

The argument of enterprise democracy is that class conflict cannot explain American history. Rather, the practice of cooperation between business, labor, and government—out of the necessity of mutual self-interest—explains the American system. Hence, while the traditional competitive spirit in America is cited as important for the development of an industrial economy, alongside competitiveness, modifying it, is the "strong strain of cooperation." The

99

feature that distinguishes modern enterprise democracy from laissez-faire capitalism is the recognition of necessary cooperation and mutual interest among society's basic groups; this includes recognition of government's positive duty to act when necessary for the varying needs of society's members. Government is different, however, from the other countervailing groups in the economy: "Its power over our freedoms, our fortunes, and our lives can be ultimate and absolute. Every other power in our society is secondary. The power of government is final. That is why we instinctively resist its increase."

The key to enterprise democracy is the role assigned to government. Sometimes called by the USIA "the Lincoln Formula," this ideology proclaims that the function of government is to do only that which needs to be done and cannot be done so well privately.

From this thesis, three corollaries are developed: (1) that more than one group should exist to act for the needs of the community; (2) that the major groups in modern industrial society do not basically conflict but rather mutually support one another (i.e., business, labor, and government); and (3) that private methods are always inherently preferable to government action. This, then, means a preference for as little governmental action "as possible." The phrase "as possible" is, of course, elastic and vague.

Other concepts that the ideology of enterprise democracy emphasizes are freedom, property, justice, individuality, group allegiance, and religion. The traditional criticisms of capitalism—competitiveness, class conflict, and inequality of income distribution—are, needless to say, not emphasized.

Essentially, enterprise democracy represents a composite or compromise ideology that, the USIA hopes, will receive a minimum of domestic criticism to let it function abroad as representative of American capitalism. But no term has been made official. Rather, local USIA officers are allowed to describe the American economic system in any terms they feel are appropriate. The basic ideology called enterprise democracy by Larson has not, however, been repudiated by the USIA or the Administration .

The main purpose of the ideology is to produce something that both the two main political parties and the other major groups in this country can agree upon for use in portraying the United States to the world. Its basic outline, therefore, cannot be thought of as inherently Democratic or Republican. If such an identification should occur, enterprise democracy as an export ideology would lose its usefulness as a propaganda instrument.

Like the classical and managerial ideologies, enterprise democracy is backed by an organized group. The main difference is that its support comes from an agency of the government—the USIA, which functions abroad as our propaganda instrument. The operation of the USIA is of tremendous scope but, even so, it is not always a match in size or strength for its Communist counterparts. Through the Voice of America, newspapers, magazines, cultural, educational, and scientific exhibits, motion pictures, and libraries, the USIA attempts to project America's image abroad. This may also explain why the enterprise democracy ideology is better known abroad than at home.

THE ESSENCE OF PRIVATE INTERESTS

The ideology's adherence to reality is a matter of opinion. Since it offers no body of economic theory, as does the classical ideology of capitalism, the way in which the various groups work out their mutual interests is left quite vague. One must assume the presence of countervailing power, a vague answer in itself. What will prevent the government from going beyond the constraints set up by the concept of limited government is indefinite. One assumes that political pressures and traditions are the constraints.

In newer, developing countries the following of such a nebulous prototype as this would present serious problems. The essentially synthetic character of the enterprise democracy ideology—since it is an attempt to mesh a number of ideological strands from the classical, managerial, countervailing power, and people's capitalism creeds—creates a number of paradoxical, contradictory elements within the ideology. This, of course, is not uncommon in ideologies. There are, however, limits of tolerance as to how many opposing strains can be fitted within the frame of a single ideology and still leave it viable and appealing.

Many observers have commented on our demand that a greater amount of laissez faire exists in nations receiving foreign aid than exists within our own country, and this attitude is occasionally apparent in our "export" ideologies. But as one studies the pressures under which the USIA must operate and the need to propagandize an ideology inoffensive to any congressman or group apt to oppose its annual budget, it becomes clear that under our present system the United States cannot expect any other type of "export" ideology, no matter how unrealistic, that is not a compromise. This fact, of course, presents certain problems for effective propaganda. Since it must inevitably attempt to incur a minimum amount of criticism in Congress rather than focusing solely on presenting American capitalism effectively to other nations, our "export" ideology may seem somewhat unrealistic to the folks at home. Perhaps even more important, however, is the question whether it seems as strange to the folks abroad.

This short perusal of the various ideologies found within contemporary America suggests reasons why we commonly have difficulty defining our economic system and specifying what the role of government should be. Without some knowledge, however, of the prevalent ideologies of capitalism in our country, it is doubtful that the basic issues and arguments within our economy can be brought clearly into the open, as they must be.

Meanwhile, it may be worthwhile to remember that American capitalism is, in one way at least, a little like electricity: Nobody knows exactly what it is, but it works—and works well.

CAPITAL AND ROUNDABOUT PRODUCTION

Eugen von Böhm-Bawerk

The end and aim of all production is the making of things with which to satisfy our wants; that is to say, the making of goods for immediate consumption, or Consumption Goods. . . . We combine our own natural powers and natural powers of the external world in such a way that, under natural law, the desired material good must come into existence. But this is a very general description indeed of the matter, and looking at it closer there comes in sight an important distinction which we have not as yet considered. It has reference to the distance which lies between the expenditure of human labor in the combined production and the appearance of the desired good. We either put forth our labor just before the goal is reached, or we intentionally take a roundabout way. That is to say, we may put forth our labor in such a way that it at once completes the circle of conditions necessary for the emergence of the desired good, and thus the existence of the good *immediately* follows the expenditure of the labor; or we may associate our labor first with the more remote causes of the good, with the object of obtaining, not the desired good itself, but a proximate cause of the good; which cause, again, must be associated with other suitable materials and powers, till, finally,—perhaps through a considerable number of intermediate members,—the finished good, the instrument of human satisfaction, is obtained.

The nature and importance of this distinction will be best seen from a few examples. . . . A peasant requires drinking water. The spring is some distance from his house. There are various ways in which he may supply his daily wants. First, he may go to the spring each time he is thirsty, and drink out of his hollowed hand. This is the most direct way; satisfaction follows immediately on exertion. But it is an inconvenient way, for our peasant has to take his way to the well as often as he is thirsty. And it is an insufficient

From Eugen von Böhm-Bawerk, *The Positive Theory of Capital* (London: Macmillan and Co., 1891), pp. 17-22.

way, for he can never collect and store any great quantity such as he requires for various other purposes. Second, he may take a log of wood, hollow it out into a kind of pail, and carry his day's supply from the spring to his cottage. The advantage is obvious, but it necessitates a roundabout way of considerable length. The man must spend, perhaps, a day in cutting out the pail; before doing so he must have felled a tree in the forest; to do this, again, he must have made an axe, and so on. But there is still a third way; instead of felling one tree he fells a number of trees, splits and hollows them, lays them end to end, and so constructs a runnel or rhone which brings a full head of water to his cottage. Here, obviously, between the expenditure of the labor and the obtaining of the water we have a very roundabout way, but, then, the result is ever so much greater. Our peasant need no longer take his weary way from house to well with the heavy pail on his shoulder, and yet he has a constant and full supply of the freshest water at his very door.

Another example. I require stone for building a house. There is a rich vein of excellent sandstone in a neighbouring hill. How is it to be got out? First, I may work the loose stones back and forward with my bare fingers, and break off what can be broken off. This is the most direct, but also the least productive way. Second, I may take a piece of iron, make a hammer and chisel out of it, and use them on the hard stone—a roundabout way, which, of course, leads to a very much better result than the former. Third method—Having a hammer and chisel I use them to drill a hole in the rock; next I turn my attention to procuring charcoal, sulphur, and nitre, and mixing them in a powder, then I pour the powder into the hole, and the explosion that follows splits the stone into convenient pieces—still more of a roundabout way, but one which, as experience shows, is as much superior to the second way in result as the second was to the first.

Yet another example. I am short-sighted, and wish to have a pair of spectacles. For this I require ground and polished glasses, and a steel framework. But all that nature offers towards that end is silicious earth and iron ore. How am I to transform these into spectacles? Work as I may, it is as impossible for me to make spectacles directly out of silicious earth as it would be to make the steel frames out of iron ore. Here there is no immediate or direct method of production. There is nothing for it but to take the roundabout way, and, indeed, a very roundabout way. I must take silicious earth and fuel, and build furnaces for smelting the glass from the silicious earth; the glass thus obtained has to be carefully purified, worked, and cooled by a series of processes; finally, the glass thus prepared—again by means of ingenious instruments carefully constructed beforehand—is ground and polished into the lens fit for short-sighted eyes. Similarly, I must smelt the ore in the blast furnace, change the raw iron into steel, and make the frame therefrom—processes which cannot be carried through without a long series of tools and buildings that, on their part again, require great amounts of previous labor. Thus, by an exceedingly roundabout way, the end is attained.

The lesson to be drawn from these examples is obvious. It is—that a greater result is obtained by producing goods in roundabout ways than by producing

103

them directly. Where a good can be produced in either way, we have the fact that, by the indirect way, a greater product can be got with equal labor, or the same product with less labor. But, beyond this, the superiority of the indirect way manifests itself in being the only way in which certain goods can be obtained. . . .

That roundabout methods lead to greater results than direct methods is one of the most important and fundamental propositions in the whole theory of production. It must be emphatically stated that the only basis of this proposition is the experience of practical life. Economic theory does not and cannot show *a priori* that it must be so; but the unanimous experience of all the technique of production says that it is so. And this is sufficient; all the more that the facts of experience which tell us this are commonplace and familiar to everybody. But *why* is it so? The economist might quite well decline to answer this question. For the fact that a greater product is obtained by methods of production that begin far back is essentially a purely technical fact, and to explain questions of technique does not fall within the economist's sphere. For instance, that tropical lands are more fruitful than the polar zone; that the alloy of which coins are made stands more wear and tear than pure metal; that a railroad is better for transport than an ordinary turnpike road;—all these are matters of fact with which the economist reckons, but which his science does not call on him to explain. . . .

In the last resort all our productive efforts amount to shiftings and combinations of matter. We must know how to bring together the right forms of matter at the right moment, in order that from those associated forces the desired result, the product wanted, may follow. But, as we saw, the natural forms of matter are often so infinitely large, often so infinitely fine, that human hands are too weak or too coarse to control them. We are as powerless to overcome the cohesion of the wall of rock when we want building stone as we are, from carbon, nitrogen, hydrogen, oxygen, phosphorus, potash, etc., to put together a single grain of wheat. But there are other powers which can easily do what is denied to us, and these are the powers of nature. There are natural powers which far exceed the possibilities of human power in greatness, and there are other natural powers in the microscopic world which can make combinations that put our clumsy fingers to shame. If we can succeed in making those forces our allies in the work of production, the limits of human possibility will be infinitely extended. And this we have done.

The condition of our success is, that we are able to control the materials on which the power that helps us depends, more easily than the materials which are to be transformed into the desired good. Happily this condition can be very often complied with. Our weak yielding hand cannot overcome the cohesion of the rock, but the hard wedge of iron can; the wedge and the hammer to drive it we can happily master with little trouble. We cannot gather the atoms of phosphorus and potash out of the ground, and the atoms of carbon and oxygen out of the atmospheric air, and put them together in the shape of the kernel of wheat; but the organic chemical powers of the seed can put this magical process in motion, while we on our part can very easily bury the seed in the place of its secret working, the bosom of the earth. Often, of course, we are not able directly to master the form of matter on which the friendly power depends, but in the same way as we would like it to help us, do we help ourselves against it; we try to secure the alliance of a second natural power which brings the form of matter that bears the first power under our control. We wish to bring the well water into the house. Wooden rhones would force it to obey our will, and take the path we prescribe, but our hands have not the power to make the forest trees into rhones. We have not far to look, however, for an expedient. We ask the help of a second ally in the axe and the gouge; their assistance gives us the rhones; then the rhones bring us the water. And what in this illustration is done through the mediation of two or three members may be done, with equal or greater result, through five, 10, or 20 members. Just as we control and guide the immediate matter of which the good is composed by one friendly power, and that power by a second, so can we control and guide the second by a third, the third by a fourth, this, again, by a fifth, and so on,—always going back to more remote causes of the final result—till in the series we come at last to one cause which we can control conveniently by our own natural powers. This is the true importance which attaches to our entering on roundabout ways of production: every roundabout way means the enlisting in our service of a power which is stronger or more cunning than the human hand; every extension of the roundabout way means an addition to the powers which enter into the service of man, and the shifting of some portion of the burden of production from the scarce and costly labor of human beings to the prodigal powers of nature.

And now we may put into words an idea which has long waited for expression, and must certainly have occurred to the reader; the kind of production which works in these wise circuitous methods is nothing else than what economists call Capitalist Production, as opposed to that production which goes directly at its object. . . . And Capital is nothing but the complex of intermediate products which appear on the several stages of the roundabout journey.

DEMAND ANALYSIS

Joel Dean

. . . DEMAND THEORY

If demand analysis is to be helpful in solving management problems, an understanding of demand theory is needed. Theory contributes both to the design of investigations that are relevant to management problems, and to the evaluation of empirical research.

What is meant by demand? What governs its behavior? There is no single, universally useful concept of demand. Instead, there are different concepts for different problems. The demand determinants, as well as their relative importance, differ for the various concepts. The notion of demand that is appropriate depends upon the precise question to be answered. For instance, the question "How much furniture will the American people buy in the next five years?" presents one setting for analysis. It calls for a look at trends in the number and size of new families (to show expansion of the market), and consideration of recent production levels (to indicate replacement demand).

Quite a different framework is presented in the question "What will our sales to dealers in Ohio be during the next six months if we cut our price eight percent next week and have the cut well advertised?" This question is one of shortrun regional demand sensitivity to price and promotion. These two questions are answered with two separate demand functions based on different data, assumptions, and approximations.

In order to shape an empirical analysis of demand so that it will answer the precise question that is relevant, it is desirable to be familiar with various concepts of demand and know which concept is appropriate for each sort of management problem. A convenient way to survey this domain of demand theory is to make several distinctions between different kinds of demand concepts.

From Joel Dean, *Managerial Economics,* pp. 145-151, © 1951. Reprinted by permission of Prentice-Hall, Inc., Englewood Cliffs, New Jersey.

Demand Schedules vs. Demand Functions

The number of television sets sold by Dumont during a particular month in 1951 was determined by many factors, among them: (1) Dumont's price, (2) prices of rival sets, (3) the effectiveness of Dumont's advertising (past as well as present and absolutely as well as relative to rivals), (4) the design of Dumont's product (relative to rivals'), (5) the amount (and distribution) of purchasing power, (6) time payment terms, and (7) people's expectations as to color television, and their guesses about the effect of war on future shortages and prices.

One of these many demand determinants, Dumont's price, has been singled out for special attention in conventional economic analysis. This price-quantity relationship is portrayed as a demand schedule (or demand curve) which shows the amounts that would be sold at various prices in a given place on a given date. Classical theorists are quite aware that price is not the sole factor determining sales, and that changes in other conditions can have important sales effects on a given price. However, the effect of changes in other conditions is viewed as a "shift" of the demand schedule, meaning that the quantity sold at each price will be different because incomes are greater, or down payments lower. To sharpen traditional analysis, these other conditions are therefore frozen in some given shape, and attention is directed at the relation of price to sales.[1]

But this price relation is not usually as important to management as an understanding of the "shifts" in the demand function. For many products price has little effect on sales volume in relevant ranges of price level. Other factors, particularly the level of business activity, have a bigger impact on sales of most products.

If these shifts in the conventional price-quantity curve can be related systematically to other demand factors, such as changes in buyers' income or advertising, we can transform the *demand schedule* into a more general *demand function* by relating sales to several independent variables, such as those listed above for television sets.

What are the factors that should be included in a demand function? There is no general answer to this question, because the determinants of demand depend on the product and on the demand situation.

It is impossible to make a list of generic demand factors that are important for every product. Nevertheless there are a few that underlie demand behavior of so many products that they deserve a place on a checklist of possible demand determinants for all consumer goods. The most common ones are: income, sales promotion, product-improvement, and price. For consumer goods, buyers' income is the factor most nearly universal, since it determines the amount of cash in buyers' hands and strongly affects their expectations of

---

[1]Classical theorists had a purpose (aside from simplifying the analysis) in concentrating on the price-sales relation: their aim was to find the determinants of value, resource allocation, and income distribution in a stationary economic environment, and for this, price was the key variable.

future income. The relations of demand to prices, advertising, competition, and speculation hinge more on the nature of the product; factors that are dominant for some products may be quite irrelevant or unimportant for others. The measurable determinants of demand for producers' goods usually differ from those for consumers' goods; they also vary considerably among products. Typically, personal income is displaced by business profits (e.g., corporate profits) or by business activity (e.g., an index of industrial production). For example there is a close relation between construction activity and the demand for plaster board. Products that are durable (whether producers' goods or consumers' goods) have demand factors that are different and more intricate than are those for perishables; and products whose demand is derived often take on the determinants of demand for the parent products. We shall discuss some of these contrasts below.

Producers' Goods vs. Consumers' Goods

Generally speaking, the reasons for expecting distinctive demand behavior for producers' goods are three: (1) buyers are professionals, and hence more expert, price-wise and sensitive to substitutes; (2) their motives are more purely economic: products are bought, not for themselves alone, but for their profit prospects; and (3) demand, being derived from consumption demand, fluctuates differently and generally more violently. However, it is easy to exaggerate the differences in demand characteristics between producers' goods and consumers' goods. In the first place, the distinction itself, being based on who buys and why, is bound to be fuzzy. Is a salesman-owned Chevrolet a producer's good? In the second place there are thousands of incidental needs in any business that are simply not worth the cost of scientific purchase planning. In the third place, the human element in business purchasing is badly underrated—high-styled equipment and personal fancy create demand for milling machinery as well as for automobiles.

Durable Goods vs. Perishable Goods

Durable products present more complicated problems of demand analysis than products that give a one-shot service. Sales of nondurables are made largely to meet current demand, which depends on current conditions. Sales of durables, on the other hand, add an increment to a stock of existing goods that dole out their services slowly over several years. It is thus a common practice to segregate current demand for durables in terms of replacement of old products and expansion of the total stock.

One characteristic of demand for durables is a volatile relation to business conditions: since current output of a durable provides only a small fraction of the total current services demanded of that kind of product, sales are hypersensitive to small changes in demand for the service. If we assume, for instance, that normal annual automobile production is used (1) to replace 10 percent of the existing stock of cars, and (2) to expand the car population by five percent, then a three percent increase in the demand for motor transportation will raise the new-car demand by about 20 percent.

But demand analysis for durable goods is by no means this simple. Both replacement and expansion have manifold sets of demand determinants. Continuing the automobile illustration, replacement demand depends on the value of existing cars as transportation relative to their value as scrap iron. When expansion demand spurts up suddenly, used-car values usually go higher than scrap values; as a result the scrapping rate, and thus replacement demand falls. If the public want fewer cars (expansion rate negative) the scrappage rate must be higher than the level of new car production. This excess scrappage is possible if scrap prices are high enough, and the obsolescence price-spread between new and old cars wide enough (a) to take the old cars off the road, and (b) to cover the necessary costs of producing new cars.

The most important replacement determinant is the obsolescence rate, which sets prices in the secondhand markets. Since many cars are abandoned without regard to salvage value, scrap iron prices play a much less important role. Obsolescence is pervasive and strategic in the American economy in determining the level of business activity, and it should be appreciated for its capricious and volatile self. Physical deterioration is rarely a deciding factor in replacement of durable goods. For consumer products—and to a surprising extent for producer goods, too—style, convenience, and income play a dominant role in demand, for even such workhorse products as home furnaces.

Occasionally a technological upheaval can produce a blast of obsolescence that wipes out any distinction between expansion and replacement. Thus the demand for Diesel locomotives is not affected by fluctuations in demand for rail transport, nor cotton pickers by cotton acreage. For such major innovations, demand depends only on cultural lags, financial exigencies, and rivalry of alternative investments.

The determinants of expansion demand for durables are not different in theory from those for nondurables. In practice, however, a decision to buy a durable good is more complicated, because guesses about the future stand out more sharply in the buyer's mind. He worries about future maintenance and operating costs in relation to his future income and other demands; he takes a guess at future sales values; and he wonders whether prices will rise or fall if he postpones his purchase. Thus for durable goods[2] not only present prices and incomes, but their current trends and the state of optimism are proper variables to include in the demand function. Expectation about improved product designs are also important: leaks dry up demand and cause price

---

[2] That is, for any purchase of a large stock of future services, such as a raw materials inventory or long-term wage contract. Price expectations play a dominant role in industrial inventory policy, but it is always called "price protection," never "speculation."

concessions in current models. This has been notable in television, where rapid obsolescence of receivers has caused a cascade of prices.

Derived Demand vs. Autonomous Demand

When demand for a product is tied to the purchase of some parent product, its demand is called "derived." Sometimes the dependent product is a component part (e.g., demand for doors derived from demand for houses). Sometimes dependence comes from complementary consumption (e.g., pretzels from beer). It is hard to find a product in modern civilization whose demand is wholly independent of all others. Demand for all producers' goods, raw materials and component parts, is derived. So "derived demand" is quite common, and for practical analysis the distinction between it and autonomous demand is arbitrary and a matter of degree.

Demand that is derived is generally supposed to have less price elasticity than autonomous demand, assuming substitutes are equally available. This is partly a result of dilution by other components whose prices are sticky. A 10 percent cut in the price of steel would cause only about a one percent change in the cost of a car, assuming all other cost prices stayed the same.

Some products are so closely tied to others in their uses that they have no distinctive demand determinants of their own. When such a product has only one use and its proportion to the parent-good is fixed (e.g., television antennas), there is no point in distinguishing it as separate from the parent. But fixed proportions are rare; more usually there is substitution leeway in the proportions as well as more than one parent use. Crude rubber demand shows both of these characteristics when related to the population of motor vehicles.

As variability in the proportions and the number of uses increases, it is hard to tie demand down to parent products. For instance, small electric motors have no primary uses, but to analyze their demand in terms of their thousands of parent uses is impossibly tedious. Sulphuric acid is another such product. Capital goods (plant and equipment) have a derived demand, but variations in the actual (and expected) intensities of use are so wide that analysis in terms of finished product demand is either too broad or too approximate to be of much help. Derived demand facilitates forecasting when proportions of the two products are fairly stable and there is a rigid time-lead in the parent product's demand. . . .

COST

Joel Dean

. . . Opportunity vs. Outlay Costs

A distinction can be drawn between outlay costs and opportunity costs on the basis of the nature of the sacrifice. Outlay costs are those that involve financial expenditure at some time and hence are recorded in the books of account. Opportunity costs take the form of profits from alternative ventures that are foregone by using limited facilities for a particular purpose. Since they represent only sacrificed alternatives, they are never recorded as such in the financial accounts.

Whenever the problem allows an opportunity to buy all input factors for cash, outlay cost is the correct concept to use. In this situation, cash is the scarce factor and the standard of value of input factors relative to all other conceivable uses of cash.

Such complete market access is almost never within the bounds of practicability, and thus some concept of opportunity cost is usually relevant. Indeed, for many problems, opportunity cost is the more important cost. In a cloth mill that spins its own yarn, for example, the cost of yarn is really the price at which the yarn could be sold if it were not woven into cloth. For the problem of measuring the profitability of the weaving operations in order to decide whether to expand them or abandon them, it is this opportunity cost— the foregone revenue from not selling the yarn—that is relevant. In periods of boom demand, the use of a versatile bottleneck factor, such as scarce steel or scarce loom capacity, for making one product, involves the opportunity cost of not using it to make some other product that can also produce profits. The opportunity cost of producing heating oil in a modern, flexible refinery, for example, is the value of the gasoline that might otherwise have been made.

From Joel Dean, *Managerial Economics,* pp. 259-260, © 1951. Reprinted by permission of Prentice-Hall, Inc., Englewood Cliffs, New Jersey.

For this reason, "gasoline equivalent" costing has considerable acceptance in this industry.

For shortrun decisions like those illustrated above, the alternatives are clear, and the opportunity cost of foregoing them is calculable. But opportunity cost has a broader meaning and a wider usefulness than is implied in these straightforward applications. It is useful for longrun decisions involving problems of major strategy. For example, the cost of getting a college education is not confined to the outlays on tuition and books, but also includes the earnings that are foregone by not working full time.

In military affairs, to cite another example, the cost of sending bombers on a particular mission is not the price of the gasoline and ammunition but, rather, the damage that they would have done the enemy had they been sent on a substitute mission. Opportunity costs also play a role in sales strategy. For example, in determining whether a gasoline station should do major automotive repair work, the owner should consider the cost of such work in terms of the amount of gasoline and oil that will not be sold because the attendant is flat on his back under a truck. Managerial skill is scarce in most companies. Ventures that demand executive time must have high productivity to cover the opportunity cost of foregone management activities.

Opportunity cost plays an important role in capital expenditure budgeting. Under conditions of capital rationing, the cost of acquiring a $100,000 gasoline station in New York City is not usually the interest that would have to be paid on the borrowed money but, rather, the profits or cost savings that could have been achieved if the $100,000 had been invested in four suburban gasoline stations, or in pipelines or refinery facilities. Investing equity money in the venture involves opportunity costs measurable in terms of sacrificed income from alternative investments. Estimates of cost of capital are esentially founded on an opportunity concept of investment return.

Opportunity cost is the cost concept to use when the supply of input factors is strictly limited. Such rigid supply may occur for technical reasons, e.g., the limited number of television channels available in a single locality; for social reasons, e.g., wartime rationing; for private reasons, such as lack of ready cash, or because the problem is too shortrun to adapt facilities to their most profitable longrun relation to the job. In business problems the message of opportunity costs is that it is dangerous to confine cost knowledge to what the firm is doing. What the firm is not doing but could do is frequently the critical cost consideration which it is perilous but easy to ignore. . . .

B.

Private Enterprise in Action

———

THE ECONOMIC ORGANIZATION OF A POW CAMP

R. A. Radford

INTRODUCTION

After allowance has been made for abnormal circumstances, the social institutions, ideas, and habits of groups in the outside world are to be found reflected in a Prisoner of War Camp. It is an unusual but vital society. Camp organization and politics are matters of real concern to the inmates, as affecting their present and perhaps their future existences. Nor does this indicate any loss of proportion. No one pretends that camp matters are of any but local importance or of more than transient interest, but their importance there is great. . . .

One aspect of social organization is to be found in economic activity, and this, along with other manifestations of a group existence, is to be found in

From *Economica* 12 (November 1945): 189-201. Reprinted by permission.

any POW camp. True, a prisoner is not dependent on his exertions for the provision of the necessaries, or even the luxuries of life, but through his economic activity, the exchange of goods and services, his standard of material comfort is considerably enhanced. And this is a serious matter to the prisoner: he is not "playing at shops" even though the small scale of the transactions and the simple expression of comfort and wants in terms of cigarettes and jam, razor blades, and writing paper, make the urgency of those needs difficult to appreciate, even by an ex-prisoner of some three months' standing.

Nevertheless, it cannot be too strongly emphasized that economic activities do not bulk so large in prison society as they do in the larger world. There can be little production; as has been said the prisoner is independent of his exertions for the provision of the necessities and luxuries of life; the emphasis lies in exchange and the media of exchange. A prison camp is not to be compared with the seething crowd of higglers in a street market, any more than it is to be compared with the economic inertia of a family dinner table.

Naturally then, entertainment, academic and literary interests, games and discussions of the "other world" bulk larger in everyday life than they do in the life of more normal societies. But it would be wrong to underestimate the importance of economic activity. Everyone receives a roughly equal share of essentials; it is by trade that individual preferences are given expression and comfort increased. All at some time, and most people regularly, make exchanges of one sort of another.

Although a POW camp provides a living example of a simple economy which might be used as an alternative to the Robinson Crusoe economy beloved by the textbooks, and its simplicity renders the demonstration of certain economic hypotheses both amusing and instructive, it is suggested that the principal significance is sociological. True, there is interest in observing the growth of economic institutions and customs in a brand new society, small and simple enough to prevent detail from obscuring the basic pattern and disequilibrium from obscuring the working of the system. But the essential interest lies in the universality and the spontaneity of this economic life; it came into existence not by conscious imitation but as a response to the immediate needs and circumstances. Any similarity between prison organization and outside organization arises from similar stimuli evoking similar responses.

The following is as brief an account of the essential data as may render the narrative intelligible. The camps of which the writer had experience were Oflags and consequently the economy was not complicated by payments for work by the detaining power. They consisted normally of between 1,200 and 2,500 people, housed in a number of separate but intercommunicating bungalows, one company of 200 or so to a building. Each company formed a group within the main organization and inside the company the room and the messing syndicate, a voluntary and spontaneous group who fed together, formed the constituent units.

Between individuals there was active trading in all consumer goods and in some services. Most trading was for food against cigarettes or other foodstuffs, but cigarettes rose from the status of a normal commodity to that of currency. RMk.s existed but had no circulation save for gambling debts, as few articles could be purchased with them from the canteen.

Our supplies consisted of rations provided by the detaining power and (principally) the contents of Red Cross food parcels—tinned milk, jam, butter, biscuits, bully, chocolate, sugar, etc., and cigarettes. So far the supplies to each prison were equal and regular. Private parcels of clothing, toilet requisites, and cigarettes were also received, and here equality ceased owing to the different numbers despatched and the vagaries of the post. All these articles were the subject of trade and exchange.

THE DEVELOPMENT AND
ORGANIZATION OF THE MARKET

Very soon after capture people realized that it was both undesirable and unnecessary, in view of the limited size and the equality of supplies, to give away or to accept gifts of cigarettes or food. "Goodwill" developed into trading as a more equitable means of maximizing individual satisfaction.

We reached a transit camp in Italy about a fortnight after capture and received one-fourth of a Red Cross food parcel each a week later. At once exchanges, already established, multiplied in volume. Starting with simple direct barter, such as a nonsmoker giving a smoker friend his cigarette issue in exchange for a chocolate ration, more complex exchanges soon became an accepted custom. Stories circulated of a padre who started off round the camp with a tin of cheese and five cigarettes and returned to his bed with a complete parcel in addition to his original cheese and cigarettes; the market was not yet perfect. Within a week or two, as the volume of trade grew, rough scales of exchange values came into existence. Sikhs, who had at first exchanged tinned beef for practically any other foodstuff, began to insist on jam and margarine. It was realized that a tin of jam was worth one-half pound of margarine plus something else; that a cigarette issue was worth several chocolate issues, and a tin of diced carrots was worth practically nothing.

In this camp we did not visit other bungalows very much and prices varied from place to place; hence the germ of truth in the story of the itinerant priest. By the end of a month, when we reached our permanent camp, there was a lively trade in all commodities and their relative values were well known, and expressed not in terms of one another—one didn't quote bully in terms of sugar—but in terms of cigarettes. The cigarette became the standard of value. In the permanent camp people started by wandering through the bungalows calling their offers—"cheese for seven" (cigarettes)—and the hours after parcel issue were Bedlam. The inconveniences of this system soon led to its replacement by an Exchange and Mart notice board in every bungalow, where under the headings "name," "room number," "wanted" and "offered" sales and wants were advertised. When a deal went through, it was crossed off the board. The public and semipermanent records of transactions led to cigarette prices being well known and thus tending to equality throughout the camp, although there were always opportunities for an astute trader to make a profit from arbitrage. With this development everyone, including nonsmokers, was willing to sell for cigarettes, using them to buy at another time and place. Cigarettes became the normal currency, though, of course, barter was never extinguished.

The unity of the market and the prevalence of a single price varied directly with the general level of organization and comfort in the camp. A transit camp was always chaotic and uncomfortable: people were overcrowded, no one knew where anyone else was living, and few took the trouble to find out. Organization was too slender to include an Exchange and Mart board, and private advertisements were the most that appeared. Consequently a transit camp was not one market but many. The price of a tin of salmon is known to have varied by two cigarettes in 20 between one end of a hut and the other. Despite a high level of organization in Italy, the market was morcellated in this manner at the first transit camp we reached after our removal to Germany in the autumn of 1943. In this camp—Stalag VIIA at Moosburg in Bavaria—there were up to 50,000 prisoners of all nationalities. French, Russians, Italians, Jugo-Slavs were free to move about within the camp; British and Americans were confined to their compounds, although a few cigarettes given to a sentry would always procure permission for one or two men to visit other compounds. The people who first visited the highly organized French trading centre with its stalls and known prices found coffee extract—relatively cheap among the tea-drinking English—commanding a fancy price in biscuits or cigarettes, and some enterprising people made small fortunes that way. (Incidentally we found out later that much of the coffee went "over the wire" and sold for phenomenal prices at black market cafes in Munich: some of the French prisoners were said to have made substantial sums in RMk.s. This was one of the few occasions on which our normally closed economy came into contact with other economic worlds.)

Eventually public opinion grew hostile to these monopoly profits—not every one could make contact with the French—and trading with them was put on a regulated basis. Each group of beds was given a quota of articles to offer and the transaction was carried out by accredited representatives from the British compound, with monoploy rights. The same method was used for trading with sentries elsewhere, as in this trade secrecy and reasonable prices had a peculiar importance, but as is ever the case with regulated companies, the interloper proved too strong.

The permanent camps in Germany saw the highest level of commercial organization. In addition to the Exchange and Mart notice boards, a shop was organized as a public utility, controlled by representatives of the Senior British Officer, on a no-profit basis. People left their surplus clothing, toilet requisites, and food there until they were sold at a fixed price in cigarettes. Only sales in cigarettes were accepted—there was no barter—and there was no higgling. For food at least there were standard prices: clothing is less homogeneous and the price was decided around a norm by the seller and the shop manager in agreement; shirts would average say 80, ranging from 60 to 120 according to quality and age. Of food, the shop carried small stocks for convenience; the capital was provided by a loan from the bulk store of Red Cross cigarettes and repaid by a small commission taken on the first transactions. Thus the cigarette attained its fullest currency status, and the market was almost completely unified.

It is thus to be seen that a market came into existence without labor or production. The BRCS may be considered as "Nature" of the textbook, and the articles of trade—food, clothing and cigarettes—as free gifts—land of manna. Despite this, and despite a roughly equal distribution of resources, a market came into spontaneous operation, and prices were fixed by the operation of supply and demand. It is difficult to reconcile this fact with the labor theory of value.

Actually there was an embryo labor market. Even when cigarettes were not scarce, there was usually some unlucky person willing to perform services for them. Laundrymen advertised at two cigarettes a garment. Battle-dress was scrubbed and pressed and a pair of trousers lent for the interim period for 12. A good pastel portrait cost 30 or a tin of "Kam." Odd tailoring and other jobs similarly had their prices.

There were also entrepreneurial services. There was a coffee stall owner who sold tea, coffee, or cocoa at two cigarettes a cup, buying his raw materials at market prices and hiring labor to gather fuel and to stoke; he actually enjoyed the services of a chartered accountant at one stage. After a period of great prosperity he overreached himself and failed disastrously for several hundred cigarettes. Such largescale private enterprise was rare but several middlemen or professional traders existed. The padre in Italy, or the men at Moosburg who opened trading relations with the French, are examples: the more subdivided the market, the less perfect the advertisement of prices, and the less stable the prices, the greater was the scope for these operators. One man capitalized his knowledge of Urdu by buying meat from the Sikhs and selling butter and jam in return: as his operations became better known more and more people entered this trade, prices in the Indian Wing approximated more nearly to those elsewhere, though to the end a "contact" among the Indians was valuable, as linguistic difficulties prevented the trade from being quite free. Middlemen traded on their own account or on commission. Price rings and agreements were suspected and the traders certainly cooperated. Nor did they welcome newcomers. Unfortunately, the writer knows little of the workings of these people: public opinion was hostile and the professionals were usually of a retiring disposition.

One trader in food and cigarettes, operating in a period of dearth, enjoyed a high reputation. His capital, carefully saved, was originally about 50 cigarettes, with which he bought rations on issue days and held them until the price rose just before the next issue. He also picked up a little by arbitrage; several times a day he visited every Exchange or Mart notice board and took advantage of every discrepancy between prices of goods offered and wanted. His knowledge of prices, markets, and names of those who had received cigarette parcels was phenomenal. By these means he kept himself smoking steadily—his profits—while his capital remained intact.

Sugar was issued on Saturday. About Tuesday two of us used to visit Sam and make a deal; as old customers he would advance as much of the price as he could spare us, and entered the transaction in a book. On Saturday morning, he left cocoa tins on our beds for the ration, and picked them up on Saturday afternoon. We were hoping for a calendar at Christmas, but Sam failed too. He was left holding a big black treacle issue when the price fell, and in this weakened state was unable to withstand an unexpected arrival of parcels and the consequent price fluctuations. He paid in full, but from his capital. The next Tuesday, when I paid my usual visit, he was out of business.

Credit entered into many, perhaps into most, transactions, in one form or another. Sam paid in advance as a rule for his purchases of future deliveries of sugar, but many buyers asked for credit, whether the commodity was sold spot or future. Naturally prices varied according to the terms of sale. A treacle ration might be advertised for four cigarettes now or five next week. And in the future market "bread now" was a vastly different thing from "bread Thursday." Bread was issued on Thursday and Monday, four and three days' rations respectively, and by Wednesday and Sunday night it had risen at least one cigarette per ration, from seven to eight, by supper time. One man always saved a ration to sell then at the peak price: his offer of "bread now" stood out on the board among a number of "bread Monday's" fetching one or two less, or not selling at all—and he always smoked on Sunday night.

THE CIGARETTE CURRENCY

Although cigarettes as currency exhibited certain peculiarities, they performed all the functions of a metallic currency as a unit of account, as a measure of value and as a store of value, and shared most of its characteristics. They were homogeneous, reasonably durable, and of convenient size for the smallest or, in packets, for the largest transactions. Incidentally, they could be clipped or sweated by rolling them between the fingers so that tobacco fell out.

Cigarettes were also subject to the working of Gresham's Law. Certain brands were more popular than others as smokes, but for currency purposes a cigarette was a cigarette. Consequently buyers used the poorer qualities and the Shop rarely saw the more popular brands: cigarettes such as Churchman's No. 1 were rarely used for trading. At one time cigarettes handrolled from pipe tobacco began to circulate. Pipe tobacco was issued in lieu of cigarettes by the Red Cross at a rate of 25 cigarettes to the ounce and this rate was standard in exchanges, but an ounce would produce 30 homemade cigarettes. Naturally, people with machinemade cigarettes broke them down and rerolled the tobacco, and the real cigarette virtually disappeared from the market. Handrolled cigarettes were not homogeneous and prices could no longer be quoted in them with safety: each cigarette was examined before it was

PRIVATE ENTERPRISE IN ACTION

accepted and thin ones were rejected, or extra demanded as a make-weight. For a time we suffered all the inconveniences of a debased currency.

Machinemade cigarettes were always universally acceptable, both for what they would buy and for themselves. It was this intrinsic value which gave rise to their principal disadvantage as currency, a disadvantage which exists, but to a far smaller extent in the case of metallic currency;—that is, a strong demand for nonmonetary purposes. Consequently our economy was repeatedly subject to deflation and to periods of monetary stringency. While the Red Cross issue of 50 or 25 cigarettes per man per week came in regularly, and while there were fair stocks held, the cigarette currency suited its purpose admirably. But when the issue was interrupted, stocks soon ran out, prices fell, trading declined in volume and became increasingly a matter of barter. This deflationary tendency was periodically offset by the sudden injection of new currency. Private cigarette parcels arrived in a trickle throughout the year, but the big numbers came in quarterly when the Red Cross received its allocation of transport. Several hundred thousand cigarettes might arrive in the space of a fortnight. Prices soared, and then began to fall, slowly at first but with increasing rapidity as stocks ran out, until the next big delivery. Most of our economic troubles could be attributed to this fundamental instability.

PRICE MOVEMENTS

Many factors affected prices, the strongest and most noticeable being the periodical currency inflation and deflation described in the last paragraphs. The periodicity of this price cycle depended on cigarette and, to a far lesser extent, on food deliveries. At one time in the early days, before any private parcels had arrived and when there were no individual stocks, the weekly issue of cigarettes and food parcels occurred on a Monday. The nonmonetary demand for cigarettes was great, and less elastic than the demand for food: consequently prices fluctuated weekly, falling towards Sunday night and rising sharply on Monday morning. Later, when many people held reserves, the weekly issue had no such effect, being too small a portion of the total available. Credit allowed people with no reserves to meet their nonmonetary demand over the weekend.

The general price level was affected by other factors. An influx of new prisoners, proverbially hungry, raised it. Heavy air raids in the vicinity of the camp probably increased the nonmonetary demand for cigarettes and accentuated deflation. Good and bad war news certainly had its effect, and the general waves of optimism and pessimism which swept the camp were reflected in prices. Before breakfast one morning in March of this year, a rumor of the arrival of parcels and cigarettes was circulated. Within 10 minutes I sold a treacle ration for four cigarettes (hitherto offered in vain for three), and many similar deals went through. By 10 o'clock the rumor was denied, and treacle that day found no more buyers even at two cigarettes.

119

More interesting than changes in the general price level were changes in the price structure. Changes in the supply of a commodity, in the German ration scale or in the makeup of Red Cross parcels, would raise the price of one commodity relative to others. Tins of oatmeal, once a rare and much sought after luxury in the parcels, became a commonplace in 1943, and the price fell. In hot weather the demand for cocoa fell, and that for soap rose. A new recipe would be reflected in the price level: the discovery that raisins and sugar could be turned into an alcoholic liquor of remarkable potency reacted permanently on the dried fruit market. The invention of electric immersion heaters run off the power points made tea, a drag on the market in Italy, a certain seller in Germany.

In August 1944, the supplies of parcels and cigarettes were both halved. Since both sides of the equation were changed in the same degree, changes in prices were not anticipated. But this was not the case: the nonmonetary demand for cigarettes was less elastic than the demand for food, and food prices fell a little. More important however were the changes in the price structure. German margarine and jam, hitherto valueless owing to adequate supplies of Canadian butter and marmalade, acquired a new value. Chocolate, popular and a certain seller, and sugar, fell. Bread rose; several standing contracts of bread for cigarettes were broken, especially when the bread ration was reduced a few weeks later.

In February, 1945, the German soldier who drove the ration wagon was found to be willing to exchange loaves of bread at the rate of one loaf for a bar of chocolate. Those in the know began selling bread and buying chocolate, by then almost unsaleable in a period of serious deflation. Bread, at about 40, fell slightly; chocolate rose from 15; the supply of bread was not enough for the two commodities to reach parity, but the tendency was unmistakable.

The substitution of German margarine for Canadian butter when parcels were halved naturally affected their relative values, margarine appreciating at the expense of butter. Similarly, two brands of dried milk, hitherto differing in quality and therefore in price by five cigarettes a tin, came together in price as the wider substitution of the cheaper raised its relative value.

Enough has been cited to show that any change in conditions affected both the general price level and the price structure. It was this latter phenomenon which wrecked our planned economy.

PAPER CURRENCY—BULLY MARKS

Around D-Day, food and cigarettes were plentiful, business was brisk and the camp in an optimistic mood. Consequently the Entertainments Committee felt the moment opportune to launch a restaurant, where food and hot drinks were sold while a band and variety turns performed. Earlier experiments, both public and private, had pointed the way, and the scheme was a great success. Food was bought at market prices to provide the meals and the small profits were devoted to a reserve fund and used to bribe Germans to provide grease paints and other necessities for the camp theatre. Originally meals were sold for cigarettes but this meant that the whole scheme was vulnerable to the periodic deflationary waves, and furthermore heavy smokers were unlikely to attend much. The whole success of the scheme depended on an adequate amount of food being offered for sale in the normal manner.

To increase and facilitate trade, and to stimulate supplies and customers therefore, and secondarily to avoid the worst effects of deflation when it should come, a paper currency was organized by the Restaurant and the Shop. The Shop bought food on behalf of the Restaurant with paper notes and the paper was accepted equally with the cigarettes in the Restaurant or Shop, and passed back to the Shop to purchase more food. The Shop acted as a bank of issue. The paper money was backed 100 percent by food; hence its name, the Bully Mark. The BMk. was backed 100 percent by food: there could be no over-issues, as is permissible with a normal bank of issue, since the eventual dispersal of the camp and consequent redemption of all BMk.s was anticipated in the near future.

Originally one BMk. was worth one cigarette and for a short time both circulated freely inside and outside the Restaurant. Prices were quoted in BMK.s and cigarettes with equal freedom—and for a short time the BMk. showed signs of replacing the cigarette as currency. The BMk. was tied to food, but not to cigarettes: as it was issued against food, say 45 for a tin of milk and so on, any reduction in the BMk. prices of food would have meant that there were unbacked BMk.s in circulation. But the price of both food and BMk.s could and did fluctuate with the supply of cigarettes.

While the Restaurant flourished, the scheme was a success: the Restaurant bought heavily, all foods were saleable and prices were stable.

In August parcels and cigarettes were halved and the Camp was bombed. The Restaurant closed for a short while and sales of food became difficult. Even when the Restaurant reopened, the food and cigarette shortage became increasingly acute and people were unwilling to convert such valuable goods into paper and to hold them for luxuries like snacks and tea. Less of the right kinds of food for the Restaurant were sold, and the Shop became glutted with dried fruit, chocolate, sugar, etc., which the Restaurant could not buy. The price level and the price structure changed. The BMk. fell to four-fifths of a cigarette and eventually farther still, and it became unacceptable save in the Restaurant. There was a flight from the BMk., no longer convertible into cigarettes or popular foods. The cigarette reestablished itself.

But the BMk. was sound! The Restaurant closed in the New Year with a progressive food shortage and the long evenings without lights due to intensified Allied air raids, and the BMk.s could only be spent in the Coffee Bar—relict of the Restaurant—or on the few unpopular foods in the Shop, the owners of which were prepared to accept them. In the end all holders of BMk.s were paid in full, in cups of coffee or in prunes. People who had bought BMk.s for cigarettes or valuable jam or biscuits in their heyday were aggrieved that they should have stood the loss involved in their restricted choice, but they suffered no actual loss of market value.

PRICE FIXING

Along with this scheme came a determined attempt at a planned economy, at price fixing. The Medical Officer had long been anxious to control food sales, for fear of some people selling too much, to the detriment of their health. The deflationary waves and their effects on prices were inconvenient to all and would be dangerous to the Restaurant which had to carry stocks. Furthermore, unless the BMk. was convertible into cigarettes at about par it had little chance of gaining confidence and of succeeding as a currency. As has been explained, the BMk. was tied to food but could not be tied to cigarettes, which fluctuated in value. Hence, while BMk. prices of food were fixed for all time, cigarette prices of food and BMk.s varied.

The Shop, backed by the Senior British Officer, was now in a position to enforce price control both inside and outside its walls. Hitherto a standard price had been fixed for food left for sale in the Shop, and prices outside were roughly in conformity with this scale, which was recommended as a "guide" to sellers, but fluctuated a good deal around it. Sales in the Shop at recommended prices were apt to be slow though a good price might be obtained: sales outside could be made more quickly at lower prices. (If sales outside were to be at higher prices, goods were withdrawn from the Shop until the recommended price rose: but the recommended price was sluggish and could not follow the market closely by reason of its very purpose, which was stability.) The Exchange and Mart notice boards came under the control of the Shop: advertisements which exceeded five percent departure from the recommended scale were liable to be crossed out by authority: unauthorized sales were discouraged by authority and also by public opinion, strongly in favor of a just and stable price. (Recommended prices were fixed partly from market data, partly on the advice of the MO.)

At first the recommended scale was a success: the Restaurant, a big buyer, kept prices stable around this level: opinion and the five percent tolerance helped. But when the price level fell with the August cuts and the price structure changed, the recommended scale was too rigid. Unchanged at first, as no deflation was expected, the scale was tardily lowered, but the prices of goods on the new scale remained in the same relation to one another, owing to the BMk., while on the market the price structure had changed. And the modifying influence of the Restaurant had gone. The scale was moved up and down several times, slowly following the inflationary and deflationary waves, but it was rarely adjusted to changes in the price structure. More and more advertisements were crossed off the board, and black market sales at unauthorized prices increased: eventually public opinion turned against the recommended scale and authority gave up the struggle. In the last few weeks, with unparalleled deflation, prices fell with alarming rapidity, no scales existed, and supply and demand, alone and unmellowed, determined prices.

PUBLIC OPINION

Public opinion on the subject of trading was vocal if confused and change-able, and generalizations as to its direction are difficult and dangerous. A tiny minority held that all trading was undesirable as it engendered an unsavoury atmosphere; occasional frauds and sharp practices were cited as proof. Certain forms of trading were more generally condemned; trade with the Germans was criticized by many. Red Cross toilet articles, which were in short supply and only issued in cases of actual need, were excluded from trade by law and opinion working in unshakable harmony. At one time, when there had been several cases of malnutrition reported among the more devoted smokers, no trade in German rations was permitted, as the victims became an additional burden on the depleted food reserves of the Hospital. But while certain ac-tivities were condemned as antisocial, trade itself was practiced, and its utility appreciated, by almost everyone in the camp.

More interesting was opinion on middlemen and prices. Taken as a whole, opinion was hostile to the middleman. His function, and his hard work in bringing buyer and seller together, were ignored; profits were not regarded as a reward for labor, but as the result of sharp practices. Despite the fact that his very existence was proof to the contrary, the middleman was held to be redundant in view of the existence of an official Shop and the Exchange and Mart. Appreciation only came his way when he was willing to advance the price of a sugar ration, or to buy goods spot and carry them against a future sale. In these cases the element of risk was obvious to all, and the convenience of the service was felt to merit some reward. Particularly unpopular was the middleman with an element of monopoly, the man who contacted the ration wagon driver, or the man who utilized his knowledge of Urdu. And middle-men as a group were blamed for reducing prices. Opinion notwithstanding, most people dealt with a middleman, whether consciously or unconsciously, at some time or another.

There was a strong feeling that everything had its "just price" in cigarettes. While the assessment of the just price, which incidentally varied between camps, was impossible of explanation, this price was nevertheless pretty closely known. It can best be defined as the price usually fetched by an article in good times when cigarettes were plentiful. The "just price" changed slowly; it was unaffected by shortterm variations in supply, and while opinion might be resigned to departures from the "just price," a strong feeling of resentment persisted. A more satisfactory definition of the "just price" is impossible. Everyone knew what it was, though no one could explain why it should be so.

As soon as prices began to fall with a cigarette shortage, a clamor arose, particularly against those who held reserves and who bought at reduced prices. Sellers at cut prices were criticized and their activities referred to as the black market. In every period of dearth the explosive question of "should non-smokers receive a cigarette ration?" was discussed to profitless length. Unfortunately, it was the nonsmoker, or the light smoker with his reserves, along with the hated middleman, who weathered the storm most easily.

The popularity of the price-fixing scheme, and such success as it enjoyed, were undoubtedly the result of this body of opinion. On several occasions the fall of prices was delayed by the general support given to the recommmended scale. The onset of deflation was marked by a period of sluggish trade; prices stayed up but no one bought. Then prices fell on the black market, and the volume of trade revived in that quarter. Even when the recommended scale was revised, the volume of trade in the Shop would remain low. Opinion was always overruled by the hard facts of the market.

Curious arguments were advanced to justify price fixing. The recommended prices were in some way related to the calorific values of the food offered: hence some were overvalued and never sold at these prices. One argument ran as follows:—not everyone has private cigarette parcels: thus, when prices were high and trade good in the summer of 1944, only the lucky rich could buy. This was unfair to the man with few cigarettes. When prices fell in the following winter, prices should be pegged high so that the rich, who had enjoyed life in the summer, should put many cigarettes into circulation. The fact that those who sold to the rich in the summer had also enjoyed life then, and the fact that in the winter there was always someone willing to sell at low prices were ignored. Such arguments were hotly debated each night after the approach of Allied aircraft extinguished all lights at 8 p.m. But prices moved with the supply of cigarettes, and refused to stay fixed in accordance with a theory of ethics.

CONCLUSION

The economic organization described was both elaborate and smooth-working in the summer of 1944. Then came the August cuts and deflation. Prices fell, rallied with deliveries of cigarette parcels in September and December, and fell again. In January 1945, supplies of Red Cross cigarettes ran out: and prices slumped still further: in February the supplies of food parcels were exhausted and the depression became a blizzard. Food, itself scarce, was almost given away in order to meet the nonmonetary demand for cigarettes. Laundries ceased to operate, or worked for £s or RMk.s: food and cigarettes sold for fancy prices in £s, hitherto unheard of. The Restaurant was a memory and the BMk. a joke. The Shop was empty and the Exchange and Mart notices were full of unaccepted offers for cigarettes. Barter increased in volume, becoming a larger proportion of a smaller volume of trade. This, the first serious and prolonged food shortage in the writer's experience, caused the price structure to change again, partly because German rations were not easily divisible. A margarine ration gradually sank in value until it exchanged directly for a treacle ration. Sugar slumped sadly. Only bread retained its value.

Several thousand cigarettes, the capital of the Shop, were distributed without any noticeable effect. A few fractional parcel and cigarette issues, such as one-sixth of a parcel and twelve cigarettes each, led to monetary price recoveries and feverish trade, especially when they coincided with good news from the Western Front, but the general position remained unaltered.

By April 1945, chaos had replaced order in the economic sphere: sales were difficult, prices lacked stability. Economics has been defined as the science of distributing limited means among unlimited and competing ends. On 12th April, with the arrival of elements of the 30th U.S. Infantry Division, the ushering in of an age of plenty demonstrated the hypothesis that with infinite means economic organization and activity would be redundant, as every want could be satisfied without effort.

AIRLINE TAKES
THE MARGINAL ROUTE

Business Week

Continental Air Lines, Inc., last year filled only half the available seats on its Boeing 707 jet flights, a record some 15 percentage points worse than the national average.

By eliminating just a few runs—less than 5 percent—Continental could have raised its average load considerably. Some of its flights frequently carry as few as 30 passengers on the 120-seat plane. But the improved load factor would have meant reduced profits.

For Continental bolsters its corporate profits by deliberately running extra flights that aren't expected to do more than return their out-of-pocket costs— plus a little profit. Such marginal flights are an integral part of the overall operating philosophy that has brought small, Denver-based Continental—tenth among the 11 trunk carriers—through the bumpy postwar period with only one loss year.

This philosophy leans heavily on marginal analysis. And the line leans heavily on Chris F. Whelan, vice-president in charge of economic planning, to translate marginalism into hard, dollars-and-cents decisions.

Getting management to accept and apply the marginal concept probably is the chief contribution any economist can make to his company. Put most simply, marginalists maintain that a company should undertake any activity that adds more to revenues than it does to costs—and not limit itself to those activities whose returns equal average or "fully allocated" costs.

The approach, of course, can be applied to virtually any business, not just to air transportation. It can be used in consumer finance, for instance, where the question may be whether to make more loans—including bad loans—if this will increase net profit. Similarly, in advertising, the decision may rest on how much extra business a dollar's worth of additional advertising will bring in,

From *Business Week,* April 20, 1963, pp. 11 ff.

126

rather than pegging the advertising budget to a percentage of sales—and, in insurance, where setting high interest rates to discourage policy loans may actually damage profits by causing policyholders to borrow elsewhere.

Whelan finds all such cases wholly analogous to his run of problems, where he seeks to keep his company's eye trained on the big objective: net profit.

He is a genially gruff, shirt-sleeves kind of airline veteran, who resembles more a sales-manager type than an economist. This facet of his personality helps him "sell" ideas internally that might otherwise be brushed off as merely theoretical or too abstruse.

Last summer, Whelan politely chewed out a group of operational researchers at an international conference in Rome for being incomprehensible. "You have failed to educate the users of your talents to the potential you offer," he said. "Your studies, analyses, and reports are couched in tables that sales, operations, and maintenance personnel cannot comprehend."

Whelan's work is a concrete example of the truth in a crack by Professor Sidney Alexander of MIT—formerly economist for Columbia Broadcasting System—that the economist who understands marginal analysis has a "full-time job in undoing the work of the accountant." This is so, Alexander holds, because the practices of accountants—and of most businesses—are permeated with cost allocation directed at average, rather than marginal, costs.

In any complex business, there's likely to be a big difference between the costs of each company activity as it's carried on the accounting books and the marginal or "true" costs that can determine whether or not the activity should be undertaken.

The difficulty comes in applying the simple "textbook" marginal concept to specific decisions. If the economist is unwilling to make some bold simplifications, the job of determining "true" marginal costs may be highly complex, time wasting, and too expensive. But even a rough application of marginal principles may come closer to the right answer for business decision makers than an analysis based on precise average-cost data.

Proving that this is so demands economists who can break the crust of corporate habits and show concretely why the typical manager's response— that nobody ever made a profit without meeting all costs—is misleading and can reduce profits. To be sure, the whole business cannot make a profit unless average costs are met; but covering average costs should not determine whether any particular activity should be undertaken. For this would unduly restrict corporate decisions and cause managements to forgo opportunities for extra gains.

Management overhead at Continental is pared to the bone, so Whelan often is thrown such diverse problems as soothing a ruffled city council or planning the specifications for the plane the line will want to fly in 1970. But the biggest slice of his time goes to schedule planning—and it is here that the marginal concept comes most sharply into focus.

Whelan's approach is this: He considers that the bulk of his scheduled flights have to return at least their fully allocated costs. Overhead, depreciation, insurance are very real expenses and must be covered. The out-of-pocket

127

approach comes into play, says Whelan, only after the line's basic schedule has been set.

"Then you go a step farther," he says, and see if adding more flights will contribute to the corporate net. Similarly, if he's thinking of dropping a flight with a disappointing record, he puts it under the marginal microscope: "If your revenues are going to be more than your out-of-pocket costs, you should keep the flight on."

By "out-of-pocket costs" Whelan means just that: the actual dollars that Continental has to pay out to run a flight. He gets the figure not by applying hypothetical equations but by circulating a proposed schedule to every operating department concerned and finding out just what extra expenses it will entail. If a ground crew already on duty can service the plane, the flight isn't charged a penny of their salary expense. There may even be some costs eliminated in running the flight; they won't need men to roll the plane to a hangar, for instance, if it flies on to another stop.

Most of these extra flights, of course, are run at off-beat hours, mainly late at night. At times, though, Continental discovers that the hours aren't so unpopular after all. A pair of night coach flights on the Houston-San Antonio-El Paso-Phoenix-Los Angeles leg, added on a marginal basis, have turned out to be so successful that they are now more than covering fully allocated costs.

Whelan uses an alternative cost analysis closely allied with the marginal concept in drawing up schedules. For instance, on his 11:11 p.m. flight from Colorado Springs to Denver and a 5:20 a.m. flight the other way, Continental uses Viscounts that, though they carry some cargo, often go without a single passenger. But the net cost of these flights is less than would be the rent for overnight hangar space for the Viscount at Colorado Springs.

And there's more than one absolute-loss flight scheduled solely to bring passengers to a connecting Continental longhaul flight; even when the loss on the feeder service is considered a cost on the longhaul service, the line makes a net profit on the trip.

Continental's data handling system produces weekly reports on each flight, with revenues measured against both out-of-pocket and fully allocated costs. Whelan uses these to give each flight a careful analysis at least once a quarter. But those added on a marginal basis get the fine-tooth-comb treatment monthly.

The business on these flights tends to be useful as a leading indicator, Whelan finds, since the off-peak traffic is more than normally sensitive to economic trends and will fall off sooner than that on the popular-hour flights. When he sees the night coach flights turning in consistently poor showings, it's a clue to lower his projections for the rest of the schedule.

There are times, though, when the decisions dictated by the most expert marginal analysis seem silly at best, and downright costly at worst. For example, Continental will have two planes converging at the same time on Municipal Airport in Kansas City, when the new schedules take effect.

This is expensive because, normally, Continental doesn't have the facilities in Kansas City to service two planes at once; the line will have to lease an extra fuel truck and hire three new hands—at a total monthly cost of $1,800.

But, when Whelan started pushing around proposed departure times in other cities to avoid the double landing, it began to look as though passengers switching to competitive flights leaving at choicer hours, would lose Continental $10,000 worth of business each month. The two flights will be on the ground in Kansas City at the same time.

This kind of scheduling takes some 35 percent of Whelan's time. The rest of his average work week breaks down this way: 25 percent for developing nearterm, point-to-point traffic forecasts on which schedules are based; 20 percent in analyzing rates—Whelan expects to turn into a quasi-lawyer to plead Continental's viewpoint before the Civil Aeronautics Board; 20 percent on longrange forecasts and the where-should-we-go kind of planning that determines both which routes the line goes after and which it tries to shed. (Whelan's odd jobs in promotion, public relations, and general management don't fit into that time allotment; he says they "get stuck on around the side.")

The same recent week he was working on the data for his Kansas City double-landing problem, for instance, he was completing projections for the rest of 1963 so that other departments could use them for budget making, and was scrutinizing actions by Trans World Airlines, Inc., and Braniff Airways, Inc. TWA had asked CAB approval for special excursion fares from Eastern cities to Pacific Coast terminals; Whelan decided the plan worked out much the same as the economy fare on Continental's three-class service, so will neither oppose nor match the excursion deal. Braniff had just doubled its order—to 12—for British Aircraft Corporation's 111 jets. Whelan was trying to figure out where they were likely to use the small planes, and what effect they would have on Continental's share of competing routes in Texas and Oklahoma.

At the same time, Whelan was meeting with officials of Frontier Airlines and Trans-Texas, coordinating the CAB-ordered takeover by the feeder lines of 14 stops Continental is now serving with leased DC-3s.

And he was struggling, too, with a knotty problem in consumer economics: He was trying to sell his home on Denver's Cherry Vale Drive and buy one in Los Angeles, where Continental will move its headquarters this summer.

129

ECONOMIC INCENTIVES
IN AIR POLLUTION CONTROL

Edwin S. Mills

Smoke is one of the classic examples of external diseconomies mentioned in the writings of Alfred Marshall and his followers. Generations of college instructors have used this form of air pollution as an illustration to help their students to understand conditions under which competitive markets will or will not allocate resources efficiently. By now, the theoretical problems have been explored with the sharpest tools available to economists. The consensus among economists on the basic issue is overwhelming, and I suspect one would be hardpressed to find a proposition that commands more widespread agreement among economists than the following: The discharge of pollutants into the atmosphere imposes on some members of society costs which are inadequately imputed to the sources of the pollution by free markets, resulting in more pollution than would be desirable from the point of view of society as a whole.

In spite of the widespread agreement on the fundamental issues regarding externalities such as air pollution, there have been remarkably few attempts in the scholarly literature to carry the analysis beyond this point. Most writers have been content to point out that the free market will misallocate resources in this respect, and to conclude that this justifies intervention. But what sort of intervention? There are many kinds, and some are clearly preferable to others.

Too often we use the imperfect working of a free market to justify *any* kind of intervention. This is really an anomalous situation. After all, markets are manmade institutions, and they can be designed in many ways. When an economist concludes that a free market is working badly—giving the wrong signals, so to speak—he should also ask how the market may be restructured so that it will give the right signals.

Thus, in the case of air pollution, acceptance of the proposition stated above leads most people to think entirely in terms of direct regulation—permits, registration, licenses, enforcement of standards and so on. I submit that this is rather like abandoning a car because it has a flat tire. Of course, in some cases the car may be working so badly that the presence of a flat tire makes it rational to abandon it, and correspondingly the inadequacies of some market mechanisms may make abandonment desirable. Nevertheless, I submit that the more logical procedure is to ask how a badly functioning market may be restructured to preserve the clear advantages of free and decentralized decision making, but to remedy its defects. Only when there appears to be no feasible way of structuring a market so that it will give participants the right signals, should it be given up in favor of direct regulation.

It is easy to state the principle by which the socially desirable amount of pollution abatement should be determined: *Any given pollution level should be reached by the least costly combination of means available; the level of pollution should be achieved at which the cost of a further reduction would exceed the benefits.*

To clothe the bare bones of this principle with the flesh of substance is a very tall order indeed. In principle, if every relevant number were known, an edict could be issued to each polluter specifying the amount by which he was to reduce his discharge of pollutants and the means by which he was to do so. In fact, we are even farther from having the right numbers for air pollution than we are from having those for water pollution.

In this situation, I suggest that any scheme for abatement should be consistent with the following principles:

1. It should permit decision making to be as decentralized as possible. Other things being equal, a rule that discharges must be reduced by a certain amount is preferable to a rule that particular devices be installed, since the former permits alternatives to be considered that may be cheaper than the devices specified in the latter.

2. It should be experimental and flexible. As experience with abatement schemes accumulates, we will gain information about benefits and costs of abatement. We will then revise our ideas about the desirable amount and methods of abatement. Control schemes will have to be revised accordingly.

3. It should be coupled with careful economic research on benefits and costs of air-pollution abatement. Without benefit-cost calculations, we cannot determine the desirable amount of abatement. We can, however, conjecture with confidence that more abatement is desirable than is provided by existing controls. Therefore, our present ignorance of benefits and costs should not be used as an excuse for doing nothing. I would place great emphasis on doing the appropriate research as part of any control scheme. A well-designed scheme will provide information (e.g., on the costs of a variety of control devices) that is relevant to the benefit-cost calculations.

MEANS OF CONTROL

We are not in a position to evaluate a variety of schemes that are in use or have been proposed to control or abate air pollution. It will be useful to classify methods of control according to the categories employed by Kneese in his discussion of water pollution:

1. *Direct Regulation.* In this category, I include licenses, permits, compulsory standards, zoning, registration, and equity litigation.

2. *Payments.* In this category I include not only direct payments or subsidies, but also reductions in collections that would otherwise be made. Examples are subsidization of particular control devices, forgiveness of local property taxes on pollution-control equipment, accelerated depreciation on control equipment, payments for decreases in the discharge of pollutants, and tax credits for investment in control equipment.

3. *Charges.* This category includes schedules of charges or fees for the discharge of different amounts of specified pollutants and excise or other taxes on specific sources of pollution (such as coal).

My objection to direct regulation should be clear by now. It is too rigid and inflexible, and loses the advantages of decentralized decision making. For example, a rule that factories limit their discharges of pollutants to certain levels would be less desirable than a system of effluent fees that achieved the same overall reduction in pollution, in that the latter would permit each firm to make the adjustment to the extent and in the manner that best suited its own situation. Direct restrictions are usually cumbersome to administer, and rarely achieve more than the grossest form of control. In spite of the fact that almost all of our present control programs fall into this category, they should be tried only after all others have been found unworkable.

Thus, first consideration ought to be given to control schemes under the second and third categories.

Many of the specific schemes under these two categories are undesirable in that they involve charges or payments for the wrong thing. If it is desired to reduce air pollution, then the charge or payment should depend on the amount of pollutants discharged and not on an activity that is directly or indirectly related to the discharge of pollutants. For example, an excise tax on coal is less desirable than a tax on the discharge of pollutants resulting from burning coal because the former distorts resource use in favor of other fuels and against devices to remove pollutants from stack gases after burning coal. As a second example, a payment to firms for decreasing the discharge of pollutants is better than a tax credit for investment in pollution-control devices because the latter introduces a bias against other means of reducing the discharge of pollutants, such as the burning of nonpolluting fuels. Thus, many control schemes can be eliminated on the principle that more efficient control can normally be obtained by incentives that depend on the variable it is desired to influence rather than by incentives that depend on a related variable.

Many of the specific schemes under *Payments* can be eliminated on the grounds that they propose to subsidize the purchase of devices that neither add to revenues nor reduce costs. Thus, if a pollution-control device neither helps to produce salable products nor reduces production costs, a firm really receives very little incentive to buy the device even if the government offers to pay half the cost. All that such subsidy schemes accomplish is to reduce somewhat the resistance to direct controls. Of course, some control devices may help to recover wastes that can be made into salable products. Although there are isolated examples of the recovery of valuable wastes in the process of air-pollution control, it is hard to know whether such possibilities are extensive. A careful survey of this subject would be interesting. However, the key point is that, to the extent that waste recovery is desirable, firms receive the appropriate incentive to recover wastes by the use of fees or payments that are related to the discharge of effluents. Therefore, even the possibility of waste recovery does not justify subsidization of devices to recover wastes.

The foregoing analysis creates a presumption in favor of schemes under which either payments are made for reducing the discharge of pollutants or charges are made for the amount of pollutants discharged. The basic condition for optimum resource allocation can in principle be satisfied by either scheme, since under either scheme just enough incentive can be provided so that the marginal cost of further abatement approximates the marginal benefits of further abatement. There are, however, three reasons for believing that charges are preferable to subsidies:

1. There is no natural "origin" for payments. In principle, the payment should be for a reduction in the discharge of pollutants below what it would have been without the payment. Estimation of this magnitude would be difficult and the recipient of the subsidy would have an obvious incentive to exaggerate the amount of pollutants he would have discharged without the subsidy. The establishment of a new factory would raise a particularly difficult problem. The trouble is precisely that which agricultural policy meets when it tries to pay farmers to reduce their crops. Jokes about farmers deciding to double the amount of corn not produced this year capture the essence of the problem.

2. Payments violate feelings of equity which many people have on this subject. People feel that if polluting the air is a cost of producing certain products, then the consumers who benefit ought to pay this cost just as they ought to pay the costs of labor and other inputs needed in production.

3. If the tax system is used to make the payments, e.g., by permitting a credit against tax liability for reduced discharge of pollutants, a "gimmick" is introduced into the tax system which, other things being equal, it is better to avoid. Whether or not the tax system is used to make the payments, the money must be raised at least partly by higher taxes than otherwise for some taxpayers. Since most of our taxes are not neutral, resource misallocation may result.

I feel that the above analysis creates at least a strong presumption for the use of discharge or effluent fees as a means of air-pollution abatement.

Briefly, the proposal is that air-pollution control authorities be created with responsibility to evaluate a variety of abatement schemes, to estimate benefits and costs, to render technical assistance, to levy charges for the discharge of effluents, and to adopt other means of abatement.

Serious problems of air pollution are found mostly in urban areas of substantial size. Within an urban area, air pollution is no respecter of political boundaries, and an authority's jurisdiction should be defined by the boundaries of a metropolitan air shed. Although difficult to identify precisely, such air sheds would roughly coincide with Standard Metropolitan Statistical Areas. Except in a few cases, such as the Chicago-Gary and the New York-northern New Jersey areas, jurisdiction could be confined to a single metropolitan area. In a number of instances, the authority would have to be interstate. In many large metropolitan areas, the authority would have to be the joint creation of several local governments. There would presumably be participation by state governments and by the federal government at least to the extent of encouragement and financial support.

Each authority would have broad responsibility for dealing with air pollution in its metropolitan air shed. It would institute discharge fees and would be mainly financed by such fees. It would have the responsibility of estimating benefits and costs of air-pollution abatement, and of setting fees accordingly. It would have to identify major pollutants in its area and set fees appropriate to each significant pollutant. The authority could also provide technical advice and help concerning methods of abatement.

Although there would be great uncertainty as to the appropriate level of fees at first, this should not prevent their use. They should be set conservatively while study was in progress, and data on the responses of firms to modest fees would be valuable in making benefit-cost calculations. Given present uncertainties, a certain amount of flexible experimentation with fees would be desirable.

Questions will necessarily arise as to just what kinds and sources of pollutants would come under the jurisdiction of the proposed authority. I do not pretend to have answers to all such questions. Presumably, standard charges could be set for all major pollutants, with provision for variation in each metropolitan air shed to meet local conditions. It is clear that provision should be made for the possibility of varying the charge for a particular pollutant from air shed to air shed. The harm done by the discharge of a ton of sulfur dioxide will vary from place to place, depending on meteorological and other factors. It is probably less harmful in Omaha than in Los Angeles. It is important that charges reflect these differences, so that locational decisions will be appropriately affected.

Consideration would also have to be given to the appropriate temporal pattern of charges. In most cities, pollution is much more serious in summer than at other times. Charges that were in effect only during summer months might induce a quite different set of adjustments than charges that were in effect at all times.

No one should pretend that the administration of an effective air-pollution control scheme will be simple or cheap. Measurement and monitoring of discharges are necessary under any control scheme and can be expensive and technically difficult. Likewise, whatever the control scheme, finding the optimum degree of abatement requires the calculation of benefits and costs; these calculations are conceptually difficult and demanding.

The point that needs to be emphasized strongly is that the cost of administering a control scheme based on effluent fees will be less than the cost of administering any other scheme of equal effectiveness. An effluent-fee system, like ordinary price systems, is largely self-administering.

This point is important and is worth stating in detail. First, consider an effluent-fee system. Suppose a schedule of fees has been set. Then firms will gradually learn the rate of effluent discharge that is most profitable. Meanwhile, the enforcement agency will need to sample the firm's effluent to ensure that the firm is paying the fee for the amount actually discharged. However, once the firm has found the most profitable rate of effluent discharge, and this is known to the enforcing agency, the firm will have no incentive to discharge any amount of effluent other than the one for which it is paying. At this point the system becomes self-administering and the enforcement agency need only collect bills. Second, consider a regulatory scheme under which the permissible discharge is set at the level that actually resulted under the effluent-fee scheme. Then the firm has a continuing incentive because of its advantage on the cost side to exceed the permissible discharge rate so as to increase production. Monitoring by the enforcement agency therefore continues to be necessary.

Of course, under either a regulatory or an effluent-fee scheme, a change in conditions will require the search for a new "equilibrium." Neither system can be self-enforcing until the new equilibrium has been found. The point is that the effluent-fee system becomes self-enforcing at that point, whereas the regulatory system does not.

PUBLIC CONTROL OF BUSINESS

Clair Wilcox

. . . THE NEED FOR CONTROL

The case for private enterprise, as it was developed by economists and expounded by teachers of economics for a century and a half, was based upon the assumption that competition would prevail. Businessmen were selfish; they would seek to maximize their profit by paying too little and charging too much. But their competitors, though equally selfish, would prevent them from doing so by paying more and charging less. Competition would thus harness selfishness and make it serve the common weal.

With the growth of big business, in later years, it has appeared to many observers that competition has declined. If this were true, the selfishness of the businessman was no longer held in check. A new defense of private enterprise was thus required. One was found in the doctrine of social responsibility. This is the view that recent changes in the structure of the corporation, the character of management, and the environment of enterprise have so transformed the motivation of businessmen that they seek, now, to serve the general interest.

In this view, social responsibility is assumed voluntarily; it is not compelled. Another theory rests upon a new form of compulsion—countervailing power. According to this theory, protection against the selfishness of big business is afforded, not by the competition of other enterprises on the same side of the market, but by the emergence of equally large units on the other side of the market. Big sellers thus find themselves confronted by big buyers, and vice versa, so that neither one can take advantage of the other.

Each of these theories argues that business will serve the general interest, whether through the discipline of competition, the assumption of social

---

Reprinted with permission from Clair Wilcox; from *Public Policies Toward Business* (4th ed.; Homewood, Ill.: Richard D. Irwin, In.), pp. 10-15.

responsibility, or the force of countervailing power. What need is there, then, for the imposition of public controls?

The Rationale of Competition

Private enterprise is justified, in the defense long offered by economists, by the service it renders to people in their capacity as consumers. Private enterprise seeks profit. But, to obtain profit, it must serve consumers, for this is the only way to profit that competition will allow. It is thus on the foundation of competition that the case for private enterprise is built.

Human wants are many and growing; the productive resources through which they can be satisfied—land, labor, capital, materials, and power—are scarce. The central problem of economics is to determine how these resources shall be allocated; to decide what goods shall be produced. The goods produced by private enterprise, in a market economy, will be those that the consumer demands. In such an economy, the consumer exercises sovereign power. Each time he spends a dollar he casts a vote for the production of the thing he buys. His dollar votes, recorded in his purchases, express the character of his demands. Where his demand for a commodity declines, its price will fall. Where demand increases, price will rise. When producers, in their turn, compete against each other to obtain resources, those with products where demand is weak will find themselves outbid by those with products where demand is strong. Resources will be diverted from the one field to the other, away from producing goods that are wanted less and toward producing goods that are wanted more. Competition is thus the regulator that compels producers to follow the guidance of consumer choice.

Competition serves the consumer in other ways. It operates negatively to protect him against extortion. If the quality of the product offered by one producer is low, the quality of that offered by another may be high. If the price charged by one producer is high, that asked by another may be low. The consumer is not at the mercy of the one as long as he has the alternative of buying from the other. More than this, competition operates affirmatively to enhance quality and reduce price. The producer who wishes to enlarge his profits must increase his sales. To do so, he must offer the consumer more goods for less money. As he adds the quality and subtracts from price, his rivals are compelled to do the same. The changes which he initiates soon spread throughout the trade. Every consumer of its products gets more and pays less. Competition also makes for efficiency. It leads some producers to eliminate wastes and cut costs so that they may undersell others. It compels others to adopt similar measures in order that they may survive. It weeds out those whose costs remain high and thus operates to put production in the hands of those whose costs are low. As the former are superseded by the latter, the general level of industrial efficiency is accordingly enhanced. Competition is congenial to material progress. It keeps the door open to new blood and new ideas. It communicates to all producers the improvements made by any one of them. Competition is cumulative in its effects. When competitors cut their prices, consumers buy more goods, output increases, and unit costs may decline. The lower prices compel producers to seek still further means of cutting costs. The resulting gains in efficiency open the way to still lower prices. Goods are turned out in increasing volume, and the general plane of living is raised.

Competition is thus held to be a stern disciplinarian. It has long been recognized, however, that there still is need, in a competitive economy, for public controls. The existence of competition is not always assured. Many firms may agree among themselves that they will not compete. Two or more firms may combine to make a single unit. One or a few firms may come to dominate an industry, through the employment of unfair methods or through the enjoyment of special advantages. If the consumer is to reap the benefits of competition, government must make sure that competition is maintained.

Opposite to the benefits of competition are the evils of monopoly. Monopoly prevents the allocation of resources in accordance with the pattern of consumer choice. The monopolist is likely to increase his profit by raising his price. He will then limit his output to the quantity that the market will take at the price that he has fixed. Consumers who would be willing to purchase larger quantities of his product at a lower price are left, instead, to buy goods that are wanted less. Resources are thus diverted from those things which the community prefers to those which are, at best, a second choice. The resources that are excluded from the superior occupation compete with others for employment in inferior ones and their productivity declines. Monopoly, moreover, affords the consumer no protection against extortion. The monopolist may persist in offering inferior quality at a high price, since the purchasers of his product lack the alternative of turning to other sources of supply. He may obtain his profit, not by serving the community, but by refusing to serve it. Monopoly inflicts no penalty on inefficiency. The monopolist may eliminate wastes and cut costs, but he is under no compulsion to do so. Through inertia, he may cling to accustomed techniques. His hold upon the market is assured. Monopoly, as such, is not conducive to progress. The large firm may engage in research and invent new products, materials, methods, and machines. But when it possesses a monopoly, it will be reluctant to make use of these inventions if they would compel it to scrap existing equipment or if it believes that their ultimate profitability is in doubt. The monopolist may introduce innovations and cut costs, but instead of moving goods by reducing prices he is prone to spend large sums on alternative methods of promoting sales. His refusal to cut prices deprives the community of any gain. Monopoly impedes the improvement of levels of living. Because it does not compel the enhancement of quality or the reduction of price, because it fails to penalize inefficiency, because it is not conducive to progress, it makes the total output of goods and services smaller than it otherwise would be.

The maintenance of competition protects the community against the evils of monopoly. But this is not enough, for harm may also be done by the behavior of competitors. Competing sellers and competing buyers may not be equally well informed, and those who possess information may take advantage of those who lack it. Sellers and buyers may not be equally able to bargain, and those who are strong may impose upon those who are weak. Sellers seeking present profits and buyers seeking present satisfactions may waste scarce natural resources, thus impairing the well-being of future generations. Government must therefore be concerned, not only with the preservation of competition, but also with the ways in which men compete. It must act to equip traders with accurate information, to protect the weak against the strong, and to safeguard future needs against present wastes. Public control is thus required to facilitate the operation of competitive markets and to protect them against abuse.

The Doctrine of Social Responsibility

Business is driven to serve the common interest, according to a view now popular with businessmen,[1] not by the force of competition, but by a sense of social responsibility. Such service is not compelled; it is rendered voluntarily.

The notion that business conduct may be influenced by moral considerations is not entirely new. Business has long had its unwritten code of ethics—pay thy debts, fulfill thy contracts, satisfy thy customers, deal fairly with thy competitors—honored sometimes in the breach but often in the observance. Associations of businessmen have also had their written codes of ethics for many years. These codes, modeled on those of the professions, give formal expression to even higher standards of social obligation. But this is often little more than window dressing. The high standards may not be observed; they cannot be enforced. And behind their facade, the codes go on to ban competitive behavior as unethical. Even in the professions, codes of ethics are designed to give protection to the members of the group. One doctor, for instance, is not to criticize the diagnosis or treatment given by another. But the professions do assume responsibility for the service rendered by their members. Doctors may be excluded from hospitals, and lawyers may be disbarred. Business, however, has none of the characteristics of a profession. It requires no common training. It does not stand in a confidential personal relationship with those it serves. Its associations assume no responsibility for the quality of the products sold by their members. They have no means of imposing professional discipline. Business codes have never been regarded, therefore, as a substitute for public law.[2]

---

[1] See Howard R. Bowen, *Social Responsibilities of the Businessman* (New York: Harper & Bros., 1953).

[2] See J. M. Clark, *Social Control of Business,* 2d ed. (New York: McGraw-Hill Book Co., 1939), Chapter 12.

The doctrine of social responsibility, in its present form, has to do only with big business. In the modern corporation, ownership has come to be separated from control. Ownership is scattered among thousands of shareholders whose contact with the enterprise is limited to filling out proxy statements and cashing dividend checks. Control is in the hands of a self-perpetuating management. Participation in management has come increasingly to require formal training. The decisions of management are made in the full light of publicity. In such a situation, the manager holds himself responsible not only—or even primarily—to the stockholders but also to suppliers, workers, consumers, and the community at large. He serves as a mediator among these groups, balancing their interests, one against another. His motivation differs sharply from that of the primitive entrepreneur. He takes little interest in immediate profit, looking rather toward the security of the corporation as an institution and its growth in the longer future. He seeks his satisfaction in the prestige that is accorded to success and progress. He wields his power benevolently, making each decision in the light of its social effects.[3]

There have been changes, says the doctrine, not only within the corporation but also in its environment. The manager, today, comes into frequent contact with labor leaders and with agencies of government. He must reckon with public opinion and with the possibility of further regulation. But these checks on his discretion are remote. The picture that is painted is that of an oligarch, held responsible by nothing but his own conscience, who is free to collect the profits of monopoly, but chooses instead to serve his fellow man.

The doctrine of social responsibility cannot be taken in disproof of the need for public control. Most men do not kill or steal, but laws against murder and theft are needed because some men do. Socially-minded men are undoubtedly to be found, in large and growing numbers, within the ranks of corporate management, but it would not be wise to assume that all managers of all corporations are of this type. Even though most managers were socially responsible, laws would still be needed to regulate the few who were not. The doctrine assumes, moreover, that the public interest is properly to be defined, and the social responsibility of business determined, by businessmen themselves. But such a view is not to be accepted; it is by society as a whole, acting through its political instruments, that these determinations should be made. Performance in the public interest should not be bestowed upon the community as a gift; it should be rendered because it is required.

The Theory of Countervailing Power

The theory of countervailing power, like the doctrine just examined, has to do with big business. As advanced by J. K. Galbraith,[4] this theory

---

[3] See A. A. Berle, *The Twentieth Century Capitalist Revolution* (New York: Harcourt, Brace & Co., 1954), Chapter 6; and J. K. Galbraith, *The New Industrial State* (Boston, Mass.: Houghton Mifflin Co., 1967), pp. 11-13.

[4] J. K. Galbraith, *American Capitalism* (Boston: Houghton Mifflin Co., 1952).

asserts that the presence of concentrated power on one side of the market will evoke the development of offsetting power on the other. Where a buyer is powerful, sellers will organize. Where a seller is powerful, strong buyers will appear. Big business, therefore, cannot abuse its power, because it must deal with those possessing equal power.

This theory does describe the situation that exists in many markets. The big employer bargains with the big union; the big milk distributor with the cooperative association of milk producers. The big meatpacker sells to the big chain stores. But there are many other markets in which strong buyers have long dealt with weak sellers; strong sellers with weak buyers. Countervailing power may emerge. But there is no reason to believe that it must necessarily do so, or that, when it does, it will be equal to the power that it was designed to offset.

Even where the power of sellers and buyers is equal, moreover, it does not follow that the public interest will be served. Instead of fighting one another, the two may join hands to exploit somebody else. The steel workers and the steel companies may agree to raise both wages and the price of steel. The producers association and the milk distributors may agree to raise the farm price and the retail price of milk. Indeed, Galbraith himself admits that in a period of inflation this is exactly what they will do. The meatpackers and the chain stores, however, are unlikely to agree to raise the retail price of meat. But this is not because sellers and buyers in the wholesale market have equal power. It is because the business of food retailing is highly competitive. If the buying power of the mass distributor is to be of service to the consumer, competition in distribution must be maintained.

The theory of countervailing power thus leaves wide scope for the exercise of public control. There is need for control where countervailing power does not exist and where power on the two sides of the market is unequal. There is also need for control to prevent powerful adversaries from resolving their differences at the expense of the ultimate consumer. . . .

ANTITRUST IN AN ERA
OF RADICAL CHANGE

Max Ways

Our sacred cow was born two-headed. Any serious examination of antitrust must start by recognizing that two distinct—indeed, contrary—policies have existed side by side. One policy has protected competition against such practices as conspiracies between firms to fix prices or limit production; this side of antitrust, exemplified by the Addyston Pipe case of 1899 and the very similar electrical conspiracy cases of 1961, has played and should continue to play a helpful part in the ever increasing liveliness and flexibility of the American market. The other antitrust policy has been fearful of change; it has frowned upon the growth of firms, especially by merger; it has sought to preserve the specific structure of markets on the assumption—long since demonstrated to be groundless—that the degree of competition is directly proportionate to the number of competitors and inversely proportionate to their average size; it has impaired the legitimate scope of freedom of contract and introduced arbitrary rigidities into the market through which we allocate our resources.

During the last 15 years the second policy has become more and more dominant in antitrust enforcement. Essentially, this other head of antitrust is anticompetitive and reactionary. Instead of relying upon the market to protect consumers and encourage progress, it substitutes the preferences of public administrators and judges as to how production and distribution should be organized. By trying to shield specific competitors against the effects of competitive innovation, it tends to reverse—or at least to inhibit—that long line of social evolution which has been described as the movement "from status to contract."

Because our economy is so resilient, the measurable practical damage done by this second kind of antitrust policy has not been great—yet. But what of tomorrow?

From *Fortune*, March 1966, pp. 126 ff. Reprinted by permission.

PRIVATE ENTERPRISE IN ACTION

We can know very little about the business specifics of 1986 or 1996. But some general statements about the next 20 or 30 years can be made with a high degree of confidence. Among them: (1) the pace of change, which broke through a sort of sound barrier around 1950, will continue to accelerate; (2) change will be made up of millions of innovations; many will be based on scientific discoveries and technological inventions; there will also be significant innovations in merchandising, finance, and corporate structure, and those patterns of coordination and decision making that we sum up in the word "management." In short, what we know of the next 20 years is that corporations will need the utmost flexibility because in each year our economy will be more and more involved with innovation. It is this prospect that urgently requires the U.S. to abandon the anticompetitive side of antitrust.

TRAUMATIC MEMORIES

Serious debate of antitrust policy is drowned out by a kind of litany. "What makes the American business system superior to the British and all others?" "Antitrust." "What slakes the public resentment of big business?" "Antitrust." "What preserves us from direct government regulation and maybe even socialism?" "Antitrust." . . .

But this thing, as they used to say in Hollywood, is bigger than all of them. The reactionary side of antitrust has a momentum that is built into court decisions, congressional investigations, and the cliches of public discussion. This trend has picked up speed during the terms of such dissimilar Presidents as Truman, Eisenhower, Kennedy, and Johnson. A White House "friendly to business" cannot reverse the way antitrust has been going. The place to clarify a fundamental national policy is Congress. . . .

Much more is at stake than the level of corporate profits, or the efficiency of the aggregate economy, or its rate of growth. The *quality* of the American future depends on the flexibility of the market framework. If our business system continues to be haunted by hallucinations lingering from American capitalism's traumatic childhood, we will deal clumsily—and perhaps disastrously—with an era of radical change. . . .

BRYAN, BRANDEIS, BIGNESS, AND BADNESS

A glance back at the origins of antitrust may help clarify the choice that now confronts the U.S. In both its good and bad aspects, antitrust was a response to the great change that began in the last third of the nineteenth century. The good side—the confidence in competition and the resolve to foster it—was a brave leap in the dark by a nation that could not be sure of the direction in which modern capitalism would evolve. The bad side—the fear of large business units, new methods, new patterns of trade—was a timid, if understandable, clinging to the circumstantial patterns of an older America.

143

Both elements, side by side, can be clearly seen in the discussion of "the trusts" that rolled through the U.S. between 1880 and 1917.

Many words conspicuous in that discussion—including "trust," "monopoly," and "competition"—had split meanings; antitrust history is an exercise in unscrambling unintentional puns. "Trust," for example, meant originally a quite specific device by which stockholders in competing companies ended competition by pooling their voting stock in the hands of a board of trustees. But "trust" was also widely used to mean *any* large business corporation. "Trusts" in the first meaning—along with price-fixing agreements and other anticompetitive practices—were regarded by many lawyers and businessmen of the day as "conspiracies in restraint of trade," which had been illegal under common law. A practical difficulty was that the courts of the states, which normally enforced such common-law principles, could not readily get their hands on these huge new combines; they leapt across state lines and operated a nationwide business system. Without an act of Congress, federal courts had no solid authority to enforce the common-law prohibition against agreements in restraint of trade. Many who supported the Sherman Act of 1890 saw it as plugging a loophole in the federal-state structure. They reasoned that in the new business world, as in the old, competition would protect the public and stimulate progress. The good side of present antitrust policy is descended from this position.

But their interpretation of antitrust fell a long way short of satisfying that part of the public clamor which used the word "trust" to mean everything that was large, new, and different in business. Theodore Roosevelt understood —perhaps sooner and better than anyone else—the political dilemma involved in the two usages of the word "trust." In 1900, as governor, he told the New York Legislature: "Much that is complained about is not really the abuse so much as the inevitable development of our modern industrial life. We have moved far from the old simple days when each community transacted almost all its work for itself and relied upon outsiders for but a fraction of the necessaries, and for not a very large portion even of the luxuries, of life. Very many of the antitrust laws which have made their appearance on the statute books of recent years have been almost or absolutely ineffective because they have blinked the all-important fact that much of what they thought to do away with was incidental to modern industrial conditions, and could not be eliminated unless we were willing to turn back the wheels of modern progress by also eliminating the forces which had brought about these industrial conditions." As a politician, T. R. was responsive to that element in popular antitrust feeling which was simply resentment of change. But when it came to practical antitrust policy he moved very cautiously because he believed that at bottom the people wanted progress even more than they wanted "the old simple days."

The young Walter Lippman, writing in 1914 and using the word "trusts" in the broad sense of modern business organizations, brilliantly described popular reaction to the change. The trusts, he said, had come "into the life of the simple American community as a tremendous revolutionary force, upsetting custom, changing men's status, demanding a readjustment for which people were unready. Of course, there was antitrust feeling; of course, there was blind desire to smash them. Men had been ruined and they were too angry to think, too hard pressed to care much about the larger life which the trusts suggested." Lippmann understood that William Jennings Bryan represented resistance to change. "Bryan ... thought he was fighting the plutocracy; as a matter of fact he was fighting something much deeper than that; he was fighting the larger scale of human life ... What he and his people hated from the bottom of their souls were the economic conditions which had upset the old life of the prairies, made new demands upon democracy, introduced specialization and science, had destroyed village loyalties, frustrated private ambitions, and created the impersonal relationships of the modern world."

This "antitrust" state of mind, which Lippmann called "conservative," had little knowledge of or faith in market competition. In the old, simple life only a small proportion of goods and services had ever passed through a competitive market. The village blacksmith was a small businessman who had a local monopoly. The village general store was a retail conglomerate, and in the absence of competition it could indulge in all kinds of administrative inefficiencies—e.g., the new clerk's ignorance that the proprietor kept the nail keg behind the pickle barrel. Louis Brandeis, one of the most influential voices in developing the reactionary side of antitrust, never really believed that, under the stimulation of increasing competition, corporate management was reducing administrative inefficiencies; instead, he seemed to feel that a thousand nail kegs would be hidden behind a thousand pickle barrels. Brandeis believed that in very big corporations inefficiencies would be multipled; therefore, if big corporations made profits this fact could be explained only by assuming that size gave them illegitimate "market power" to insulate them from their small competitors.

THEY RAN HARDER

This sort of thinking widened the split that had opened between two meanings of the word "monopoly." Originally, it had meant an exclusive right, granted or protected by the Crown, to do business in a certain commodity in a defined area. (All enduring European cartels were to have this element of government protection.) In the U.S. of 1880-1917, however, monopoly began to take on a very different meaning, which is at the root of many of our present antitrust difficulties. Section 2 of the Sherman Act is directed against "every person who shall monopolize, or attempt to monopolize or combine or conspire with any other person or persons, to monopolize any part of the trade or commerce among the several states...." Does "monopolize" refer to a set of practices intended to erect artificial walls against competition? Or does the statute forbid a company to attain in the course of the competitive race a large share of a line of trade? Under the influence of the Bryan-Brandeis type of "conservatism," the word "monopolize" has tended to move more and more toward the latter meaning. *Fortune*'s proposition is intended to move it back toward the first meaning.

The greatest source of confusion, however, lay in the different applications of the word "competition." When in the late nineteenth century the U.S. entered a genuine market economy, businessmen were not immune to the general feeling of insecurity. The late nineteenth century's notorious conspiracies in restraint of trade were efforts to flee the rising uncertainties of intensified competition. These conspiracies all broke down, either because they had been outlawed by Section 1 of the Sherman Act or because of technological developments.

But the main line of U.S. development in the twentieth century found very different answers to "the problem of competition." The corporation, with the principle of limited liability, compensated for the mounting risks that had become too great for individual proprietors and unlimited partnerships. If accelerating change undermined the security of a company, the company's response was to run faster—not to try to stop the change. If the new technology required huge investment, the corporation's response was to grow by plowing back profits, attracting new capital and by mergers with other companies. If huge technological plants required specialization, the corporation was to develop professional managers to coordinate the specialists. In short, twentieth-century business evolved in exactly the opposite direction from the repressive spirit of suppressing innovation in order to raise prices, modern corporations place a tremendous emphasis on increasing sales volume by vigorous merchandising, by the search for new markets, by cutting costs; they spend billions on research and development to create new products and services; they rely on the diversification of product lines, rather than on the suppression of innovation, to defend the company against the increasing vulnerability of *any* product to competition.

THE RISE OF CONSUMER POWER

The economy of 1900 was dominated by trade in the necessities of life. A family needed food, clothing, fuel, in quantities that could not be produced and distributed at a cost far below the family's income. There was not much consumer choice—or "power"—in that situation. The family could not resist a rise in the price of bread by shifting its purchasing to overcoats, even if the price of overcoats was falling. Demand in all three markets was "inelastic." A monopoly position in any one of them could by raising prices siphon off what little difference there might have been between family income and the cost of subsistence.

The twentieth century's enormous increase in productivity—and therefore in real wages—changed all that. In the U.S. today the basic subsistence requirements of 1900 can be purchased for less than 20 percent of an average family's income. We have raised our standard of "necessary" purchases to include home furnishings, non-utility clothing, etc. In this area of "secondary

146

needs" today's consumer can at least postpone purchase if he finds the current price of one "need" less attractive than another. Above this, now, lies a third level, the vast domain of "discretionary" goods and services. Competition in this area jumps over the old market boundaries; as the economists say, these discretionary markets are subject to a high degree of "cross elasticity of demand." The beer competes with the candy; the trip to Miami competes with the violin lessons for Junior. This increase in demand elasticity—and therefore in the buyer's power to resist monopoly—has far outstripped any increase in "market power" that may have accrued to large corporations.

Back in 1902 an economist, Simon N. Patten, foresaw that the power of the great corporations would be limited by "the consumers' power of substitution." The chemists, among others, vindicated him. Synthetics hover menacingly over just about every raw material except gold, which is protected—at a low level—by some rather odd governmental arrangements. Progress has done most of antitrust's work by sharply reducing the chance that "market power" can arbitrarily raise prices.

By ignoring the whole range of fundamental changes that have come over the U.S. economy and by looking only at the percentage shares of large companies in narrowly defined markets, the Brandeis tradition insists that competition has been decreasing. In order to make it appear that a given company has an inordinately large share of a market, the government's usual tendency is to define "market" as narrowly as possible. If you assume that aluminum wire doesn't compete with copper wire (the Alcoa-Rome Cable case, 1964), that a commercial bank doesn't compete with another commercial bank twenty miles away (Philadelphia Bank, 1963), that a retail shoe market could be arbitrarily defined as any city of 10,000 with its "immediately surrounding areas" where both the merging companies had stores (Brown Shoe, 1962), then of course, you can prove quite a lot of "concentration." By setting up the rules of proof as if the U.S. market today were as tightly compartmentalized as in 1890, you can give some color of truth to the charge that U.S. business has become oligopolistic. Antitrust policy is still riding on a quest to rescue the maiden, Economic Freedom; but the girl has long since been liberated by other hands and now has fourteen daughters livelier than their mother.

THE GREAT SCOURING-PAD CASE

Don Quixote wasn't exactly crazy; he had just arranged his mental life so that he could see what he wanted to see. Sometimes events in the actual world of business intrude abruptly upon antitrust's *La Mancha*. The government had no sooner won the Paramount Pictures case, after years of complicated market analysis, than television came on the scene to prove that the movie industry as a whole was not exactly immune from competition. Within a few years television not only changed the structure of the entertainment industries but also caused an upheaval throughout the world of advertising.

147

Television is the biggest and best-known postwar example of the effect of innovation on the U.S. economy. But every year there are tens of thousands of smaller examples of how innovation can transform a relatively stagnant business situation into one marked by agitated competition. Frequently, the increased liveliness is triggered by a merger.

Consider the great scouring-pad case pending, as this was written, before the Federal Trade Commission. For many years two medium-sized companies, S.O.S. and Brillo, doing a nearly equal business, accounted for more than 95 percent of the steel-wool pads sold to housewives for cleaning pots and pans. During this period the competition between Brillo and S.O.S. does not appear to have been intense; there were few important changes in product design or in production or merchandising methods. At the end of 1957, General Foods, which had not previously been in the household cleanser business, bought S.O.S. No challenge came from Washington. During the next two years sales of S.O.S., relative to Brillo's, slumped.

General Foods then took several steps to revive its ailing property, steps that did not depend upon General Foods' vast size or market power but simply on its managerial brains. It turned the S.O.S. account over to a different advertising agency; then it followed the agency's recommendations for some changes in the product and the advertising pitch. Because investigators found that housewives associated the red soap in S.O.S. pads with rust, the soap was changed to blue; to call attention to the sizable amount of soap in S.O.S., a TV commercial showed a soap pad being whipped into a sort of meringue in an electric mixer. Brillo fought back with a plastic pad called "Dobie" and a disposable pad called "Paddy." General Foods, after a fumble with something called "Handigrips," countered "Paddy" with "S.O.ettes." General Foods' tactics worked. S.O.S. overtook Brillo and spurted ahead, even making big gains in the New York market, where Brillo's share had run as high as 84 percent.

Clearly, competition was heating up in scouring pads. But the FTC was not pleased. In 1963 it issued a complaint charging that the six-year-old merger of General Foods and S.O.S. violated the Clayton Act because it "tended to create a monopoly." In its complaint the FTC had little to say about what was actually going on in scouring pads. Instead, it stressed the size of General Foods and carried on about such matters as the company's possession of more than 50 percent of the markets in coconut and "edible gelatins (excluding ready-to-mix desserts)." The FTC displayed its solicitude for the status quo ante by asserting that the merger had "upset and realigned adversely, and threatens to upset and realign further, the competitive structure of the household steel wool industry." This fell deed, said the complaint, had been achieved through General Foods' "economic power, merchandising prowess and extensive advertising and promotion." S.O.S.'s share of the steel-wool scouring-pad market had risen from 51 percent at the time of the merger to 57 percent at the time of the complaint. The FTC asserted that monopoly was on the march.

But was it? At the initial hearing before the FTC's examiner, evidence showed that innovation had been breeding in another part of the teeming forest of American business. Scouring pads made with materials *other than steel wool* were attracting a rising share of the housewife's money. General Cable had a copper pad called "Chore Girl"; Kurly Kate Corporation had a plastic pad called "Flip" and two copper pads called "Kurly Kate" and "Kopper Kate"; Du Pont was in there with "Combo," made of nylon; Colgate-Palmolive had test-marketed a nylon pad called "Colgate-Ajax"; General Mills had a plastic pad called "Ocelo"; Minnesota Mining & Manufacturing was marketing "Scotch-Brite" and building a plant to make "Rescue" (both of nylon). Lever Brothers, Procter & Gamble, American Home Products, and a host of small firms were reported considering getting into the cleaning-pad free-for-all. Some monopoly!

The FTC's examiner was not impressed. He defined the market in which S.O.S. was sold as that for "steel wool scouring pads." He cited the indubitable fact that the physical properties of steel-wool pads are different from those of nonsteel pads. But do their *uses* differ? The FTC's lawyers say "we must conclude" that nonsteel pads are used only for cleaning china and glassware, but the lawyers did not produce evidence to back this up. General Foods denies that it is the case. Store managers, who probably know more about housewives than do FTC lawyers, mingle steel-wool pads and nonsteel pads on their shelves, indicating that they think it's all one market. Advertising for the nonsteel pads directly attacks steel pads as out of date. Prices of several nonsteel pads are obviously set up to compete (on a per-time-used basis) with steel pads. In short, against a mountain of evidence that all scouring pads compete with all other scouring pads in an exceedingly lively market, the FTC's lawyers and the examiner, intent on showing monopolistic concentration, decided that steel wool stands impregnably alone in its ability to clean pots and pans. If so sweeping a claim were publicly made on behalf of S.O.S. or Brillo, the FTC would probably crack down on it for deceptive advertising.

ON THE POINT OF A NEEDLE

Many government briefs and judicial opinions contain ingenious economic analysis and show an impressive ability to relate old legal precedents to new sets of facts. Yet these admirable exercises are suffused with unreality. Everybody now laughs at the medieval schoolmen who engaged in complicated speculation on how many angels could dance on a needle's point. The schoolmen did this as a kind of mental calisthenics; they were not attempting to regulate a seraphic oligopoly. The FTC, the Antitrust Division, and the federal judges, however, aren't kidding.

The trouble is that the sophisticated analytical techniques they employ, though impressive in a purely academic sense, are being hopelessly outstripped by the increasing fluidity and complexity of the U.S. economy.... The mind reels at the prospect of antitrust lawyers and economists arguing over whether X's lasers really compete with Y's masers.

It is significant that market-structure analysis as used in antitrust cases always distorts the facts in one direction—toward a simpler, more primitive, more stagnant economic picture than the situation that actually exists. In the present state of the science, economic analysis cannot handle more than a small fraction of all the variables and contingencies needed for a sound *legal* judgment on changing market structure in any particular "monopoly" case. And the analysis tends to ignore the element around which competition in fact increasingly centers—managerial brains.

THE CREATIVE GALE

The economist who best appreciated the central role of management in the modern economy was Harvard's great Joseph Schumpeter. Writing in the 1930s and 1940s, he foresaw that the future U.S. economy would live in a self-generated "gale of creative destruction." He believed that the excellence of an economy would and should be measured by its innovative capacity rather than its size. As Schumpeter used the term, innovation did not mean the ability of science to discover new truths or of technology to invent new things. His "innovation" is an *economic* act by which a new product or a new service or a new production or merchandising method is introduced to actual use. One of management's most important functions is calculating the relative risks and rewards of possible innovations. At any point in time there are millions of potential innovations, many of them arising from advances in science and technology. These compete with one another for birth. A decision to attempt a certain innovation is based on calculations about how it will fare in competition with other offerings, old and new. Before and after the decision, management assembles and coordinates the work of scientists and technicians from many specialized fields, along with the judgments of merchandisers and of men who deal with the markets for capital. Rivalry between corporations centers on management teams that compete with one another to find new ways of cutting costs, increasing volume, modifying old products and introducing new ones. The general market "allocates resources" by awarding different levels of profits to the winners and losers of this race.

Given Schumpeter's views about the decisive role of management, it is not surprising that he expressly foresaw the importance of mergers for American business. He understood, of course, that some operations require heavy capital investment under a unified management; but his thought on mergers went much further than a justification of bigness. Schumpeter's view of the innovating society puts the accent on flexibility. The merger technique is one that a management can use to develop the abilities it has, or to acquire abilities it needs to take advantage of new opportunities, or to protect itself by product diversification when the "gale of creative destruction" blows hard upon its existing business. In the innovating society, no company can expect to maintain indefinitely a given product line or a given market position or a given technology or a given set of marketing methods or a given set of financing arrangements.

Here is an example of a merger where present antitrust policy would play down the socially valuable motives while inputing "monopolizing" motives.

Company A has a group of scientists and engineers who have developed a narrow line of products in a specialized field of electronics. Starting from scratch six years ago, company A has achieved a profitable volume of $20 million a year. Its product line looks safe over the next three or four years—but beyond that, who knows? Its research and development people, still fecund with ideas, may come up with another series of inventions; but this second series, unlike the first, may not find an avidly waiting market. The second series may require vigorous selling, a skill that company A has not needed to develop. The second series may require financing on a scale unknown to the brief history of company A. It may require a great increase in numbers of employees, bringing problems of union negotiations of which company A is innocent.

Company B is also in electronics. It is older and bigger—say, $250 million a year. Some of its products compete directly with the present products of company A. Company B has a vigorous merchandising arm and a good reputation in the markets for capital. Its present product line looks fairly safe over five or six years. But its R&D seems tired, sterile. It decides that acquisition of company A will stimulate its research, while it can supply the broader managerial deficiencies of company A.

Antitrust policy, as now practiced, would tend to ignore all these considerations of managerial balance and efficiency and concentrate upon one fact: A and B are competitors in certain markets; therefore a merger between A and B is a horizontal merger that would "reduce competition"—meaning only that it would reduce the number of competitors in a narrowly defined market. Antitrust policy would say that if company A needs merchandising and financing expertise, let it go into the executive market and hire the men individually; if B needs scientists, let it do the same. This answer displays an ignorance of how work is organized in this society. A first-rate R&D department is far more valuable than the sum of the individual skills that make it up. So is a first-rate sales department or a treasurer's office. Company A's inventiveness might be aborted long before it could build, man by man, its merchandising and financial skills. And company B's capacity for introducing innovations might be wasted for lack of technological inventiveness.

Merger of A and B can be defended as socially desirable on grounds of efficiency. In a static economy this desideratum might be overbalanced by the danger of monopoly. But on the actual line of this economy's movement the danger that a merged A and B could garner the fruits of monopoly approaches zero. . . .

THE "SOCIAL AND MORAL" ARGUMENT

The trustbuster has in his arsenal one reserve weapon that transcends economics. When he fails by economic analysis to show that some company, escaping the competitive discipline, has damaged the public, he can always shift his ground to the "social and moral" argument against bigness—an argument that goes all the way back to the William Jennings Bryan era. This argument rests upon one interpretation of "equality" as a social goal. It prefers a society of many small producers because it fears "the concentration of political or social power in the hands of a few men."

In antitrust law the classic expression of this fear of bigness is a passage in Judge Learned Hand's opinion in the Alcoa case. He brushed aside as irrelevant Alcoa's attempt to show that it had not *acted* as if it were a monopoly, that it had not engaged in "predatory practices" or gouged the public. Moving to the "higher" ground, Judge Hand said: "Congress . . . did not condone 'good trusts' and condemn 'bad' ones; it forbade all. Moreover, in doing so it was not necessarily actuated by economic motives alone. It is possible, because of its indirect social or moral effect, to prefer a system of small producers, each dependent for his success upon his own skill and character, to one in which the great mass of those engaged must accept the direction of a few."

This quotation encapsulates fundamental mistakes about the nature of the modern corporation. It assumes that today's business unit is simply a magnification of the village general store where the proprietor "directed" his obedient clerk; this way of looking at modern business inevitably results in a picture of concentrated power.

But the regimentation and loss of freedom that Hand feared is not a characteristic of largescale business. The actual development of the modern corporation disperses power to many individuals within a unified decision making structure. The head of a modern corporation is hedged about with new limitations upon his power. He is rarely, for instance, in any significant sense the owner of the business. The rise of professional management, distinct from the shareholders but answerable to them, has created a fundamental check-and-balance situation unknown to early capitalism and to the old law of private property. A more recent and equally important trend has been the dispersal of power *within* management. In a complex modern organization subordinate is not the "agent" of his boss. Managers far below the top level of a large contemporary corporation have power that inheres in their skills rather than in the delegation of a superior. They are not so much "directed" as given responsibility and opportunity to initiate, to decide, and to coordinate activities that a chief executive officer would be quite helpless in handling. More and more work that is entirely "directed" from above is performed by machines and computers. Millions of little managers within large modern corporations have more actual scope for individual choice and decision than the "independent" small farmers, artisans, and small tradesmen of the nineteenth century had.

The U.S. public, which may be more in touch with reality than antitrust lawyers, seems to sense that business power is not being concentrated "in the hands of a few men." Once upon a time every banker and bootblack knew the names of Vanderbilt, Rockefeller, Morgan, Harriman, Carnegie. He knew what business each was in and what kind of man each was. These men were giants in the land and their tremendous concentration of economic power carried with it a threat of inordinate political and social influence. But the man in the street today is not likely to know the names of Frederic G. Donner, Michael L. Haider, Fred J. Borch, Albert L. Nickerson, and Donald J. Russell, who are the chief executive officers of companies doing an annual business in excess of $10 billion—a sum that makes the sales of the old Standard Oil Trust look like a hot-dog stand. If your barber can identify the companies headed by the names above, he should stop cutting hair and come write a gossip column for *Fortune.* . . .

SOCIAL RESPONSIBILITY
IN BUSINESS

Arthur J. D. Cook and C. E. Gilliland, Jr.

The question of the social responsibility of business has become increasingly important in American business life as the complex problems of an industrial-urban society become more evident. While the conservative business man may still feel that he best serves American ideals by running a prosperous business, many leading industrial figures seek to make business executives aware of the influences, both for good and bad, that apparently purely economic decisions may have on the general environment. In line with this belief, a *Wall Street Journal* editorial, during the United Automobile Workers' strike against General Motors, bemoaned a proposed price increase in the following terms:

In view of the risks involved it is perhaps unrealistic to ask a single company to take an anti-inflation initiative. But GM is the nation's largest manufacturer. Evidence that it was exercising forbearance on prices would have been impressive to the public. It might also have been impressive to Congress, which in recent years has passed tough safety and anti-pollution bills aimed at the auto industry partly because of widespread accusations that the industry is insensitive to public needs."[1]

Such indications that responsible decisions by management can no longer be made in an economic vacuum require that any consideration of management policies include this new, important area if all facets of the problem are to be covered. Also it requires understanding that the modern concept of social responsibility goes far beyond the old public relations ideal of presenting a favorable image to the public. It is no longer sufficient to "keep one's

---

From a chapter in a forthcoming book entitled *Business Policy*.

[1] Editorial, "GM's Price Increase," *Wall Street Journal* (September 19, 1970), p. 20.

skirts clean" and do no wrong. It requires positive action on the part of management that can be seen by society as aiding or helping the solution of the nation's complex social problems.

From this point of view, economic justification for management's actions fails completely as a standard because most of these activities are not measurable in any profit or loss statement. They require new standards of measurement and new justifications which go far beyond the traditional fields of business interest and involvement. It is still too early to predict whether or not, in the long run, this new concept of business responsibility will gain general acceptance, but it is difficult to deny that the success or failure of a business or economic system will eventually depend on the success or failure of the general society in which it operates. Anything that strengthens American society as it now operates will strengthen the business system and, as such, the majority of the individual firms operating within the system. Anything that weakens it will tend to undermine those very same firms.

Assuming the above statement to be correct, it becomes necessary to examine the concept of social responsibility in greater detail and attempt to develop criteria which may be useful to the manager in making decisions in this area. Before this, however, consideration of the historical background of the problem seems pertinent.

Originally, with the development of classical economic theory, the problem of social responsibility was nonexistent. Adam Smith recognized the inherently selfish nature of business decisions but considered the power of competition sufficient to bend these decisions to the public good. Thus the "invisible hand" served to guide the profit-making decisions of the individual businessman in the best interests of society because his best interests could only be served by providing more, better, and cheaper goods than his competitors.

This concept, which assumes a high degree of competition, was not seriously challenged until the development of the modern corporate form, which, by allowing for the concentration of great wealth, allows for the concentration of economic power and reduces competition. The reaction to this condition was primarily legal as first the state governments and then the federal governments used legislation to prevent the most flagrant abuses of the public by the corporations.

Also involved was the switch from a production-oriented society to a distribution one. While production was the main problem, any firm engaged in production naturally did improve the general welfare, but once basic needs were satisfied, firms grew by intensive market activity. The ability to influence consumers by promotion and advertising tended to reduce price competition because the process of offering the buyers greater value as a means to success became less important.

The list of such legislation is long and includes efforts to protect the individual as a producer, consumer, and investor. In some cases this protection is provided by interposing the regulatory power of government between the individual and business. In others it is achieved by allowing for group action as a countervailing power to the economic power of the corporation.

Among the more important laws protecting the individual as a producer are child labor laws and laws protecting women at work, workmen's compensation, and the series of acts setting minimum wages and hours of work, and those regulating and encouraging collective bargaining as a means of determining working conditions and wages. Consumer protection laws are less extensive but include pure food and drug laws and the newer wave of legislation to protect consumers from false labeling and advertising. As investors the public is protected by the New Deal legislation reforming the stock market and the regulations imposed by the Securities Exchange Commission. The present trend is to demand protection for the individual, not in any specialized area of his life, but in his total environment.

Legislation to control business behavior was but an addition to previously established controls. Society had evolved behavioral modes for interpersonal economic dealings which can be traced partially to religious teachings and partially to the economic requirements for the general welfare of the public. These patterns have evolved as conditions within the society have changed and demanded new patterns of behavior. The change from an agricultural to a commercial society, for example, placed a premium on the fulfillment of contractual agreements, fair dealings, and being true to one's word.[1]

The attitude of corporate management toward its responsibilities has changed dramatically since the days of the robber barons. This change has not been completely a result of legal action but is also tied to the increasing professionalism of management and the more enlightened attitudes that result. The difference between the past and the present is especially apparent when the concern for customers, employees, and stockholders by many modern corporations is contrasted with the actions of management in the nineteenth century. This concern, however, cannot yet be regarded as a complete protection for the public even though it is generally extended to include the communities within which the corporation operates.

Recognizing the fact that United States business management has developed a changed attitude toward its responsibilities, it is pertinent to recall that this concept of responsibility has its impact on the decision-making process of management. Because of the uncertainty usually associated with management decisions, the actual impact of a decision may produce results that differ very markedly from those intended and which may be considered as irresponsible by society in general. Judgment on the decision should be based not only on results but also on the desired objectives, which may or may not indicate responsibility by the decision makers according to the ethical and moral standards of the society in which the firm operates. The higher these standards are

---

[2] It is worth noting that many U.S. businessmen and government officials find it difficult to deal with members of less developed societies where an agreement or contract may only be binding as long as it is convenient to either side.

among the management personnel of the firm, the greater probability that the objectives will reflect the concept of social responsibility.

Crucial to this problem is the recognition that social responsibility becomes another objective in the decision-making process. This, under conditions of uncertainty, adds to the problem by increasing the number of variables that must be considered and may make reasonable planning more difficult. Under any conditions, by adding to the number of constraints that must be satisfied, the introduction of the concept of business responsibility narrows the choices and may make the satisfactory attainment of other objectives more difficult or impossible. It is not to be wondered at, therefore, that many executives look upon social responsibility as an added burden which they seek to avoid.

The General Electric Company problem with violations of antitrust laws is an example of this. Upper management was firmly committed to the federal guidelines on antitrust action but lower echelons of management found the constraints imposed by this policy made the achievement of other objectives difficult. Thus, the policy was ignored with the resultant scandal that rocked the business world.[2]

The imposition of changed conditions as business developed and grew necessitated the development of new standards beyond those of ordinary morality by which to judge management behavior. The ones most commonly accepted by the business community are those of legality and profitability. Each of these will be examined in greater detail as providing standards so that it was possible to judge top management.

LEGALITY

A valid measure of responsibility in the decision-making process is provided by the law as a minimum standard for action. This excludes decisions which have been made to deliberately flout the law because there is reason to believe that it will not be sustained by the judiciary. It merely considers the law as setting boundaries within which decisions must conform, but leaves unanswered the questions about the appropriate action in the presence of an undesirable or unjust law.

Does the fact that a law is considered undesirable by an individual or a group of individuals alter the basic premise that actions must be consistent with the law? Some critics consider certain laws to be anachronisms which are generally disregarded and must eventually be modified to be in line with reality. Despite these opinions, restraints imposed by law cannot be ignored at the whim of a few, or even many individuals, and executives must consider them as responsible guides to policy. Means are provided in the structure of the government by which laws unsatisfactory to the majority may be modified and an orderly effort can be made to correct legal inadequacies.

---

[2] Richard Smith, "The Incredible Electric Conspiracy," *Fortune* (April 1961).

Because of the fragmented legal structure in the United States, it is often possible to circumvent an undesirable law by physical relocation beyond the jurisdiction of the particular law to another state or another community. This, of course, may be expensive, but the alternative of lawlessness is unacceptable because this would lead to anarchy, and anarchy is not only destructive of ordered society but also of the economic order. Management may seek to change the law by political means, or void the effects of the law by judicial means, or escape the law by relocation, but it can never ignore the law and still be considered as acting in a legal manner.

Under the standard of legality as a test for social responsibility, management has complete freedom of action as long as it does not break the law. Management is not responsible for any deleterious effects of its decisions as long as these decisions are not contrary to the legal rules of society. It is obvious, of course, that in many areas legislation lags behind the needs of society and that by taking this view management is seeking a refuge in a strict interpretation of its responsibilities. In addition, it must be considered that in many areas legislation is difficult, if not impossible, to enact and this leaves a wide area for freedom of action by management with few or no constraints.

RESPONSIBILITY FOR PROFITABILITY

Profitability has always been regarded as the prime objective of business and it has long been considered that providing for profits is a prime responsibility of management. Thus legality of actions had to be coupled with profitability in judging management performance.

From an economic point of view, this standard is fully justified. Under a system of free enterprise and profit motive, the market mechanism is assumed to function to provide the most efficient allocation of resources. As long as each firm's management is seeking the longrun maximization of profits, they will purchase and apply resources to this end. The result is the optimization of economic activities through the efficient allocation of resources. Responsible action on the part of management requires longrange planning for profit maximization. Otherwise, the mechanism for the best allocation of resources cannot function properly.

Milton Friedman, the noted conservative economist of the University of Chicago, regards the concept of social responsibility as a subversion of the market economy. He believes that the voluntary acceptance of social responsibility by management means that noneconomic factors will enter into purely economic decisions and that the end result will be a misallocation of resources.[3] He assumes, of course, that management decisions are made on exclusive economic grounds and that noneconomic factors such as friendship, familiarity, habit, or lack of knowledge never influence these decisions.

---

[3] Milton Friedman, *Capitalism and Freedom* (Chicago, Ill.: The University of Chicago Press, 1963), p. 134.

PRIVATE ENTERPRISE IN ACTION

The assumption that management seeks to maximize profits, either in the longrun or the shortrun, is one that must be examined more carefully. Although it is part of the economic theory of business firms, there is considerable doubt that businessmen base their decisions on the attainment of this objective. Other than studies that indicate the more mundane objective of "fair profits" to be most common, the practical difficulties involved in developing a demand curve for a product, the need to maintain stability of prices, and the lack of precise cost information needed to use marginal analysis makes maximization of profits, even in the shortrun, an impossible dream.

It must also be realized that many actions of business cannot be quantified in any meaningful sense because actual results are so diffuse. Many types of business activity reflect upon the public image of the firm and may, thereby, directly effect the fundamental profit position of the firm. For these reasons, a socially responsible management may take actions because of longrun profitability objectives, even though it is not attempting to maximize these profits and even though the total effect of its action on these profits cannot be directly measured. Management must always keep clearly in mind its profit responsibilities since the life and future well-being of the business depends on this, but this does not require ignoring social responsibility, since it too may have a bearing on the life of the enterprise.

THE PUBLIC RELATIONS ERA

The concepts of profitability and legality may have sufficed to salve management's conscience, but it has failed to protect either workers or the public from the exploitation of business. The introduction of mass production and technological change was made with no consideration to those who suffered from the results. As long as the economy enjoyed the spotty prosperity of the 1920s business was not attacked. But, with the advent of the depression of the 1930s, the shortcomings of the business system became a favorite target for reformers.

Business responded by turning to the struggling new profession of public relations to rebuild its public image. Unfortunately, this was a fumigating process rather than a reforming one. The attempt was made to present a favorable image of business, whether merited or not, rather than to change the practices that were creating the unfavorable image. This attempt failed, as it should have, but more advanced thinking in public relations is responsible for emphasizing the need for good relations with employees, the community, customers, and stockholders. This thinking also stressed the need to improve business behavior as a means of improving its public image.[4]

---

[4]Glenn Griswold and Denny Griswold, *Your Public Relations* (New York: Funk and Wagnalls Company, 1948), pp. 6,7.

THE DEVELOPMENT OF NEWER CRITERIA

Other elements, particularly those relating to the concentration of economic power, are now becoming part of the evidence demanding a show of business responsibility on the part of management. When the 500 largest corporations are producing nearly half the goods and services that are available annually in the United States, the concentration of economic power assumes a significance that cannot be overlooked. It is no longer the unilateral behavior of the individual buyer and seller controlling the market as is propositioned in economic theory. The business decisions of a corporate spokesman have a vastly more widespread impact on the economy than decisions of the same type by the same individual but applied only to his personal affairs.

Recognition of this impact and the resulting need for social responsibility on the part of business has been expressed by many business leaders. Lawrence I. Wood, Vice-President, General Counsel, and Secretary of the General Electric Company, stated the concept as follows, "Far more, we must sense and be responsive to the social demands of the public as well as the market place and recognize the social consequences of economic decision making."[5]

The recognition by business and industry that a large corporation does not and cannot play the role of an individual buyer and seller in the market place means the recognition that the concept of competition has been distorted within the United States economy. It is no longer possible for such corporations, whether large or small, to seek only their own welfare and await the action of the "invisible hand" to guide their decisions in the interests of public welfare. The need for new criteria, beyond those already discussed, to establish policies becomes evident in this largely new and unexplored field of public responsibility.

Despite growing demands for greater social responsibility in management decisions, business has not been defenseless before this onslaught. The theories of one critic of business, John Kenneth Galbraith of Harvard University, on countervailing power and the unparalleled success of the United States economy in providing material goods to the society have served to defend existing business practices.

THE THEORY OF COUNTERVAILING POWER

Under a system of competition the seller of a product is kept from exploiting the consumers, not by the resistance of the consumers to outrageous prices, but by the eagerness of his competitors to sell to those consumers. The seller who charges too high prices loses sales to competitors who lure his customers away with lower prices. In the same way, a large buyer of products

---

[5] As quoted by C. E. Gilliland, Jr., in *Readings in Business Responsibility* (Braintree, Mass.: D. H. Marks Publishing Co. 1969), p. 4.

or labor who wishes to pay too low prices finds his suppliers drifting to the competition that is willing to pay a higher price. The constraints on sellers are from other sellers and on buyers from other buyers.

The rapid disappearance of competition from the economy, which is fostered by the growth of large corporations, has necessitated the development of some other power to control selfish business decisions. Galbraith has called this the Theory of Countervailing Power, which briefly states that private economic power is held in check by the countervailing power of those who are subject to it. The concentration of industrial enterprises has developed not only strong sellers but also strong buyers who carry enough economic power to prevent their being exploited.[6]

While countervailing power has not meant that business executives have had to consider the social consequences of their decisions, it has served as a strong brake to their unilateral power to make decisions since other than selfish considerations are important. This power, while not exercised in the interests of the consumers, has, nevertheless, served to protect them, particularly when used by large retailers, since retailing is still one of the more truly competitive fields still to be found in the United States economy.

Countervailing power has thus served as a restraining influence on business and prevented the development of practices that would have brought about a greater public outcry. As such, it has been an important factor in maintaining a favorable ideological climate for the United States concept of free enterprise.

IDEOLOGIES

One element that has helped mute criticism of the lack of social responsibility on the part of management has been the almost uncontested ideological acceptance by the general public of the business position. While it is easy to forget this in light of the present youthful revolt against United States materialism, it must be remembered that the productive record of the United States economy and free enterprise system during the World War II and in the immediate postwar period gave it great stature in the eyes of the public. Business leadership and business objectives passed the test of national emergency and only a small radical minority cared to question an evidently successful system.

The New Deal reform of the 1930s undermined much of the radical outcry against the system. Historically, competing ideologies had clamored for public attention and often sought to amend or even overturn the concept of private ownership of the production process. The exploitation of labor in the past gave rise to a socialist, reformist labor movement that was hostile to the wage system and to the business economy. The separation of ownership and

---

[6]John Kenneth Galbraith, *American Capitalism* (New York: Houghton Mifflin Co., 1956), chapter 10.

mangement, often accompanied by flagrant stock price manipulation by managers and speculators, gave rise to the hostility of the stockholders, which found expression in government action, first on the state level with blue sky laws and finally on the federal level with the Securities Exchange Act. The *caveat emptor* attitude of much business leadership before the depression of the 1930s provided ample grounds for public indignation.

From the period following the end of the World War II until late in the 1960s there was an absence of significant antibusiness proposals. During this time some voices from within the business community were raised in favor of social responsibility. But the majority of business leaders were satisfied, knowingly or not, to follow the Friedman dictum that criticism of the existing system only serves to undermine it and open it to attacks on the profit motive.[7] Nevertheless, the revolt of youth with its radical antibusiness minority and distrust of the establishment suggests that business has time limits and that it must prove its concern for the general welfare by constructive action.

Two new standards for measuring business responsibility have been suggested. The theory of legitimacy seeks to place modern management within the framework of modern society, while the theory of responsibility provides a justification for social responsibility.

THE THEORY OF LEGITIMACY

The management of the modern corporation is generally clearly separated from ownership and is, except in the rare cases of a stockholders' revolt, self-perpetuating. This condition creates problems about one of the concepts of the free enterprise system—the right of the owner to manage and dispose of his property as he wishes. In the modern corporation this is no longer true; it is the managers, not the owners, who determine objectives and policies and prescribe the distribution of profits between dividends and retained earnings. Yet the fiction still remains that power rests with the owners and that management acts as agents in their behalf according to their policy guidelines.

Economic theory does not recognize this condition, and while the diversity between theory and fact is generally accepted by practitioners, it is not generally known by the public. This has created in the minds of many management personnel the need to buttress their position in some manner that will make their deeds and influence acceptable to the public. This quest for legitimacy has been aided by the concept of social responsibility. If the responsibility of management is greater than that given solely to the owners, their position of power is necessitated by this greater responsibility.

Since managers have the power that should legitimately be exercised by the owners, the managers contend that they have a broader responsibility in the exercise of this power, that of the public welfare. As managers they are

---

[7]Milton Friedman, "The Social Responsibility of Business is to Increase Profits," *The New York Times Magazine* (September 13, 1970), p. 126.

simply representatives of the owners' interests, they assume a third-party role in seeking those goals that are the legitimate aims of society. In this view, the inadequacies of economic theory as an idealogical basis for the power position of the manager has influenced many executives to legitimize their self-perpetuated positions by promoting the concept of broadened business responsibility. Social acceptance of the concept could assure the continuation of their power position. The separation of ownership and management has thus promoted a purely defensive ideology that seeks to legitimize management's power position within the society.[8]

THE IRON LAW OF RESPONSIBILITY

The "Iron Law of Responsibility" proposed by Davis and Bloomstrom serves as the last factor in the defense of social responsibility.[9] The concept involved is that the avoidance of social responsibility leads to the gradual erosion of social power as other institutions step into the vacuum thus created. When business fails to recognize its social responsibilities, its freedom to act in the matter will be curtailed and action will be prescribed by society through legislation or other social constraints. There are many specific illustrations of this from the past, ranging from child labor laws of the nineteenth century to presentday consumer protection laws. The important consideration here is that the lack of social responsibility by business can lead to legal controls and reform or to fundamental changes in the system of ownership even without violent revolution. By nationalizing key industries, the British Labor Party has set an example of the possible extent of such changes.

In this context, business leaders must be fully aware of the need to accept social responsibility or face the probability that society will act to deny them the opportunity of freedom of action in those areas. Thus, in considering any particular decision, management must not only look upon it from the long and shortrun aspects of the return to the particular firm but also from the long and shortrun effects it will have on society in general. The rising clamor over the pollution of our environment by industry indicates this most clearly, and if management does not wish to have regulation imposed upon it, it must act to make public action unnecessary.

The concepts involved in the "Iron Law of Responsibility" are, of course, not universally held and this places the exponents of business responsibility at a competitive disadvantage. The firm that takes the problems of pollution seriously and seeks to dispose of its wastes without endangering its environment is undoubtedly subject to greater costs than the firm that ignores these areas. Equally difficult for the idealist may be the extent of responsibility

[8]Earl F. Cheit, ed., *The Business Establishment* (New York: John Wiley & Sons, Inc., 1964), pp. 164-65.

[9]Keith Davis and Robert Bloomstrom, *Business and Its Environment* (New York: McGraw-Hill Book Co., Inc., 1966), p. 174.

required. Since the results are almost impossible to measure financially, how does management determine the amount that it is proper to invest in cleaner air for a community? If social responsibility is to be directed particularly at employees and employee problems, for example, at what point does it become paternalism and harmful in itself?

Milton Friedman, who apparently takes only a shortrun view of the problems of social responsibility, conceives expenditures for social purposes as a form of taxation without representation. The business man decides whom to tax, the amount of the tax, and how to spend the proceeds as if he were an elected public employee rather than an agent serving the interests of the stockholders. If he thus usurps power, the stockholders are justified in dismissing him after his policies of social responsibility have undermined the firm to the point it is no longer competitive.[10]

Refusal to act on these grounds, however, does not deny the workings of the "Iron Law of Responsibility" and the executives of the large corporations are the only ones in a power position who can accept this responsibility. The fiction that they are the representatives of the owners is only true in economic theory—business practices show few examples of top company executives being held accountable by the stockholders. The traditional method of voting against management is by selling one's stock, not by trying to replace it at the next stockholders' meeting.

CONCLUSIONS

The concept of social responsibility for business is becoming more and more important despite the criticism of theoreticians, such as Friedman, and some business leaders. This new emphasis is necessary since the old standards of management behavior such as profitability and legality are no longer sufficient because of the increased economic power of the large corporations. It is also evident that the growing criticism of the selfishness inherent in the system of private ownership of the means of production requires more than legal enforcement of social responsibility requirements. Those among the young that are disenchanted with the system are not seeking to reform it but to overturn it and any defense by business leaders that they are acting legally in polluting the environment will only serve to convince a larger segment of the population that a revolutionary change in the system is needed.

It is obvious that large corporations have greater power and influence and that their actions will have a greater effect, but even the small business executives must consider the social and physical environment in which he operates. Profit must still be the primary objective of business, but business leaders must also consider social costs in addition to monetary costs. In planning

---

[10]Milton Friedman, "The Social Responsibility of Business Is to Increase Profits," *Op. Cit.,* p. 122.

operations, the total effect of the decisions, not just the monetary effects, must be considered and immediate profit may have to be sacrificed, as it is on many occasions, for longrun objectives. When incorporated into the planning, the cost of many of these decisions becomes less important than if they are ignored by management and law later forces their inclusion.

THE POWER OF
POSITIVE PERSUASION

John Kenneth Galbraith

One of the few reassuring things about economics is its tendency to adopt, on occasion, the sensible ideas of the ordinary citizen. Sometimes the citizen is well out in front.

One striking example. For many years before the decade of the Great Depression, amateurs argued that depressions were caused by a shortage of purchasing power. And this being so, they naively held that the government could provide a remedy by increasing its own spending. Almost without exception, economists reacted with horror to such heresy.

Early in the Depression, Presidents Hoover and Roosevelt and the Hearst press all urged such a policy. Something was assumed to have gone wrong with their mental development.

Then in the mid-Thirties Lord Keynes made the notion of a shortage of demand and the resulting prescription of government spending respectable. In less than a decade, what had been a heresy had become the conventional wisdom. It is now called the New Economics.

What happened before could, obviously, happen again. And, unless I am mistaken, a major revolution in economics is now under way.

Since the instinct of the average citizen has much to commend it, I hope all who admit to only average knowledge of economics will remain with me for the argument. What I am about to argue will seem astonishingly sensible.

The part of economics that has now become suspect is a proposition that, like the succession of day and night to astronomers, is considered by economists to be almost as fundamental as life itself. It is that in the non-Communist economy the individual is ultimately in charge—he is possessed of what all economic textbooks celebrate as consumer sovereignty.

From *Orlando-Sentinal Star's* Florida Magazine, Famous Author Series 12, no. 23.

In accordance with this hallowed proposition, wants originate with the individual. Then, as a consumer in the market, the individual by buying this product instead of that makes the one product more profitable and the other less so. This reflects the consumer will to the producer. It tells him how he can make the most money, and in responding, he responds to the consumer will.

In a parallel process, the citizen chooses one candidate for public office instead of another and his choice reflects to the government his preferences as to public goods—his choice as between education, law enforcement, clean streets, a new ABM or MIRV or lower taxes.

Admittedly, this part of the process can be a bit occluded and unreliable but the broad tendency is what counts. And this ruling tendency is what distinguishes the Western industrial system from the planned economics where, alas, the state decides what the consumer will have and then graciously allows him to have it, always assuming that it is available.

This view of matters, comforting though it is, is increasingly unreal. In much of the modern industrial economy, the large producing corporation is far more powerful than this orthodox vision allows. And this power is more or less inherent in highly organized, highly technical production. More important, numerous of the problems that currently oppress us can be understood only when we see that consumer and citizen sovereignty has given way to the sovereignty of the large corporations that supply us.

Specifically, as the means by which things are produced become more complex and costly, production is carried on by corporations of ever increasing size. These firms do not wait to be instructed by the consumer; indeed, given their investment in plant and organization, they cannot afford to be subject to the whims of the consumer. Instead they set their prices and go on to persuade the consumer as to what he (or she) should buy.

This means, obviously, that wants are no longer original with the consumer but with the producer.

It was not a consumer but a producer who discovered that white sheets which are whiter than any other white sheets enhance the social standing of the woman who displays them and presumably sleeps between them and that a particular chemical contributes to this purity.

Similarly it was a tobacco producer, not a consumer, who discovered that Salems promote seduction in wholesome outdoor surroundings. And it was an automobile company that first learned that an automobile, through its horsepower, contributed to a rewarding feeling of dominance and controlled destructivity.

Much money and art are spent on this persuasion. A further result is a profound belief in the importance of goods for happiness. This causes people to take goods with the utmost seriousness and insures that after achieving a certain income, they won't goof off and enjoy more leisure. Instead they will continue to work and consume and thus remain at the service (i.e., in the power) of the producer.

167

This same persuasion also helps to insure that the community will measure its achievement by the amount that it produces—the size of its Gross National Product. This means that the needs of the producer (for industrial sites, power lines, water, air, raw materials, research and development) will have a triumphant claim on government and community.

Producers are also sovereign as regards public goods. If one believes in consumer sovereignty, one supposes that the citizen instructs his congressman as to the weapons systems and space probes that he wants from the federal government.

Given producer sovereignty, it will be agreed that the large weapons firms and the armed services as producers of defense services have the decisive power. They instruct the legislators as to what their constituents will have in the way of weapons. The constituents pay.

Thus we see the change. Sovereignty has come to be exercised not by the consumer or citizen but by the organizations that were once assumed to serve him.

Organization in the form of the great corporation identifies or defines the need and then persuades (or in the case of public goods, more or less commands) the individual to want what it provides. The individual has the myth of power on his side, but organization has the reality of power.

This view is not wildly attractive to the big organizations in question—to General Motors, General Electric, General Dynamics, or the generals who comprise the Joint Chiefs. To have the reality of power while sheltering behind the myth that the consumer or citizen is really in charge is to have the best of all worlds. But the truth is often disturbing. It may not comfort the afflicted but it does afflict the comfortable.

And in this case the truth marvelously illuminates our present problems and discontents.

The young are commonly held to be oppressed by the feeling that they live in a world which has scant respect for the individual. Big government and big corporations have big impersonal purposes of their own—the spilling out of civilian goods that seem not to be terribly important, a military budget of uncontrollable scale, the purchase of weapons regardless.

In a world where the individual is in charge, no such conflict could arise; people cannot be at war with themselves. But if organization is sovereign—if big private corporations, big public bureaucracies pursue purposes of their own—such conflict is inevitable.

Other things are put in a new light once we accept the idea of producer sovereignty.

The cities are clogged with automobiles and have been extensively devoured by highways and freeways. Mass or commuter transit is slow, unreliable, uncomfortable, and filthy.

If the consumer is sovereign, that, presumably, is the way he wants it; one sighs and knuckles under to the popular taste. But if the producer is sovereign and the automobile companies, as seems likely, are considerably more sovereign than most, we have here a reflection not of consumer but producer preference.

PRIVATE ENTERPRISE IN ACTION

Our quarrel is not with ourselves but the auto companies.

Similarly if the air is nearly lethal and the riparian waters are thick with industrial excrement but the consumer is sovereign, we have a marvelous formula for social indifference. The consumer wants cheap goods. That is his preference even if the price is a ghastly or dangerous environment.

But if the producer is sovereign, the destruction of the environment reflects producer convenience. That convenience cannot be defended as an expression of public will—especially if the organization men scurry off to some grassy suburb well out of sight and smell of the mill, once day is done.

If the consumer is sovereign, society must bow to the consumer's will. He is the final authority. If he wants two automobiles instead of one and three instead of two, they must be supplied. This will be true, however burdened the streets or the air.

But if the multiplication of automobile use reflects not consumer choice but artful stimulation by the producer, then questions must be asked about such consumption.

This is import. For a considerable range of products, of which tobacco, the internal combustion engine, numerous chemicals and electric power are all examples, we are reaching the socially tolerable limits of consumption.

Within the next decade, control of such consumption will be the liveliest of issues. Circumstance is forcing an issue, the reality of which economics—assuming consumer sovereignty—denies.

I come to a final and very practical point. If the consumer is sovereign, the economy can be controlled by influencing his exercise of power. If he is spending too much for goods and thus causing prices to rise, his taxes can be increased or his borrowing discouraged. This will bring things back into balance. Such is the present strategy for preventing inflation.

But when the producing firm is sovereign, its power includes that of setting its prices. If unions are pressing or other costs are rising, it can almost always raise prices and pass the added costs along to the public. It will not be possible to control inflation by nudging the consumer, for that is not where the power lies.

Here is the most important reason—why, after a year of solemn promises to control inflation, prices are continuing to rise as rapidly as ever.

The administration is conservative in its economics. Accordingly and quite appropriately, it adheres to the old vision of consumer sovereignty. Through control of public spending, the surtax and high interest rates, it has been nudging the consumer (and also the smaller, more competitive and less powerful producer.)

But power lies elsewhere—with the large and sovereign producers who cannot be so nudged and who can and do continue to raise prices and wages. And so promises to control inflation continue and so do the prices increase.

Only a considerable recession will curb this manifestation of producer sovereignty. It is the deep conviction of all reputable men that the world in the end will somehow conform to their vision of it. Were it only so.

The new view of the economic system, it will be evident, drastically alters our view of public policy.

Given consumer sovereignty, there is a presumption against public inter-ference with the economy. Things are broadly in accord with public wish and need; before the state intervenes, there has to be a strong showing that the public taste has been ignored or is remarkably depraved.

But if producer sovereignty and convenience is assumed, the burden of proof is very different. Shocking as it seems at first glance—a measure of the hold which consumer sovereignty has on our psyche—the presumption favors intervention. Unless society intervenes to defend itself, it may not survive in comfort or even decency.

But again the presumption accords with reality. For the problems of urban transportation, of ghetto housing, of the environment, of the weapons culture are surely hard to reconcile with public desire.

They do reflect, as a deeper instinct tells us, the power of the organizations that are presumed to serve us and now serve themselves or their convenience.

Once again the popular instinct is leading and the formal ideas of econ-omists are struggling to come abreast.

THE PASSION THAT
RULES RALPH NADER

Richard Armstrong

On a recent visit to Marymount College in Arlington, Virginia, Ralph Nader arrived at the school gymnasium an hour late. But he then proceeded to pacify an overflowing crowd of restless students—and earn a lecture fee of $2,500—by denouncing America's big corporations in venomous language. Afterward one question from the audience brought a rousing and spontaneous burst of applause. When, the questioner asked, did he plan to run for President?

A slightly more measured assessment of the Nader phenomenon came from Bess Myerson, New York City's commissioner of consumer affairs, when she introduced him as star witness at a recent hearing on deceptive advertising. "Mr. Nader," she said, "is a remarkable man who, in the last six years, has done more as a private citizen for our country and its people than most public officials do in a lifetime."

The remarkable thing about this tribute is that it is literally true. In the seven years since he moved to Washington from Winsted, Connecticut—without funds and with a narrow base of expert knowledge in a single subject, automobile safety—Nader has created a flourishing nationwide movement, known as consumerism. He is chiefly responsible for the passage of at least six major laws, imposing new federal safety standards on automobiles, meat and poultry products, gas pipelines, coal mining, and radiation emissions from electronic devices. His investigations have led to a strenuous renovation at both the Federal Trade Commission and the Food and Drug Administration. And if the quality and convenience of American life do not seem dramatically improved after all that furious crusading, Nader can point to at least one quite tangible result. Last year, for the first time in nine years, traffic fatalities in the U.S. declined, to 55,300 from 56,400 in 1969. Unless the decline was a

From *Fortune*, May 1971, pp. 144 ff. Copyright 1971. Reprinted by permission.

fluke (and officials at the Highway Traffic Safety Administration do not think it was), then for those 1,100 living Americans, whoever they may be, Nader can be said to have performed the ultimate public service.

MORE THAN TEN KREMLINS

And yet, despite all this, it is easy to conclude after a conversation with Nader that he is not primarily interested in protecting consumers. The passion that rules in him—and he is a passionate man—is aimed at smashing utterly the target of his hatred, which is corporate power. He thinks, and says quite bluntly, that a great many corporate executives belong in prison—for defrauding the consumer with shoddy merchandise, poisoning the food supply with chemical additives, and willfully manufacturing unsafe products that will maim or kill the buyer. In his words, the law should "pierce the corporate veil" so that individual executives could be jailed when their companies misbehaved. He emphasizes that he is talking not just about "fly-by-night hucksters" but the top management of "blue-chip business firms."

The lawyers who provide legal cover for all these criminal acts are, to Nader, nothing but "high-priced prostitutes." As for the advertising profession, Nader recently served up the following indictment: "Madison Avenue is engaged in an epidemic campaign of marketing fraud. It has done more to subvert and destroy the market system in this country than ten Kremlins ever dreamed of." With the certainty of the visionary, Nader would sweep away that shattered market system and replace it by various eccentric devices of his own, such as a government rating system for every consumer product.

If, on the one hand, Nader has advanced the cause of consumer protection by his skillful marshaling of facts in support of specific reforms, he has, on the other hand, made reform more difficult through his habit of coating his facts with invective and assigning the worst possible motives to almost everybody but himself. By some peculiar logic of his own, he has cast the consumer and the corporation as bitter enemies, and he seems to think that no reform is worth its salt unless business greets it with a maximum of suspicion, hostility, and fear.

Nader is a strange apparition in the well-tailored world of the Washington lawyer. His suits hang awkwardly off his lanky frame, all of them apparently gray and cut about a half size too large. His big brown eyes in their deep sockets have a permanent expression of hurt defiance, and before a crowd he blinks them nervously. The eyes, the bony face, and a small, set chin give him, at 37, the look of an underfed waif.

Nobody has been able to explain the deep personal anger that erupts when Nader begins to speak about corporations. He himself simply denies that he is antibusiness. "People who make that charge are escalating the abstraction," he told an interviewer recently, his long hands clasped together, his brown eyes flashing. "They don't dare face the issues." But anger of some kind is unmistakably there. It seems to spring out of some profound alienation from the comfortable world he sees around him, and perhaps dates back to his early days in the conservative little town of Winsted, where he was something of an oddball, the son of a Lebanese immigrant, the boy who read the Congressional Record. He recalls proudly that his father, who kept a restaurant and assailed customers with his political views, "forecast the corporate takeover of the regulatory agencies back in the 1930's." Princeton and Harvard Law School trained Nader's brilliant mind, but their social graces never touched his inner core. There seems something of the desert in him still, the ghost of some harsh prophet from his ancestral Lebanon.

According to one old friend, Nader has always had a conspiratorial view of the world, and when General Motors put private detectives on his trail in 1965 just before the publication of *Unsafe at Any Speed* that view was strongly reinforced. "He thought somebody was following him around," says the friend, "and then, by gosh, somebody *was* following him around." Apparently, at the time, Nader was convinced that GM planned to have him bumped off. He still moves about Washington in great secrecy from one rendezvous to the next.

THE FIFTH BRANCH OF GOVERNMENT

In his role as scourge of the regulatory agencies, Nader is aggressive and ill-mannered as a matter of calculated policy. "Rattle off a few facts so they will know you can't be bluffed," he tells his teams of young investigators setting out to interview government officials. "Get on the offensive and stay there." Says Lowell Dodge, who runs Nader's Auto Safety Center: "If somebody is messing up, Ralph wants to embarrass them."

But Nader can be an engaging fellow when he chooses. He takes care to maintain good relations with Washington journalists—parceling out news tips with an even hand—and many of them pay him the ultimate tribute of calling him the best reporter they know. To these men he seems to serve as a sort of ghost of conscience past, a reminder of investigations not pursued and stables left uncleansed. Both reporters and professional politicians find him extremely useful. "Nader has become the fifth branch of government, if you count the press as fourth," says a Senate aide who has worked with Nader often in drafting legislation. "He knows all the newspaper deadlines and how to get in touch with anybody any time. By his own hard work he has developed a network of sources in every arm of government. And believe me, no senator turns down those calls from Ralph. He will say he's got some stuff and it's good, and the Senator can take the credit. Any afternoon he's in town you still see him trudging along the corridors here with a stack of documents under his arm, keeping up his contacts."

What Nader gets out of the intercourse is power—not the trappings but the substance—more of it by now than most of the senators and congressmen on whom he calls. When an important bill is pending he is quite capable of playing rough, threatening to denounce a representative to the press unless he goes along on a key amendment. "Does Ralph like power?" The Senate aide laughed at such a naive question. "Good gracious, yes. He loves it." Compared to other powerful men in Washington, Nader enjoys a rare freedom of action, flourishing as a sort of freebooter who is able to pick his targets at will, unconstrained by an electorate or any judgment but his own. "You will find sensitive people around town who are saying it's time to take a second look at this guy," says the Senate aide. "There are people who wonder whether he ought to be the final arbiter of safety in autos or in the food supply. Nader has something the companies don't have—credibility—especially with the press. There is a danger that people will be afraid to go up against him for that reason alone."

REGRETS TO DAVID SUSSKIND

By any measure, Nader's power is still growing. He remains absolute master of his own movement, but he is no longer alone. "When I think of all the lean years Ralph spent knocking on doors—" says Theodore Jacobs, who was Nader's classmate at both Princeton and Harvard Law School and now serves as a sort of chief of staff. Jacobs had just concluded a telephone call that, from his end, had consisted only of various expressions of regret. "That was Susskind. He's got a new show, he wants Ralph, and I had to turn him down. Ralph hates New York—all that traffic and pollution—and I can't get him up there unless it's imperative. I spend a lot of my time saying no. Among other problems, he's got two people on his tail right now who are writing full-length biographies. He has to husband his time. He's down for the *Today* show next Tuesday, but that's right here in town. If there is an important bill pending in committee and they need some input, he'll be there. He'll duck anything else for that."

Jacobs presides, loosely, over a modern suite of offices in downtown Washington housing the Center for the Study of Responsive Law. This is home base for the seven most senior of Nader's "raiders" and is one of the three organizations through which Nader now operates. The other two are located a few blocks away: the five-man Auto Safety Center and the Public Interest Research Group, staffed by 12 bright young graduates of top law schools, three of them women. In addition, there are the summertime student raiders, who this year will number about 50, only one-quarter as many as last year. The program is being cut back, Jacobs explains, because the students are a mixed blessing, requiring a good deal of nursemaiding by the full-time staff. "But we still think it's useful for the regulatory agencies to see a fresh batch of faces wafting through."

One of the center's main functions is to handle a flood of crank calls. "No, I'm afraid Mr. Nader isn't here," says the young girl at the switchboard. "Can you tell me what it's about?" After a protracted conversation, she explains with a grin: "He said it was something so big he didn't dare put a word on paper. No name either, but still he wants to speak to Ralph." Nader drops by for a few minutes every day or so, and the other raiders emulate his casual example; by the switchboard, message boxes improvised out of brown paper are filled to overflowing with notices of calls never returned.

The Center for the Study of Responsive Law is tax-exempt, supported by well-known foundations, such as Field, Carnegie, and Stern, and by wealthy benefactors such as Midas muffler heir Gordon Sherman and Robert Townsend, author of *Up the Organization.* (Townsend gave $150,000.) On a budget of $300,000 a year, the center is able to pay its raiders a stipend of up to $15,000 each. "A far cry from five years ago," says one of the veteran Raiders, Harrison Wellford, 31, "when Ralph was being trailed by GM gumshoes and we would meet at night at the Crystal City hamburger joint on Connecticut Avenue to compare notes. We'd work our heads off and then get gunned down by someone from Covington & Burling [a large Washington law firm] who had been on an issue for a corporate client for 10 years."

Consumers Union is the biggest single donor to the Auto Safety Center, which operates on a slender budget of $30,000 a year. The Public Interest Research Group, or PIRG as it is called, is Nader's own nonprofit law firm, and he pays all the bills out of his own pocket, including the stipends of $4,500 a year to the 12 young lawyers. It is an irony that must warm Nader's heart that the money comes out of the $270,000 he netted in the settlement of his lawsuit against GM for invasion of privacy. Since PIRG's budget is $170,000 a year, Nader is obviously going through his windfall at an unsustainable clip.

CONSCIOUSNESS III DOESN'T GIVE A DAMN

Nader calls his own organization "a big joke really, a drop in the bucket compared to the size of the problem." It is in his nature to conceive of the enemy as being enormous, pervasive, and exceedingly powerful. "How many public-interest lawyers would it take to oversee the Pentagon? A hundred? Multiply that by the number of departments and agencies. This country needs 50,000 full-time citizens, including 10,000 public-interest lawyers. And I could get that many applicants if I had the money." Last month Nader began a campaign to raise $750,000 from students in two states, Connecticut and Ohio, where the money would be used to set up Nader-like centers for investigating state and local government. Students in two other states, Oregon and Minnesota, have voted to donate $3 each from their college activities funds to finance similar organizations. Nader hopes that one plan or another will spread across the country.

To the young, Nader is a hero of great stature. Thousands of students in law, medicine, engineering, and every other field want to "conform their careers and their ideals," as he puts it, by going to work for him. They are the mass base of his movement, and he is able to pick and choose among them for his staff. (They say on campus that getting a job with Nader is "tougher than getting into Yale Law School.") And yet this appeal is in many ways hard to fathom. Nader has no use at all for the "counterculture," and he abhors drugs. "There's a conflict between living life on a level of feeling on the one hand and Ralph's product ethic on the other," admits Lowell Dodge. "To produce, to have an impact—that's what Ralph admires. Consciousness III doesn't give a damn about the FTC. Ralph does." Dodge thinks Nader is growing ever stronger on campus as revolutionary ideas begin to fade. "There's more interest in change *within* the system, and Ralph is the most effective example of an agent for change."

Nader hectors students mercilessly about their public duties, about their "anemic imaginations," about their "thousands of hours on the beach or playing cards." And they seem to love it. "Suppose students would engage in one of history's greatest acts of sacrifice and go without Coke and tobacco and alcohol, on which they spend $250 each a year?" he asked a student audience at Town Hall in New York. "They could develop the most powerful lobby in the country. Write to us! We'll tell you how to do it." Hands dived for pens as he called out his address in Washington.

It is possible to question, nevertheless, whether this enthusiasm would survive a close association with Nader. Although most of the members of his full-time staff plan to stay in public-interest legal work, many of them talk with enthusiasm about the day when they will be leaving Nader. One reason, of course, is money. "On $4,500 a year, it's tough," says Christopher White, one of the young lawyers at the Public Interest Research Group. And then these young people are blither spirits than Nader and have a spontaneity and graciousness he lacks. Although they refrain from criticizing him directly, the picture that emerges is of a boss at least as dictatorial as any they would find in a private law firm. "The emphasis is on production," one of them says. "Ralph thinks that if a brief is 90 percent right, it's a waste of time to polish it." Nader tells them that a work week of 100 hours is "about right." He lectures them about smoking, refuses to ride in their Volkswagens, and never has time to waste socializing. Lowell Dodge got a call from Nader last Christmas Eve, but only because Nader had a question to ask about work in progress.

The warmth and empathy so important to the young are not to be found in any relationship with Nader. Robert Townsend's daughter Claire, a pretty blonde student at Princeton, says with unblushing candor that she became a raider last summer partly because "I had a terrible crush on Ralph. All the girls have crushes on Ralph." But Nader apparently never has crushes on them. He still lives monk-like in a rented room. His most pronounced concession to cravings of the flesh comes in appeasing a voracious although picky appetite. He is leery of most meats but often tops off a meal with two desserts. It is somehow typical of the man that when the soon-to-be-famous blonde detective tried to pick him up, back during his fight with GM, she found him in a supermarket buying a package of cookies.

176

NOTCHES ON NADER'S GUN

The Automobile. An auto-safety enthusiast while at Princeton and Harvard Law School, Nader went to Washington in 1964 to work on his pet subject as an aide to Daniel Patrick Moynihan, then Assistant Secretary of Labor, who happened to be interested in a field far removed from his assigned duties. Bored with office routine, Nader quit the following year and wrote *Unsafe at Any Speed* in 10 weeks. During the Senate hearings on auto safety, he came out a clear winner in a much-publicized confrontation with James Roche, president (now chairman) of General Motors. The publicity assured passage of the Motor Vehicle Safety Act of 1966, establishing a government agency to set mandatory vehicle-safety standards, of which there are now 34.

Unsanitary Meat. For his second campaign, Nader found readymade evidence in a study done by the Department of Agriculture of state-regulated packing plants, considered to be in intrastate commerce and so not covered by federal law. Many of the plants were filthy and rodent infested, but apparently nobody of any consequence had ever bothered to read the study's report. Nader did. The result was the Wholesome Meat Act of 1967, giving states the option of bringing their inspection programs up to federal standards or having them supplanted by federal inspection. In 1968 the provisions of the act were applied to poultry products.

Federal Trade Commission. A team of student raiders assigned by Nader to the FTC in 1968 found one official at the agency literally asleep on the job, others frequenting nearby saloons during working hours, and still others who seldom bothered to come to work at all. President Nixon commissioned a study of the FTC by an American Bar Association panel, which confirmed the major findings of the Nader report: low morale, lack of planning, preoccupation with trivial cases and timidity in pursuing important ones. Outcome: new faces and new vigor at the FTC.

Food and Drug Administration. Student raiders studying the FDA in the summer of 1969 compiled evidence on two important regulatory blunders: approval of cyclamates and monosodium glutamate for unrestricted use in the food supply. Alerted by the raiders, the news media covered both stories with unrestrained enthusiasm until the FDA banned cyclamates from soft drinks and manufacturers voluntarily stopped putting monosodium glutamate in baby food In December, President Nixon fired the three top officials at the FDA.

Other Doings. Legislation inspired by Nader: Natural Gas Pipeline Safety Act (1968), Radiation Control for Health and Safety Act (1968), Coal Mine Health and Safety Act (1969), Comprehensive Occupational Safety and Health Act (1970). Published reports: *The Chemical Feast* (on the FDA); *The Interstate Commerce Omission* (it recommends abolishing the ICC); *Vanishing Air* (a critical look at air-pollution-control laws and industry compliance); *What To Do With Your Bad Car* ("an action manual for lemon owners"); *One Life—One Physician* (on the medical profession). Reports in progress on: the Department of Agriculture, nursing homes, water pollution, Du Pont, First National City Bank of New York, the Washington law firm of Covington & Burling, land-use policies in California, supermarkets, and "brown lung" disease in the textile industry.

TRYING TO FIND FREE ENTERPRISE

What young people admire in Nader is a dark and uncompromising ideal-ism, coupled with a system of New Left economics that he is able to shore up with all sorts of impressive-sounding facts. They think he has got the goods on "the system." And he is completely free of any humdrum sense of propor-tion. A conversation with Nader makes the consumer society sound as gory as a battlefield: motorists "skewered like shish kebab on noncollapsible steering wheels"; babies burned to death by flammable fabrics improperly labeled; a little girl decapitated because a glove-compartment door popped open in a low-speed collision; "thousands of people poisoned and killed every year through the irresponsible use of pesticides and chemicals."

The corporate criminals responsible for this slaughter always go un-punished. "If we were as lenient toward individual crime as we are toward big-business crime we would empty the prisons, dissolve the police forces, and subsidize the criminals." The regulatory agencies are "chatteled to business and indifferent to the public," and Congress is "an anachronism, although a good investment for corporations." As for the market economy, it is rapidly being destroyed by the same corporate executives who are always "extolling it at stockholder meetings."

"Where is the free-enterprise system?" Nader asks, a sly smile lighting up his face. "I'm trying to find it. Is it the oil oligopoly, protected by import quotas? The shared monopolies in consumer products? The securities market, that bastion of capitalism operating on fixed commissions and now provided with socialized insurance? They call me a radical for trying to restore power to the consumer, but businessmen are the true radicals in this country. They are taking us deeper and deeper into corporate socialism—corporate power using government power to protect it from competition."

DOWN TO ZERO PROFITS

Nader is not exactly the first social critic to be astonished at the functions —and malfunctions—of a market economy, and to render them in overtones of darkest evil. But sinister tales of this sort, while they go down well enough with college crowds, throw no light at all on the issues Nader claims to want to face. It is true enough that unless consumers themselves are concerned about product safety, corporations have no particular bias in its favor. This is due, however, not to corporate depravity but rather to the economics of the case: an extra margin of safety is an invisible benefit that usually increases costs. When products, automobiles for example, are too complicated for con-sumers to make independent judgments as to safety, government must usually set standards if there are to be any—and it is a measure not just of business power but also of consumer indifference that safety standards for autos came so late.

178

Government must also counter the ceaseless efforts of corporations to escape from the rigors of competition through the acquisition of monopoly power, through tariff protection, import quotas, and the like. Granted that government hasn't done a very good job of this. All the same, most corporate executives, obliged to immerse themselves daily in what feels very much like competition, would be surprised to learn from Nader how free of it they are supposed to have become.

Given Nader's own diagnosis, it might be thought that he has been spending his time battling restraints on trade, but this is far from the case. He has instead been devoting his considerable ingenuity to devising new schemes for regulating and "popularizing" business, by such means as a federal charter for all corporations, "which would be like a constitution for a country," publication of corporate tax returns, and the election of public members to corporate boards. He would require an attack on pollution "with maximum use of known technology and down to zero profits."

Nader denies any desire to take the country into socialism, and in this he is apparently sincere. One of his raiders, Mark Green, told the *New York Times* recently that when Nader thinks of socialism "he doesn't think of Lenin but of Paul Rand Dixon," former Chairman of the FTC and, in Nader's mind, the quintessential bureaucrat. Yet Nader seems never to have grasped that when he talks about operating on "zero profits" he is talking not about a market economy but about a confiscatory, state-imposed system that would inevitably bring in train a host of other controls.

In his "consumer democracy" of the future, as he outlines it, everybody could order business around. Tightly controlled from above by the federal government, business would be policed at the local level by what would amount to consumer soviets. Nader thinks it will be easy to organize them, by handing out application forms in the parking lots of shopping centers. "Then collectively you can bargain with the owners of the center. You can say, 'Here are 18,000 families. We want a one-room office where we can have our staff within the center that will serve as a liaison between us and you. And we're going to develop certain conditions of our continuing patronage on a mass basis.' It might take the form of banning detergents with phosphates, improving service under a warranty, or holding down prices." Nader's product-rating system, including a telephone data bank for easy reference, would force manufacturers, he says, to abandon their present policy of "severe protective imitation" for one of "competition on price and quality." (Nobody has been able to explain just how such a system would make the millions of decisions the market makes now, many of them involving subjective judgments as to quality or value.)

While otherwise holding business in low esteem, Nader seems to have a blind faith in instant technology, insisting that if corporations are given tough enough deadlines, on antipollution devices or on proving the safety of food additives, they will somehow manage to comply. While it is true that some corporations plead ignorance as a convenient alibi for doing nothing about

179

pollution, it is also true that feasible systems have not yet been developed to control a number of crucial pollutants, including sulphur dioxide. On the question of food additives, James Grant, deputy commissioner of the Food and Drug Administration, says, "Scientific advances solve problems but also raise new questions. We can prove that certain chemicals are unsafe, but we can never prove, once and for all, that *anything* in the food supply is safe. We frequently are obliged to make absolute decisions on the basis of partial knowledge. If I have one criticism to level at the consumer advocates, it's that they're unwilling to take scientific uncertainty into account."

DOES SEARS, ROEBUCK CHEAT?

Economics, clearly, is not Nader's strong suit. He seems to think of figures as weapons, to be tossed around for maximum effect. To cite one of his current favorite examples of business fraud, he says that the orange-juice industry is watering its product by 10 percent, and thus bilking the public out of $150 million a year. And he adds: "You may wish to compare that with what bank robbers took last year in their second most successful performance to date: $8 million." Nader says he arrived at the 10 percent figure on the basis of "insider information." He applied it to total sales of the citrus industry and, lo, another "statistic" on business fraud. Even if the industry were watering, which it strenuously denies, it does not follow that the public is being gypped out of $150 million. On a water job of that scale, the price would reflect the water content, and if water were eliminated the price would have to go up.

Another of Nader's current favorite targets is Sears, Roebuck & Co. "Nobody thinks Sears, Roebuck cheats people. But they charge interest from the date the sales contract is signed rather than from the date of delivery—a few pennies, millions of times a year." But Sears no longer has ownership or use of the merchandise once the contract is signed, and could not, for example, apply any price increase that might subsequently be decided upon. The contract is perfectly open and aboveboard and should be considered in the context of the total transaction, price versus values received.

Nader quotes and endorses an estimate by Senator Philip Hart of Michigan that the whole gamut of business fraud and gouging, from shoddy merchandise to monopoly pricing, costs the consumer some $200 billion a year, "or 25 percent of all personal income." That utterly fantastic figure is also more than four times as large as all corporate profits in 1970. For a clipping of that magnitude to be possible, even theoretically, it would have to run as a sort of inflationary factor through the whole economy—wages as well as prices—and thus the argument becomes something of a wash, but a grossly misleading one all the same.

Like reformers before him, Nader is extremely reluctant to admit that any progress at all has been made in any area of consumer protection, even where he has helped write new legislation. "Very little progress, really," he sums it up. "It's a push-and-shove situation." He still refers to the nation's meat supply as "often diseased or putrescent, contaminated by rodent hairs and other assorted debris, its true condition disguised by chemical additives." This is the identical language he used three years ago to arouse Congress and propel passage of the Wholesale Meat Act. Since then the Department of Agriculture has declared 289 packing plants "potentially hazardous to human health," and has told state authorities to clean them up or shut them down. The department says "much remains to be done" to eliminate unsanitary conditions—but perhaps not as much as Nader seems to think. Similarly, despite the 34 automobile safety standards enforced by law and 701 recall campaigns, Nader says that "the changes are purely cosmetic."

SHOCK WAVES AT THE AGENCIES

The most impressive documents to come out of the Nader movement are the reports on the regulatory agencies. In most respects they are detailed and thoughtful, written with surprising skill by various groups of amateurs working under Nader's direction. And they have sent shock waves through Washington's bureaucracy. Since their publication, agency awareness of the public interest has greatly increased, and a certain distance has crept into the previously cozy relations between the regulators and the regulated. That distance, however, is still not nearly great enough to please Nader, who wants industry policed with eternal suspicion. "Sharpness" is one word he uses to describe the proper attitude. Jail terms for executives, he says, would be far more effective than the voluntary compliance on which the agencies now mostly rely. "Jail is a great stigma to a businessman, and even a short sentence is a real deterrent," explains James Turner, who wrote the FDA report. "You would get maximum compliance with a minimum of prosecutions."

That may well be so. But in the atmosphere of hostility that would result, regulation might actually be less effective than at present. The agencies can now make sweeping judgments—that a rate is "discriminatory" or a trade practice "deceptive"—on the basis of a simple hearing. "If criminal penalties were involved, our statutes would be interpreted in a much less flexible way," says Robert Pitofsky, the new head of FTC's Bureau of Consumer Protection. Most regulatory matters are exceedingly complex, and the agencies have trusted the industries concerned to furnish the data. If this system were replaced by a program of independent government research on countless topics, the sums expended could be huge enough to dent the federal budget. "It has to be a cooperative effort," argues Administrator Douglas Toms of the National Highway Traffic Safety Administration, which sets auto safety standards. "We're not going to get anywhere with an ugly, persistent confrontation, where the two sides try to outshout each other. We'd be pitting a tiny government agency against the worldwide auto industry."

At the FDA, a new leadership is attempting to stay on cordial terms with the $125-billion food industry while attacking the two key problems documented in great detail in the Nader report, *The Chemical Feast.* First, the FDA is undertaking comprehensive review of the hundreds of chemicals added to the food supply as preservatives, colorings, or flavorings. "None of these chemicals, perhaps, has been put to the most rigorous testing that presentday science could muster," admits Deputy Commissioner Grant, one of the new men at the agency. Second, the FDA has also acted on mounting evidence that many prepared foods are deficient in nutritional values, and is now setting guidelines for their fortification with vitamins and minerals. "In many ways the FDA was a bar to progress," says Grant, "and we are attempting to turn that around."

CONFESSIONAL FOR SINNERS

Among the agencies Nader has investigated, the FTC comes closest to the tough, proconsumer point of view that he is pushing for. Under its new leadership the FTC has filed a flurry of complaints on deceptive advertising, and in a number of these cases it has gone far beyond the traditional cease-and-desist order (known around the FTC as "go and sin no more"). To the dismay of the advertising profession, the FTC now seeks what it calls "affirmative disclosure"—that is, an admission in future advertising, for a specific period, that previous ads were deceptive. Howard Bell, president of the American Advertising Federation, says this amounts to "public flogging."

"Somebody is going to take us to court on affirmative disclosure, and they should," Pitofsky cheerfully admits. "It is a substantial expansion of FTC power." The FTC is also insisting that claims be based on evidence. "We're not after something that 'tastes better,'" Pitofsky says. "That's just puffery. But if you say it's twice as fast or 50 percent stronger, we will take that to mean faster or stronger than your competitor's product, and it better be so."

By swinging to "a fairly stiff enforcement of the law," as Pitofsky puts it, the FTC hopes to encourage self-regulation by industry. "Voluntary compliance comes when companies see that they are better off cleaning house themselves than letting government do it for them." And that is what seems to be happening. Warning of "the regulatory tidal wave which threatens to envelop us," the American Advertising Federation is trying to establish a National Advertising Review Board, which would set standards for ads, seek voluntary compliance with the standards, and refer ads it finds deceptive to the FTC for action.

In all this unaccustomed bustle, the agencies are, of course, just doing what they were supposed to be doing all along. To say only that, however, is to ignore the extraordinary difficulty of the regulatory function when there is no counterpressure to the steady, case-by-case intervention of skilled lawyers with specific and valuable corporate interests to protect. Congress, like the agencies, responds to the pressures applied—it's a case of "who's banging on the door," in Nader's words. Yet the pressures applied by individual corporations in individual cases can work to subvert the larger interests of the business community as a whole. "Intriguingly enough," says the FDA's Grant, "the overwhelming majority of the food industry believes that it is better off with a strong FDA, because all get balanced treatment." It is Nader's accomplishment, and no small one, that he has given the agencies the other constituency they need, the public. "Until we came along," says Nader, "the people at the agencies had forgotten what citizens looked like."

Nader will bend all of his lobbying skill this year to persuade Congress to pass a bill that would give the consumer permanent representation before regulatory bodies. The consumer agency to be established by the bill would, in fact, attempt to do just the sort of thing that Nader is doing now, but with the help of government funds and powers. A number of other consumer bills have broad support this year, including regulation of warranties and power for the FTC to seek preliminary injunctions against deceptive advertising. But Nader says, "I'd trade them all for the consumer agency."

THE PROBLEM OF MAINTAINING CLOUT

But can a movement like consumerism, powerful and yet amorphous, really be institutionalized? Certainly the passion and craft of a Nader cannot be. Nor would the director of a consumer agency enjoy Nader's complete freedom of action. A Senate aide who helped draft the bill predicts that the new office might "have its time in the sun, like the Peace Corps or OEO. Then it will carve out a rather cautious domain of its own and become part of the bureaucracy."

That being so, there will still be opportunities for Nader, always provided that he can stay in the sun himself. His support is volatile, a matter of vague tides of public opinion. "His problem is maintaining clout," says Douglas Toms, the Traffic Safety Administrator. "He has a strange kind of constituency, people with a burr under their saddle for one reason or another. He has to constantly find vehicles to keep him in the public eye." Financing will continue to be a problem. Nader himself is well aware of all these difficulties. He says that a basic error of reform movements is expecting to succeed. "You will never succeed. All you're trying to do is reduce problems to the level of tolerability."

Nader's answer to that question about the presidency is this: "I find that I am less and less interested in who is going to become President. A far more interesting question is, who's going to be the next president of General Motors?" Despite any such disclaimers, it is easy to imagine the movement going political and Nader running in some future year as, say, a candidate for the U.S. Senate from Connecticut. Nader might do well in politics, as a sort of latterday Estes Kefauver. A recent Harris survey revealed that 69 percent of the people think "it's good to have critics like Nader to keep industry on its toes," while only five percent think he is "a troublemaker who is against the free enterprise system." This is the sort of public response that most politicians, including Presidents, yearn for in vain.

183

Judging Nader on the basis of the specific reforms he has brought about, it would be hard to disagree with this public verdict. There has been some cost, however, and this cannot be measured. He has visited his own suspicions and fears upon a whole society, and in the end his hyperbole may prove to be a dangerous weapon. But this year at least, the public apparently expects its crusaders to be twice as fast and 50 percent stronger.

IV.

CONTEMPORARY
ISSUES

Economics is relevant. Most students of economics (particularly in their first year), have difficulty accepting this idea. Once the nature of economic scarcity is fully comprehended, however, one realizes that as a central economic problem, scarcity, is an ongoing, contemporary concern.

The solution to this central dilemma entails achieving efficient utilization, i.e., optimal return, of society's resources. The form of social organization selected to achieve this solution may, broadly speaking, be one of three: tradition, command, or market. Considering the criterion of efficiency, the proven champion is the market system. This solution of scarcity, achieved via the market, while quite good, is not perfect. Problems still exist. To some degree they are problems inherent in the system itself, but to a larger extent they are problems of the times, reflecting themselves as inefficiencies in the economic solution. The specific nature of inefficiency in this system is best seen by separating the problem into the two basic resource areas—human and nonhuman.

185

Part A encompasses the human resource area. The human resource, designated by President John F. Kennedy as the "basic" resource,[1] stands at the base of the economic system. Inefficient utilization of this resource is multiplied throughout the system, since all other resources must be combined with some portion of human resources to produce output. The readings chosen for this section are representative of the major areas of human resource inefficiencies and areas of concern.

Part B concerns itself with the nonhuman resource area, or perhaps more accurately, the problem of economic growth. It may at first seem incongruous to speak of growth "problems" when referring to a nation with the highest standard of living in the world. Only very recently has the average American considered the possibility that unchecked economic growth might well be a thing of the past. The nature of these growth problems and the potential constraints imposed on future United States economic advances is presented by a careful selection of key articles about this subject.

Considering the various problems facing the U.S. economy today, it is only logical to raise as a final issue, in Part C: "What will the future bring?" While economists do not possess any crystal balls, they do attempt some predictions based on events that have transpired. Two such attempts are presented as concluding comments to both this section and the anthology as a whole.

---

[1] *Manpower Report of the President,* (Washington 25, D.C.: U.S. Government Printing Office, March 1963), p. xii.

A.

Human Resources

ECONOMIC DEVELOPMENT AND INDIVIDUAL OPPORTUNITY

Council of Economic Advisers

The unprecedented prosperity of the past seven years has brought great economic progress to most Americans. Poverty has been significantly reduced; educational attainment is rising; the quality of public service has improved; and far more jobs are available to the previously disadvantaged.

But not all Americans have shared in the Nation's prosperity. About one-seventh of the population remains in poverty. And the plight of the poor is ever more sharply contrasted with the comfortable standards of living most Americans enjoy in an era of growing and widening abundance. This contrast has awakened the social conscience of the nation; at the same time, the nation's ability to assist the disadvantaged minority has reached new heights. The majority of our people have now achieved incomes which make the elimination of poverty a concrete, realistic, and attainable goal in our

---

From Council of Economic Advisers, *Economic Report of the President, 1968,* chapter 4.

generation. For the first time in any society, the United States can afford to eliminate poverty; indeed, it cannot afford to do otherwise.

The reduction of poverty has been a continuing process in our society, fundamentally reflecting the longterm growth of output per worker—which in turn has derived from progress in technology and management, from a labor force ever better educated and more adaptable, and from the provision of more and better capital per worker. Economic growth brings great rewards; but because it comes unevenly it can be a highly disruptive process. Some industries, some occupations, some regions undergo dramatic expansion; others decline relatively or even absolutely. Whole new industries and occupations arise; many older ones are completely transformed or disappear entirely.

Many of the structural changes that lie at the heart of progress do not force individuals to change their occupations or residences. The adjustment comes as sons and daughters take up occupations different from their parents' or move to new areas. But rapid and uneven change often cannot be fully accommodated in this way. Many individuals are uprooted or find their livelihoods threatened. Some cannot make the transition which provides the opportunity for improvement. And even an adjustment occurring between generations often creates hardship when childhood background and training are inadequate or unsuited to the needs of the new order.

Thus the process which has reduced poverty has sometimes created it. It has redistributed both affluence and poverty, and in many cases has concentrated them—geographically, occupationally, and by demographic category. As those able to respond to opportunity have moved out of poverty, those left behind are increasingly the ones whose opportunities were restricted; the immobile, the aged, the disabled, the handicapped, the broken family, the poorly educated, the victim of discrimination.

Significant reduction in the number of poor people has occurred only when the economy is expanding. When economic growth is slow, poverty diminishes slowly—and often actually increases. The years from 1948 through 1953 saw rapid reduction in poverty, as have the years since 1964. By contrast, the number of individuals in poverty declined very slowly during the latter half of the 1950s.

The first part of this chapter focuses primarily on the geographical aspects of the process by which poverty has been both eliminated and redistributed—the transformation of agriculture, the growth of the city, and the redistribution of opportunity and of poverty within the city.

The second part of this chapter largely abstracts from the geographical dimensions of poverty. It deals with programs offering solutions to poverty, wherever the poor may be found.

Programs for the reduction of poverty are—and should be—in part the responsibility of local organizations and units of government. Nevertheless, even though concentrations of poverty are local, the problem is national and must be a national responsibility. Indeed, it is a national problem just because of its concentration. The forces which produce poverty in particular areas are largely beyond the influence of local governments. And the remedies needed to lift citizens from poverty cannot be successfully applied by individual communities acting alone.

THE CHANGING STRUCTURE OF OPPORTUNITIES

The social scientist needs a yardstick to measure progress in reducing economic deprivation. For statistical purposes, households are defined as poor if their income falls below the cost of a certain minimum consumption standard—$2,185 in current prices for a nonfarm couple under 65 years of age, $3,335 for a nonfarm family of four, and so on. A reduction in numbers by this definition is only a rough measure of progress, since social and psychological conditions associated with poverty may persist after incomes rise above the poverty line. Moreover, the income levels used in the definition cannot provide for much more than minimum necessities. Nevertheless, measured changes in the incidence of poverty over time provide a reasonable criterion of achievement, and are employed frequently throughout this chapter.

Between 1959 and 1966, the number of poor declined sharply from 38.9 to 29.7 million, or from 22.1 to 15.4 percent of the population. Substantial progress was recorded for almost every population group, but the reduction in the number of poor farm households was especially marked. This progress, though encouraging, should not conceal the magnitude of the remaining problems nor the fact that they fall with disproportionate severity on certain groups.

Geographically, poverty is today concentrated in the central cities of our large metropolitan areas and in certain rural districts. While the proportion of poor farm households remains above the national average, the great bulk of rural poverty today is found among the rural nonfarm population. The distribution and extent of poverty have been influenced by the changing structure of employment opportunities and the massive internal migrations encouraged by these changes. One of the most significant of these changes has occurred in farming.

CHANGES IN THE FARM ECONOMY

The most pervasive influence affecting employment in agriculture has been a growth of labor productivity substantially in excess of the growth of markets. Between 1940 and 1966, aggregate production inputs used in farming increased by only eight percent, while farm output increased by 61 percent. The overall ratio of output to inputs increased 50 percent, and the ratio of output to labor input increased by a spectacular 347 percent.

The demand for farm products has consistently increased less rapidly than the growth of incomes. Combined with sharp increases in productivity, this fact has greatly diminished the need for labor resources in farming. Further, the revolutionary increase in labor productivity could be realized only through mechanization. Because many machines could be efficiently utilized only on large farms, the full benefits of mechanization were not available to farms of smaller size. Since 1940, the number of farms has been reduced by almost one-half and the average size of farms has more than doubled. The farm population meanwhile has fallen by almost two-thirds; after remaining virtually unchanged in the preceding 20 years, it declined from 30.5 million in 1940 to 11.6 million in 1966.

As a result of the trends in demand and in productivity, the number of farms with sales valued at $10,000 or more per year has been increasing, while the number of farms with annual sales under $10,000 has declined almost one-third since 1959 (Figure 1). There is a movement up the income ladder within farming as some operators of smaller farms acquire additional resources to expand their sales. But operators of the smallest farms have become increasingly dependent on off-farm employment to supplement their incomes. Farm incomes are benefited both by Government price-support operations and by direct payments. These benefits, of course, do little for farmers who have little to sell. Despite the growing prosperity of large farmers, many small farmers and farmworkers cannot earn a decent income in farming.

Industrial expansion offered many farmers and farmworkers an opportunity to raise their incomes by accepting nonfarm employment. Several studies show that movement out of farming is much more closely related to employment opportunities and income in the nonfarm sectors than to earnings in farming. The experience of the 1960s again confirms this. Rapid economic growth was accompanied by sharp reductions in the farm population.

Poverty in the Farm Population

Farm poverty remains a serious problem, especially since most of the farm poor are ineligible for income maintenance programs as presently organized. As recently as 1959, 63 percent of all farm families had less than $5,000 in sales and averaged less than $3,500 of total family income (Figure 1). The number of farmers in this sales class has declined sharply since then, and their off-farm earnings have increased. Operators of the smaller farms tend to be older than those of large farms, and have on the average almost three years less of formal education. The remaining poverty on farms is concentrated among those operators of small farms. By 1966, however, only 600,000 farm households were in poverty, a sharp drop from 1.8 million in 1959. Much of the reduction in farm poverty has resulted from migration. Some of those who moved have become members of the nonfarm poor, but the bulk of the younger migrants have increased their income potential. It is likely that many of the older farmers who left farming remain in poverty. This is reflected in the fact that, between 1959 and 1966, the number of aged poor nonfarm households outside metropolitan areas remained nearly constant.

Hired farmworkers are also very likely to be poor. In 1966 there were 757,000 persons who had hired farmwork as their primary employment. They

Figure 1. *Number of Farms and Farm Income, by Value-of-Sales Classes, 1959, 1964, and 1966*

Value-of-Sales Class and Year	Number of Farms		Cash receipts Plus Government Payments; Percentage Distribution	Farm operator Family Income		
	Thousands of Farms	Percentage Distribution		Total Income	Realized Farm Income	Off-Farm Income
All farms:						
1959	4,097	100.0	100.0	$4,844	$2,773	$2,071
1964	3,472	100.0	100.0	6,196	3,747	2,449
1966	3,252	100.0	100.0	7,787	5,049	2,738
Sales under $5,000:						
1959	2,576	62.9	13.9	3,493	1,115	2,378
1964	2,030	58.5	9.3	3,860	946	2,914
1966	1,769	54.4	6.7	4,492	1,071	3,421
Sales of $5,000-$9,999:						
1959	693	16.9	15.5	4,705	3,160	1,545
1964	530	15.3	10.7	5,202	3,434	1,768
1966	446	13.7	7.9	5,902	3,989	1,913
Sales of $10,000-$19,999:						
1959	503	12.3	21.5	6,413	5,091	1,322
1964	488	14.0	18.8	7,482	5,984	1,498
1966	510	15.7	17.1	8,463	6,869	1,594
Sales of $20,000 and over:						
1959	325	7.9	49.1	13,420	11,506	1,914
1964	424	12.2	61.2	17,146	14,979	2,167
1966	527	16.2	68.3	19,791	17,539	2,252

Source: Department of Agriculture.

averaged 212 days of farmwork and an added 13 days of nonfarmwork with total wages from both sources averaging $2,102 for the year. The hired farm work force contains a disproportionate number of nonwhites—27 percent in 1966; this contrasts with 13 percent of nonwhites in both the total farm and the total U.S. population.

The largest concentration of low-income farms and farmworkers is in the South. In 1964, 55 percent of all farms with less than $5,000 in annual sales—but 44 percent of all U.S. farms—were located in the South. Moreover, in that year more than 53 percent of the hired farmworkers lived in the South.

Despite the revolution in agricultural technology and the attendant migration, the transformation of agriculture is not complete. The farm population will continue to decline, creating serious problems for some rural communities. The young, rather than the older farmers, will continue to be the primary migrants. This will leave behind a progressively aging population, especially among the farm poor. As a result, the natural rate of increase of the farm population will continue to fall. In 1950 the natural increase of the farm population totaled 392,000 and net emigration came to 1.5 million. By 1966 the natural increase had been reduced to 90,000 and net emigration to 858,000.

THE GROWTH OF NONFARM JOBS

The decline of employment opportunities in farming has been accompanied by a rapid growth of jobs in manufacturing and service industries. Initially concentrated in or near the large northern cities, these jobs attracted millions of migrants from rural areas.

During the economic expansions accompanying World War II and the Korean war, manufacturing employment remained highly concentrated in the heavily metropolitan areas of the industrialized States of the North—Massachusetts, New York, New Jersey, Pennsylvania, Ohio, Michigan, and Illinois. With less than 40 percent of the U.S. population, these seven States provided about 55 percent of manufacturing employment in 1953, about the same share as in 1939 when the national total was approximately half as large.

The pattern of growth in manufacturing employment changed significantly during the late 1950s. Technological advance in transportation, construction of interstate highways, expansion of trucking, construction of long distance pipelines, and the extension of coordinated electric power grids reduced the advantage of potential manufacturing sites in the large metropolitan centers. This trend was accelerated by the rapid growth of industries such as technical instruments, electronics, and small consumer appliances, whose products have high value per unit of weight and volume and thus can be shipped at relatively low transport cost. As a result, the location of industry was increasingly determined by other factors, such as relative wage rates, labor availability, local taxes, climate, and land costs.

These developments shifted the growth in manufacturing employment away from the North. Between 1956 and 1966, U.S. manufacturing employment increased 1,840,000 (11 percent). Meanwhile, in the seven industrialized States mentioned above, manufacturing employment increased only 37,000 (less than one-half of one percent). By contrast, during the same period, manufacturing employment grew 465,000 (26 percent) in the West and 1,026,000 (33 percent) in the South.

Nonfarm job opportunities have grown less rapidly in metropolitan areas—especially in the giant ones—than in the rest of the Nation. From 1962 to 1966, private nonfarm employment grew five percent a year or more in nonmetropolitan counties, regardless of the size of the largest urban center; in comparison, it rose four percent yearly in metropolitan counties. In the same period, total nonagricultural employment increased less than three percent in the 13 largest metropolitan areas.

While these figures show a general relative improvement in nonagricultural employment opportunities in the less densely settled areas, many nonmetropolitan areas were stagnant or declining. Between 1959 and 1964, there were 1,315 nonmetropolitan counties in which private nonfarm employment either declined or increased by less than 100 jobs. Large contiguous blocks of counties with declining populations are found in Appalachia, the northern portions of the Lake States, the Great Plains, and the Southwest.

The process of economic growth has been and continues to be very uneven in rural areas and in smaller cities. These are the areas where, because of dependence on one or two industries—frequently resource-based industries such as agriculture, forestry, or mining—the greatest adjustments are needed in response to shifts in the pattern of demand, technological change, or the exhaustion of resources. This uneven growth has been responsible for major shifts in population.

RECENT CHANGES IN POPULATION DISTRIBUTION

In the past 10 years, significant changes have occurred in the pattern of migration and in the growth and distribution of population in the United States. These changes have both affected and been affected by the changing pattern of demand and productivity in an expanding economy. They have served both as an engine whereby poverty has been reduced and as a force contributing to its redistribution.

Migration

The shifts in the geographical distribution of jobs noted above have been paralleled by changes in the pattern of migration. Migration to the North and to the largest metropolitan areas soared during the economic expansion of the 1940s and early 1950s, but has slowed markedly in the last 10 years. Since

Figure 2. Components of Population Change by Area, 1950-65

Period and Area	Percentage Increase per Year in Population	Population Changes (thousands of persons)			
		Natural Increase	Net Gains from Migration		
			Total	Foreign[1]	Domestic[2]
1950 to 1960:[3]					
Total	1.7	25,337	2,660	2,660	--
Metropolitan areas[4]	2.4	16,336	8,634	1,955	6,679
Nonmetropolitan areas	.5	9,002	−5,974	705	−6,679
1960 to 1965:[5]					
Total	1.5	12,626	1,846	1,846	--
Metropolitan areas[4]	1.7	8,589	2,436	1,357	1,079
Nonmetropolitan areas	1.1	4,037	−590	489	−1,079

[1]Distribution of net foreign migration is estimated to be the same as distribution of gross migration from foreign countries during 1962-66.
[2]Estimated migration among 50 States and the District of Columbia.
[3]April 1950 to April 1960.
[4]Metropolitan areas as defined in 1967.
[5]April 1960 to July 1965.

Sources: Department of Commerce and Council of Economic Advisers.

1960, the 12 largest metropolitan areas (those with more than 1,700,000 population in 1960) have grown only slightly more rapidly than their natural excess of births over deaths. In the North-Central States, the largest metropolitan areas grew 1.8 percent a year during the 1950s, but only 1.0 percent a year so far in the 1960s. They are now experiencing more emigration than immigration. In most regions, the metropolitan areas under 250,000 population are growing considerably more rapidly than the largest ones.

Net domestic migration to metropolitan areas declined from 668,000 a year during the 1950s to 216,000 a year in the first half of the 1960s. As Figure 2 indicates, during the latter period domestic migration contributed less to the growth of metropolitan area population than did foreign migration. Metropolitan areas are still growing faster than nonmetropolitan areas, but the difference in growth rates is narrowing. Furthermore, in the 1960s the non-farm population was growing about as fast outside as inside metropolitan areas.

From 1960 to 1965, only the North-Central region lost more migrants—foreign and domestic combined—than it gained (Figure 3). This was the result of a large net loss of whites through domestic migration, which was offset only slightly by the much reduced net domestic immigration of nonwhites. During the same period the Northeast gained population through migration, although the region experienced a net emigration of domestic whites. The West continued to receive the largest gains from migration, and was the only

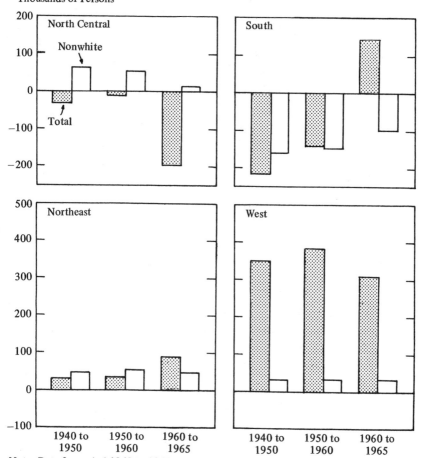

Figure 3. Average Annual Net Migration by Regions

Note: Data for period 1960 to 1965 not strictly comparable with other data.
Sources: Department of Commerce and Council of Economic Advisers.

region to gain more domestic migrants than it lost. The South was the only region in which emigration exceeded immigration among nonwhites. The South's gain through total migration was due to a large inflow of white foreign immigrants, which offset a net outward movement of both domestic whites and nonwhites.

The growth of the nonwhite population in metropolitan areas averaged 3.9 percent a year in the 1950s, but it slowed to 3.1 percent a year in the 1960s. Nonetheless, this latter rate was about twice as fast as the rate of increase of the white population, partly because the nonwhite rate of natural increase was double that of the white. In the 1960s, 32 percent of the increase in nonwhite population in these areas was attributable to migration, compared with

43 percent in the 1950s. Not since the 1940s has migration accounted for more than half of the growth of nonwhite population in metropolitan areas.

Racial Distribution Within Metropolitan Areas

Like the European immigrants of earlier times, the Negroes from the South came to the cities looking for better jobs, housing, and schools for their children. To a greater degree than their immigrant predecessors, Negroes met severe discrimination in housing. Because most of them were poor, the housing they could afford was usually in the older sections of the metropolitan area and usually in the central city. And because of discrimination, this area became a segregated ghetto. The only way in which the segregated but rapidly growing Negro community could obtain additional housing was through encroachment on the white neighborhoods at the borders of the ghetto. Racial tensions increased as the process continued. The more affluent whites moved to the suburbs, where Negroes were largely excluded.

Thus, within metropolitan areas, the nonwhite population has become increasingly concentrated in the central cities while the white, middle- and upper-income population has become increasingly suburban. Since 1960, the white population in central cities has declined, while the nonwhite population has grown by 3.6 percent a year. Meanwhile, the growth rate of suburban populations has been six and one-half times the rate for central cities, and that growth has been overwhelmingly among the white population. Less than one suburbanite in 20 is nonwhite, and the white suburban population is growing more than twice as fast as nonwhite. Between 1960 and 1966, there was an exodus of more than 3.5 million whites from central cities. Over the same period, net migration added one million to the nonwhite population of central cities, and natural increase added another 1.5 million. As a result of these shifts, not only particular city areas or neighborhoods, but entire cities and counties, are becoming increasingly segregated by race.

Economic Aspects of the Transformation

Businesses, as well as the white middleclass, have found suburban locations increasingly attractive. Cheaper land permits manufacturing firms to construct one- or two-storied buildings, which are usually more efficient. The suburbs also provide some escape from central city traffic congestion. Following the shift of population and manufacturing, other industries—construction, retail trade, and other services—have also grown rapidly in the suburbs. Employment gains in central cities have been largely limited to clerical, managerial, and professional positions.

The decline of the central city as a place of employment relative to the suburbs has been most typical of large northern metropolitan regions. New

196

York City is a case in point. Between 1956 and 1966, manufacturing employment declined 15 percent in the city but increased 35 percent in the New York State suburbs. In the city, only financial institutions, State and local government, and miscellaneous service industries experienced substantial gains in employment.

Redistribution of job opportunities in metropolitan areas has increased the distance between the residence of the less-skilled, lower-income individual, often a Negro, and the potential jobs available to him. Metropolitan transit systems characteristically do not provide adequate service between central city poverty areas and the sites of suburban employment.

Changes in the Distribution of Poverty

Many migrants to the cities in recent decades were poor when they arrived. Yet, as a proportion of all households in metropolitan areas, poor households declined from 19.6 percent in 1959 to 14.9 percent in 1966. This seven-year decline in the incidence of poverty in metropolitan areas was comparable to the reduction from 29.1 percent to 23.6 percent in the incidence of poor households in other nonfarm areas. Thus, metropolitan areas continue to have less than a proportionate share of the poor; they contain 69 percent of the total nonfarm population but only 56 percent of the nonfarm poor. Within metropolitan areas, poverty is much more common in central cities than in suburbs. In 1966, the suburban population outnumbered that in central cities by 15 percent, yet there were 9.5 million poor living in central cities and 5.8 million in suburbs. About two-thirds of the metropolitan poor are white. While the white poor were distributed about equally between suburbs and central cities, about four times as many nonwhite poor lived in central cities as in suburbs.

PROPOSALS FOR CHANGE

Council for Economic Development

In this chapter, we summarize the main conclusions of several major studies of poverty made over the past few years by presidential commissions and other groups. On the basis of these studies and our own analysis of the poverty problem, we have developed recommendations regarding the approaches that we feel are likely to prove most useful and efficient in bringing about an equitable and uniform welfare system.

MINIMUM NATIONAL STANDARDS

In 1966, the Advisory Council on Public Welfare, which had been appointed by Anthony J. Celebrezze, Secretary of the Department of Health, Education, and Welfare, reported to his successor, John W. Gardner, that the federal government should "set a minimum standard for welfare payments below which no state may fall and below which no family would be required to live." Among many other recommendations, it urged that public assistance be a matter of "right" and that "need" be the sole criterion. It further recommended that the federal government assume full financial responsibility for the difference between the state's share and the total cost of the program.[1] Essentially the same recommendations were made in February 1969 by a task force appointed by President Nixon.[2] These studies and others in recent years have emphasized the need for minimum national standards as a first step in reforming the present system.

On December 2, 1969, the Advisory Commission on Intergovernmental Relations recommended that the federal government should assume "full

---

From Council for Economic Development, *Improving the Public Welfare System,* April 1970, pp. 54-63.

[1] *Having the Power, We Have the Duty,* (Washington, D.C., 1966).

[2] Not released publicly.

financial responsibility" for all public assistance programs including Medicaid. This 26 member commission was established by the Congress in 1959 to offer advice on the "most desirable allocation of government functions." Its bipartisan membership includes Administration officials, members of the Congress, governors, state legislators, mayors, county executives, and private citizens.

FAMILY ALLOWANCES VERSUS NEGATIVE INCOME TAX

The Arden House Conference on Public Welfare, in which many CED Trustees participated, was convened by Governor Rockefeller of New York in 1967 and spent almost 18 months studying the problem. In addition to position papers prepared especially for their consideration, this group had made available to it many of the major studies previously published containing recommendations for welfare reform. In reporting its findings, the Steering Committee concluded that the public interest would be served if a practical system of income maintenance could be devised that would replace the present system of welfare payments and provide some benefits to all who live below the poverty line, instead of only the persons now on the welfare rolls. Such a system should contain incentives to work, should provide greater administrative efficiency and effectiveness than now exists, and should incorporate regional cost-of-living differentials.[3]

The Arden House group spent a substantial amount of time studying two major income maintenance proposals. One was a system of universal family or children's allowances. The second was a negative income tax. Here are its main findings:

Family Allowances. One of the committee's major findings was that under a family allowance system about 70 to 80 percent of the funds would go to families who need it least, with the government then recouping this money through the tax system. Other weaknesses noted in that system were that no provision is made for individuals or couples without children who are in need, that the payments proposed would be inadequate as an anti-poverty measure and that the inclusion of a work incentive principle would be difficult.

Negative Income Tax. Because this offers the possibility of achieving automatically two longsought but heretofore unattainable goals—*need* as the basis for financial assistance and a uniform national minimum standard—the committee indicated that it "leaned" toward the negative income tax. It said that the nation was at a stage in its history when it could afford to give serious consideration to an income maintenance plan which would raise all Americans to at least the poverty level. Its recommendation therefore was that

---

[3]*Report from the Steering Committee of the Arden House Conference on Public Welfare* (New York, 1968).

Congress pass legislation which would enable those states which wished to experiment with various income maintenance proposals to do so.[4]

In summing up its position, the Arden House group said that it was less concerned with the kind of income maintenance that is finally evolved than it was with the acceptance, as a national goal, of the objective that basic economic support, at the poverty level at least, be assured all people. The report also applauded the appointment in early 1968 by President Johnson of the President's Commission on Income Maintenance, headed by Ben W. Heineman of Chicago, as a move in "the direction this committee believes must be taken."

$2,400 FOR A FAMILY OF FOUR

The Heineman Commission submitted its report to President Nixon in November 1969.[5] On the major issues involved in improving the welfare system, the Arden House and the Heineman Commission recommendations are in substantial agreement. The commission's main recommendation is for "the creation of a universal income supplement program financed and administered by the federal government, making cash payments to all members of the population with income needs." The payments would vary by family size and would provide a base income for any needy family or individual. The report specifically urges that single persons and childless couples be covered by federal assistance. It recommends the eventual elimination of all categorical assistance.

The commission urges that the federal government provide a minimum annual income of $2,400 to a family of four, an amount that, in its opinion,

---

[4]Considerable data is being gathered that will assist any attempts along these lines. The Office of Economic Opportunity has been experimenting since 1968, under the supervision of the University of Wisconsin, with 1,000 families in New Jersey in an income maintenance experiment that most closely resembles a negative income tax, and which also includes some work incentive as a part of the experiment. Professor Harvey Brazer, chairman of the Department of Economics of the University of Michigan, has published a variety of papers dealing with aspects of income maintenance and negative income tax. His work includes a concept of working within a framework of the present $600 exemption in the present income tax law, but reversing the benefit so that the maximum accrues to the low income tax payer and the minimum to the highest-bracket tax payer. (*Tax Policy and Children's Allowances,* Harvey E. Brazer, Chairman, Department of Economics, University of Michigan, 1967.) The Brookings Institution has also sponsored a number of studies on the subject of the negative income tax. (*Negative Taxes and the Poverty Problem,* Christopher Green, The Brookings Institution, Washington, D.C., 1967.)

[5]*Poverty Amid Plenty: The American Paradox* (Washington, D.C., 1969).

could be "implemented promptly." A clear preference is declared for an entirely *cash* income, with no income in-kind, which the commission regards "as a poor substitute for providing adequate cash incomes to the poor." The report urged that "special programs providing food to poor families should be phased out and equivalent assistance given in cash. Income supplements, when they approach adequate levels, also would allow housing programs to be phased out as soon as the market could meet the demand for low-cost housing."

The Heineman Commission proposals incorporate a system of income incentives that "would always result in significantly higher income for those who work than for those who do not." However, it challenges the assumption that sufficient income from work is within the reach of most poor people. In the commission's view, largely because of the false assumption that everyone who is employable could work at adequate wages, no federal income transfer programs have been enacted to supplement the earnings of the employed poor. Yet, continues the report, "one-third of all persons in poor families in 1966 lived in families headed by full-time employed male workers. If the head of a family of four worked 40 hours a week, 52 weeks a year, at the minimum wage of $1.60 per hour, family income would still fall below the poverty line." Since nearly one-half of the working poor families have six or more members, the report pointed out, full-year employment at more than $2.00 per hour would be required for them even to reach the poverty level. The commission estimates that there are at least 10 million jobs in this country—including some state and municipal government jobs—which pay less than the current federal minimum wage.

There are, of course, differences in emphasis and detail between various of the major recommendations in the Arden House and Heineman Commission reports, and in at least two instances there are sharp divergences in policy. As to the matter of differentials in the minimum income based on regional variations in the cost of living, the Heineman Commission argues against these differentials on the grounds that "available data do not indicate clearcut regional variations," and that it might be wiser policy not to encourage regional differences where they exist but to "induce more advanced levels of income and standards of living throughout the United States." In regard to day-care centers, the commission feels that such a system based on the stipulation that mothers accept work or training would be "costly, narrowly conceived, and coercive." A preference is indicated for providing enriched day-care facilities on an ability-to-pay basis for both welfare recipients as well as others. (... the Heineman Commission opposes a mandatory work requirement not only for women heads of households under the AFDC program but for all welfare recipients.)

The commission's welfare proposals would extend coverage to some 36 million Americans as compared with the 25.4 million persons it is estimated would be affected by the Administration's proposals. The commission estimates that the overall annual added federal cost of its recommendations, including training programs, would be somewhat less than $10 billion.

A UNIFORM NATIONAL APPROACH

Having described earlier in this statement the broad principles that we believe must underlie an effective reform of the present welfare system, we now turn to a consideration of the appropriate administrative, institutional, financial, and other measures required to accomplish the broad goals that have been outlined.

We concur fully with the view that a uniform national approach to the problem of welfare is essential to the reform of the system. *We view as practical and realistic the proposal that the level of federal income maintenance be set to provide a minimum of $2,400 for a family of four at the present time.*

The $2,400 figure for a family of four could consist of $1,600 in cash allotments with the remainder being provided through the Food Stamp Program. . . . The Food Stamp Program is a mechanism already in being for distributing assistance to the needy, and though at the present time it reaches only about 15 percent of the needy, it has gained increasing public acceptance and is being enlarged substantially.[6] Because it offers promise as a practical means for supplementing the nutrition of the poor, we feel that the food stamp plan should be enlarged and improved with a view to making it an efficient adjunct to the welfare system.

We approve the use of the Food Stamp Program as additional to the welfare cash allotment and believe that it should be extended for the immediate future to all who qualify for income supplementation. However, we recommend that it be subject to periodic review and evaluation in order to ascertain whether the efficiency of the program can be improved and also whether cash payments might not better achieve the objectives of the program.

Harnessing the food stamp subsidy program with the welfare cash allotment would have the salutary effect of raising the income floor for welfare recipients by about 50 percent in the case of those totally dependent on welfare. At the same time, however, the two schedules in combination would *reduce* the incentive to increase incomes by working.

The welfare cash allotment proposal, which allows full retention of the first $720 of annual earnings and retention of 50 percent of earnings over that

---

[6]The Food Stamp Program is still limited and is not in existence in hundreds of counties, in large part because of local indifference or outright resistance. In fiscal 1969 there were only 3.2 million recipients, the face value of the stamps distributed was some $600 million, and since they were sold on a sliding scale according to incomes of recipients, the federal subsidy amounted to only $247 million. The Administration proposes to increase the number of people covered to 5.4 million by the end of 1970, at a cost to the federal government of $575 million. By the end of 1971, 7.5 million people are to be covered at an annual cost of $1.25 billion.

amount up to a cutoff point, is a considerable improvement over the present incentive plan for AFDC families, which allows retention of only 30 percent of earnings above the first $360. The food stamp plan, when combined with the proposed welfare allotment, would reduce by about a third the exemption of the first $720 earned, and for families in some income brackets would allow retention of only about a third of additional earnings.

We recommend that in combining welfare cash and food subsidy programs for income maintenance, the incentive element be set so that the recipients retain an adequate percentage of earnings (centering around approximately half of earnings) above a minimum allowance (such as $720 a year) up to an appropriate cutoff point. Some additional costs would be incurred by such improvement in the incentive schedule, the magnitude depending on the particular plan adopted.

As noted earlier in this statement, a minimum of $2,400 income for a family of four hardly equals the barest subsistence level and is well below the so-called poverty threshold of $3,700 set in 1969. Those unable to augment their incomes through employment obviously are consigned to a very barren existence.[7] *We believe that a priority claim against future available federal funds should be invoked to raise total assistance to more acceptable levels.*

So long as the minimum level of income maintenance for a family of four remains in the $2,000 range, no problem is posed in terms of difference in costs between regions and areas. However, as the minimum income level rises toward a more realistic level, which we believe should occur, distortions very likely will begin to occur. Therefore, *we recommend that as the minimum income level rises, consideration be given to adjustments for cost differentials where appropriate between various regions of the country and between urban and rural communities.*

That the federal government must bear an increasing share of the financial burden of welfare is evident. Granted that some states have been derelict in their responsibility toward their helpless and poor, even failing in some instances to take advantage of federal funds available to them, these and other states would find great difficulty in raising sufficient revenues to finance their share of the new national welfare system now proposed. At the same time, the wealthier states, particularly those that have attempted to meet their welfare obligations and are already carrying a very heavy and disproportionate financial load, will be increasingly penalized as welfare costs rise. Various formulas have been devised through which the federal government could assume a greater proportion of this financial burden. One such formula, put forward by the Administration, combines fiscal relief under the welfare

---

[7]Even on the basis of data that is frequently inadequate and outdated, about three-quarters of the states presently set the cost standard for the basic needs of a family of four under the AFDC program at more than $2,400 a year.

proposal together with revenue-sharing with the states through block grants.[8] We find that such proposals suffer from various defects in that they are either inadequate or highly complex, or they tend to perpetuate present inequities among the states or to create new ones.

The concept of a truly uniform national system of public assistance based on income maintenance requires that the federal government not only assume an increasing share of the necessarily increasing cost, but that it eventually undertake the entire burden. *As an objective to be attained as soon as fiscally feasible, we recommend that the federal government undertake a substantially higher proportion of the financing of public assistance with a phased takeover by the federal government of state and local public assistance costs over the next five years as the goal.*

A corollary of the federal government's assumption of full responsibility for the financing of public assistance is a matching full responsibility for the administration of such a national system. Several compelling considerations are present here. A basic principle is that the full underwriting of costs without close surveillance and tight control over costs is to invite maladministration, waste, and inefficiency. Of even greater importance from a human standpoint is the need to establish uniform national administrative procedures, standards, and regulations, applying impartially and equitably to all recipients of public assistance.

Therefore, *we recommend that as the federal government takes over responsibility for financing public assistance payments, it likewise assume a commensurate responsibility for administering such assistance in order to assure efficiency as well as to provide all recipients equitable, uniform treatment.*

As interim steps along this way, we offer a final set of recommendations aimed at the two objectives—greater efficiency and greater protection for the human rights of welfare recipients—set forth above.

The entire procedures for investigating and determining the qualifications of individuals for public assistance programs not only are demeaning but also cumbersome, costly, and time-consuming. The present system should be replaced by a far simpler and more direct method of certification by affidavit, which has now been adequately tested but which should be subject to periodic review. *We support the certification method of determining welfare eligibility for both federal and state portions of the system.* With spot checks sufficient to catch and prevent abuses, this will be less costly, more efficient, and have the effect of freeing case workers to help people get off the assistance rolls instead of making certain they should stay on the rolls.

---

[8]CED's Research and Policy Committee has studied this problem in an earlier Statement on National Policy, *A Fiscal Program for a Balanced Federalism,* June 1967. Inasmuch as the uses to which states and local governments can put these funds are unlimited and likewise have no direct relationship to public welfare, we have eliminated revenue sharing from consideration in the present statement.

The present methods are particularly needless and wasteful where the aged, blind, and disabled are concerned. Once those who are eligible have been qualified, there is little point in repeating the process. Therefore, *we recommend that the administration of the assistance programs for the aged, blind, and disabled be handled within the Department of Health, Education, and Welfare by federal payments in a manner similar to that used for Social Security payments.* This does not mean that monies from the Social Security Trust Fund would be used for these programs, nor does it mean that this inclusion for administrative purposes would in any way impair the integrity of the Social Security Administration. Under this recommendation, funds appropriated from general revenue for the assistance programs would be kept separate from the Social Security Trust Fund.

We are most concerned that adequate job and wage standards for determining initial and continuing eligibility of persons for public assistance be included in the training-job component of any proposed welfare system. *We recommend that a specific safeguard for the federal level be included to insure the following:*

a. Uniform local administration in determining eligibility in conformance with standards set by federal law, particularly those specifying wages and other conditions pertaining to a suitable job.

b. Prevention of punitive actions by local administrators in the termination of eligibility of local recipients.

c. Establishment of machinery for appeal of local administrative decisions concerning eligibility outside the administering local department, with details of these procedures clearly stated to each recipient.

The Administration's welfare proposals provide for a complicated appeals machinery under which the Secretary of Labor can recommend revocation of benefits while the appeal must be made to the Secretary of Health, Education, and Welfare. This cumbersome procedure is apparently dictated by realization that the training and job portions of the bill will be operated through state departments that never have had a social casework component and that rarely have demonstrated an ability to deal with social problems other than those of a straight employment situation.

THE COSTS OF
ECONOMIC GROWTH

U. S. Chamber of Commerce Committee
on Economic Policy

Perhaps most of the best things in life are free, but economic growth is not. There are costs to pay, sacrifices to make, in order to maintain high rates of growth, or any growth at all. It is not possible to say, therefore, as many somewhat hysterical and unthinking publicists seem to be saying, that the more growth the better.

We must balance the benefits of growth against the costs of achieving various growth rates and determine the point at which the increased benefits of more growth are just outweighed by the increased costs; this point represents the optimum rate of growth, which may be high or may be low, depending upon the value we place on its benefits and the efficiency with which we engineer growth in the economy.

Very definitely, the optimum rate of growth is not the maximum rate. We might, indeed, vastly accelerate growth for a time by housing the population in crowded barracks, placing them on minimum rations, extracting maximum effort by golden promises for future delivery or by force and terror, and devoting all surplus thus obtained to research and investment.

WORK VERSUS LEISURE

The rate of economic growth at any point in time depends largely upon the share of resources diverted from current consumption for investment purposes. Investment must be broadly interpreted to include any economic activity which increases the total supply of productive resources or improves their quality. Productive resources include managerial and labor supplies and skills, as well as plant, equipment, raw materials, and the like. Investment,

From *The Promise of Economic Growth* (Washington, D.C.: Chamber of Commerce of the United States, 1961), pp. 13-21.

therefore, includes education and research as much as power plants and steel mills. Given the share of production devoted to investment, or to increasing future output, the actual amount of investment depends upon the level of current output. There are, then, two ways of increasing the rate of growth: raising the share of current income allocated to investment, and increasing current income itself.

Current income can be increased through more intensive utilization of existing productive resources. This is a one-shot approach to growth; once maximum utilization is achieved, no further gains in income can be wrested. But a permanently higher level of resource utilization means a large pie to be divided at any time, and a larger amount available for investment without reduction in the amount or share of income devoted to consumption. In terms of labor, more intensive utilization may mean a higher level of employment, a larger labor force (higher labor force participation rates), longer hours, or a speedup of work pace.

The cost of increased growth, then, is to be measured in terms of a sacrifice of leisure; the price we must pay for growth depends upon the value we attach to the leisure foregone. To the extent that the increased utilization of labor is a reduction in unemployment or idleness, rather than a sacrifice of leisure, growth, so far as the worker is concerned, is costless.

Leisure is a form of income. Idleness, on the other hand, is the deprivation of income. The distinction between the two, however subjective and difficult, must nevertheless be made, for it is at the core of the definition of employment and unemployment.

A rule of thumb measure of individual full employment is one's reaction to the opportunity to vary slightly one's hours of work *at the current wage rate.* If one chooses to work longer, he is underemployed. If one chooses to work less, he is overemployed.

Employment and leisure are the two alternative desirable uses of human time and effort. They are not to be measured in time alone. A worker may have a choice of distributing time between these two activities. He may also have the option of varying the degree of intensity with which he works (and with which he enjoys his leisure activities). A man may opt for more leisure, not by reducing his workweek, but by reducing his work pace. Or, he may reduce his workweek without reducing work effort by increasing his pace. Leisure and work have other dimensions. The different types of work between which a worker may choose once he is in mid-career may be extremely limited, but he always has a wide option in his choice of leisure activities.

Some leisure activities are complementary with work, because they require the expenditure of money earned by more work effort. Other leisure activities may be considered substitutes for work in that they either (1) produce some money income, or (2) provide goods and services directly which the man of leisure would otherwise have purchased on the market.

These possible income-yielding aspects of leisure activity raise thorny definitional problems. Would a man raise his own vegetables in his spare time, even if he did not save money as a result? Some would, and their gardening qualifies clearly as a leisure activity. Others may not, or may work less in their own kitchen gardens; their gardening is not, or not exclusively, a leisure-time activity. But what shall we call work performed for pay which is so enjoyable for the worker that he would choose to continue it, even if he were to receive substantially less remuneration?

Can we expect that, with the growth in labor force skills and reduction of tedium in many employments, the worker's preference for leisure will be weakened, his demands for shorter hours reduced? Can we anticipate that, if lesure-time activities develop a larger do-it-yourself component, the demand for work and its income will diminish? What if leisure-time activities are devoted more and more to education and other efforts which will widen occupational choice and increase the worker's market value?

In admitting the possibility that work may be enjoyable and that leisure may yield income, or may even be a kind of investment, we not only blur the distinction between work and leisure, but we also deny that either can be interpreted wholly in terms of a means-end relationship. Each is both end and means in varying degrees.

Idleness, by contrast, is neither a substitute nor a complement for work; it is involuntary, not a matter of choice. It yields no income; it has no uses.

If we consider leisure as one of our goals, one of the goods and services (real income) for which we work, we must place some value on it. Who can then say that a five percent rate of growth in output of goods and services is better than a three percent rate of growth? The latter, which provides more leisure, may indeed be preferable, and, for that matter, higher. Who can say that in all countries at all times, growth as measured in national income statistics is better than no growth? For national income data which serve as bases for computing growth rates have two glaring omissions: the value of leisure, expressed in terms of income obtainable from alternative work uses of time, and the contribution which some leisure activities make to the total supply of goods and services. The loss of these values for the sake of more rapid growth must be counted among the costs of growth.

CONSUMPTION VERSUS INVESTMENT

Any increase in output per capita, which is not the result of temporary increases in the intensity of resource utilization, requires some curtailment of current consumption. A part of current income must be saved and invested. Savings may be done by individuals, by corporations or other institutions, or by governments through taxation. The agencies and mechanisms differ greatly, but the essence is the same. Part of current income is withheld from consumption, and the resources released are devoted to increasing the supply of consumer goods at future times.

An acceleration in the rate of growth in output and, therefore, in income available per capita, requires a reduction of current consumption. This consumption foregone (or consumption postponed) is, in part, a second major cost of growth. Its calculation is somewhat easier than the calculation of value of leisure foregone, because prices of consumer goods and services are daily determined on the market, whereas the price of leisure is not so easily estimated.

The relationship between an increase in investment and acceleration in the rate of growth is not a simple or necessarily a very rigid one. So-called capital/output ratios have been computed for a number of countries at various periods of time. These ratios express a relationship between investment in capital and increases in output which result from this investment. For a number of countries, the capital/output ratios have been estimated at about three to one; that is, increase in investment of $30 should yield an increase in annual income, once the investment is completed, of $10. The capital/output ratio varies from country to country and from time to time, and more important, it may vary considerably from industry to industry. The ratio which may be pertinent for the United States in the near future depends upon the kind of industry whose capacity and output would be expanded.

Investment is not restricted to production and use of tangible plant and equipment. It includes development of human resources and research into new materials, products, and techniques. The productivity of education is much more difficult to calculate than the productivity of investment in fixed plant and equipment. The relationship between time and money spent by a man in acquiring skills and increasing knowledge, and the increased income he may expect as a result over his working life (and, indeed, increase in his working life which he may anticipate) has not been accurately calculated. The return on college education may exceed the rate of return on investment in manufacturing equipment and plant, if subsidies to education are omitted, and fall slightly short of the productivity of investment in manufacturing plant and equipment, if private and public subsidies to education are included in its cost.[1]

The productivity of income and effort devoted to research is even more difficult to estimate than the productivity of investment in human skills. Investment in research, whatever its direct returns, is fundamental to economic growth in that it provides the longrun basis for the increased income to be obtained by investment, both in fixed capital and in human skills.

In considering the productivity of investment, it is not sufficient to think of it in the technical terms of capital/output ratios. Investment in education, for example, not only yields benefits in terms of greater productivity and higher income for the future; it can be undertaken entirely for its own sake. The individual, or many individuals, would be willing to undertake the effort and expense of acquiring an education, even if they expected no benefit in the form of higher income. Education for such people is a desirable form of consumption.

---

[1] Solomon Fabricant, *The Study of Economic Growth* (National Bureau of Economic Research, Inc., 39th Annual Report, May 1959), p. 6.

Some types of investment, although productive in the technical sense, may add little or nothing to welfare or income. Defense is the most important example. Although each American obtains some psychic income in terms of national security provided by our defense expenditures, it is not true that the degree or amount of security is, in any necessary way, related to the amount of defense spending. Increased defense spending, although it may raise the GNP, may not increase security at all, since our security is relative to USSR defense efforts (and aggressive intentions) and not to our own efforts in isolation.

Another type of investment whose technical productivity may greatly overstate its contribution to welfare is that which implements the transfer of functions to business firms and governments which were formerly performed by individuals and households. Such investment adds to the GNP, but may or may not increase real income. Its effect on real incomes depends on the relative efficiency with which the functions are performed by institutions and by households and the relevant utilities and dis-utilities.

Lastly, investment, whatever the capital/output ratio, contributes to welfare only if the forthcoming goods and services are ultimately wanted and demanded by consumers. Investment creating large agricultural surpluses for which there are no markets may contribute nothing to our welfare; indeed, it may subtract from welfare by wasting resources which might have been usefully employed in other ways.

PRESENT VERSUS FUTURE

For the sake of growth, we must curtail our present consumption or present leisure, or in all probability, cut down the level of both. The greater the rate of growth, the greater the sacrifice we must make in leisure, in consumption, or in a combination of both. This sacrifice, however, is not a net cost of economic growth, for we are not giving up for all time the leisure and consumption which we forego today. We merely defer such leisure and consumption for the future, or, at least, we defer the opportunity to increase our consumption and our leisure on more favorable terms at some future time.

It does not follow that economic growth (defined as an increase in output per capita) is always a net gain, no matter what the rate of growth, simply because at some future date we will be able to enjoy all of the consumption and all of the leisure which we sacrifice in order to achieve growth. Future income or future consumption never has as great a value as the same income and consumption today. The depreciation or discounting in the value of income and consumption, as they are deferred into the more and more distant future, decreases the benefits of growth relative to the costs, until the point is reached where further increase in growth costs more than it is worth in terms of the increased future benefits.

The benefits of economic growth depend on (1) the size of the increments in future income and consumption which a given present sacrifice of consumption and leisure may provide (the capital/output ratio); (2) upon how long we must defer this increment in consumption, leisure, and income; and (3) the rate at which we discount the future.

THE PROCESS OF CREATIVE DESTRUCTION[2]

In previous pages, we have discussed the relevance of the level of resource utilization to the rate of economic growth and to the cost of achieving this rate of growth. If resources are fully employed, a larger amount can be devoted to investment without reducing the amount or the share of consumption out of current income. There is, however, another side to this picture. The process of growth itself creates temporary underemployment or unemployment of productive resources, and the more rapid and pervasive the growth, the greater the amount of resource underemployment which is likely to occur.

Economic growth, by necessity, takes place in spurts. If a steel mill is under construction in a locality, large numbers of construction workers will be employed. Once the mill is completed, demand for construction labor, equipment, and materials will drop rather suddenly, very greatly, and perhaps permanently. On the other hand, once the steel mill is completed, demand may just as suddenly develop for steel workers to place this mill in operation. From the viewpoint of the locality alone, there has been sudden unemployment in the construction industry and sudden increase in the employment of steel workers who previously were unemployed in this locality or more likely had to be attracted from other localities by suitable wage offers. Such discontinuities in the investment process and in the associated demand for labor, materials, and equipment are typical. In a large and highly diversified economy, many of these sudden increases and decreases in demand cancel each other out. But in particular localities, in particular industries, in particular occupations, the fluctuations are often large and of serious implications for employment stability and income maintenance.

In the process of economic growth, old sources of supply may be gradually exhausted or new sources of supply quickly developed, leaving stranded mining communities. Old industries may change their location in pursuit of materials or in pursuit of markets which move with shifting population. New industries may arise which replace old; new materials may be developed, new products, new markets, all of which will create unemployment problems in some areas, industries, and occupations. The more rapid the change in the location of economic activity, in the composition of products, in the nature of markets, in the choice of materials, the more numerous the depressed industry, depressed area, depressed occupation problems which will crop up in the wake of economic growth.

---

[2] See J. A. Schumpeter, *Capitalism, Socialism, and Democracy,* 3rd ed. (New York: Harper & Bros., 1950), chapter 7.

The problem of underemployed resources is only partly encompassed in terms of unemployed labor. Capital facilities of all kinds—mines, factories, and the capital invested in highly specialized human skills—rapidly lose their value and may become permanently unemployed. The opportunities for converting a coal mine into an oil well are much more limited than those of converting a coal miner into a worker with another skill in greater demand. A revival in the demand for carriage makers, blacksmiths, and glass blowers could only be the result of economic catastrophe. Obsolete machines are replaced by newer, more efficient models long before they are worn out. Rapid obsolescence is a measure of economic growth. It entails no longrun cost to the community, however serious the loss to the owner.

Fluctuations in economic activity, frictional and technological unemployment, depressed areas, obsolete capital and skills, are not then necessarily a drag on growth; to some extent they are indices of growth, its unavoidable consequences. The argument that rapid growth is necessary to provide new job opportunities for workers displaced by technological change is entirely contradictory. Rapid technological change is practically the same thing as rapid growth in output per capita. If growth is slow, technological change is slow, and the number of technologically unemployed workers is small. Full employment is quite possible without growth in per capita output. Some economic insecurity, on the other hand, is inevitable in any dynamic economy. For maximum security we must turn to a static economy and a status society.

BALANCING COSTS AND BENEFITS

The costs of economic growth, then, are three in number. First, we sacrifice current leisure for current work. Second, we sacrifice present consumption for present savings and investment. The burden of sacrifice may be borne exclusively in terms of present consumption, or in terms of present leisure (itself describable as a consumer good); more likely, however, we sacrifice some of each today for the sake of more of each in the future. The third sacrifice is stability of income and employment, security of the value of assets and skills, for more rapid growth in income and levels of living.

The costs are concentrated in the present; the benefits accrue indefinitely into the future. The costs of unemployment, in terms of obsolescence of skills and capital, are concentrated in particular regions, industries, and occupations; the benefits are broadly distributed.

The optimum rate of growth is determined ultimately by the Law of Value, which sets upper limits to the desirable rate of growth. The Law of Value states that the worth of any unit of a good or service to us is inversely related to the number of identical units in our possession. Thus, if our workweek is short, and our leisure long, we do not find a few more hours of work ·particularly irksome, nor miss much the loss of a few hours of leisure. If our work is long and our leisure short, however, we become extremely reluctant to cut down further on our leisure or to increase further our working week.

The same relation applies to the relative values of consumption and savings (investment). We may willingly do without trifles and luxuries in order to save and invest, but hesitate to trim on near-necessities and essentials; likewise, we become increasingly averse to further increases in our savings and investment once they have reached respectable amounts. Only the miser regards a maximum amount of savings and investment as the optimum amount, and conversely with the maximum amount of consumption. Only the prodigal or wastrel gives no thought for the morrow but seeks to consume as much as he can today. Thus, most individuals achieve an optimum equilibrium somewhere between the extremes of all work and all play, and all consumption and all savings.

The equilibrium point further depends upon the rate at which the present value of future consumption and leisure decline as we postpone them further into time. For a second Law of Value states that the value of any unit of income or item of consumption depends upon the time of its availability; the more remote the future when the income or consumer good will be available, the lower its present value. The optimum rate of growth depends, in other words, on the rate of discounting the future relative to the present. It is not enough to say that a dollar invested today will be worth two dollars in 10 years. Are two dollars 10 years hence worth more, or worth less, than one dollar right now? How many birds in the bush are worth one bird in hand?

As an abstraction, we can say that the market rates of interest express the rate at which we discount the future. Of course, other factors influence interest rates, and no interest rate measures the discount functions of any one individual. For each of us has his own unique outlook; the relative weight we attach to the immediate, intermediate, and remote future; to the future within our lifetime and within the lifetime of our children. Each of us has various time horizons, for we are more reluctant to sow that which we shall not live to reap than to sow the seed whose fruits we expect to enjoy.

Knowing the efficiency of investment in adding to the future supply of goods and leisure, we can determine the optimum rate of growth. The greater the efficiency of investment, the higher the optimum rate of growth. The choice, however, requires complex valuation, not single measurement of tons of steel or housing starts.

WHAT IS AN EDUCATION WORTH? A DOLLAR-AND-SENSE EVALUATION

Melvin C. Fountain

"Money talks," according to a timeworn cliche; and to this, someone has added, "It's the only conversation worth listening to when you're out of a job."

Few would argue that money is the exclusive incentive to work. Nevertheless, because money is "real" and can be measured and handled, it serves as a powerful vehicle for satisfying a never-ending stream of less definitive physical, social, and egotistical needs. Our economy relies heavily upon the magnetism of money to allocate work among industries and jobs. For decades, economists have pondered over the exact nature of this admittedly imperfect allocation phenomenon. They generally agree, however, that supply and demand forces are involved in wage and income determinations, as is a worker's relative contribution to society.

With each passing year, education has become more highly valued in the determination of a man's actual or potential contribution to society. The relationship between education and income is shown in the table on the next page of Census Bureau estimates of lifetime income for men.

Clearly, the data seem to bear out the theme, "If you want a 'good' job, get a good education." In 1966, men with college degrees could expect to earn more than a half million dollars in their lifetime, an amount nearly three times the $189,000 likely to be earned by workers who had less than eight years of schooling, and nearly twice that earned by workers with only one to three years of high school. However, these figures should be interpreted with caution. They reflect a tendency for persons with higher levels of intelligence to gravitate toward upper educational levels. Thus, while greater earnings may be associated with higher levels of schooling, education is in some degree associated with aptitude for learning.

From *Occupational Outlook Quarterly* 12, no. 4 (December 1968). Reprinted by permission.

214

HUMAN RESOURCES

Years of school completed	1966 income (age 18 to death)
Total	$321,000
Elementary: Less than 8 years	189,000
8 Years	247,000
High school: 1 to 3 years	284,000
4 years	341,000
College: 1 to 3 years	394,000
4 years or more	542,000
4 years	508,000
5 years or more	587,000

Source: *Current Population Reports, Consumer Income,* Series P-60, No. 56, August 14, 1968, Bureau of the Census, p. 9.

Graduation pays a special dividend in lifetime earnings. The worker who had one to three years of high school could expect to earn only about $37,000 more than the worker with an elementary school education. But the high school graduate could look forward to a $94,000-income advantage over his elementary school counterpart. A similar parallel exists at the college level.

What, specifically, does a worker learn in his graduation year that makes him worth so much more than a dropout? One employer had this to say:

In some fields, such as law and some of the other professions, the final year of schooling either is required by law or so useful that we wouldn't think of hiring a professional without it. Where the connection between education and contribution is less clear (such as in the case of a liberal arts graduate), I suppose it is true that a graduation requirement is more a convenient cutoff point than a productivity factor; other employers seek graduates and we follow the pack. But at least we know that the graduate has met certain minimum academic standards. With the dropout, we are unsure—unsure of his capabilities, unsure of his ability to see a job through, unsure of the breadth of his education. So long as the supply of graduates is sufficient, it is just not feasible to consider each applicant on his merits, especially since this procedure requires qualitative judgments that we like to avoid wherever possible.

Admittedly, we pass over some very capable workers who, perhaps through no fault of their own, were unable to finish their education. But the economics of employee selection do not usually warrant efforts on behalf of exceptional situations.

A CREDIBILITY GAP?

Managers, officials, and proprietors; sales workers; and clerical workers all had about the same level of education in 1966—about 12.5 years. Yet, lifetime earnings data by occupational group show that, on the average, workers

215

in the managers, officials, and proprietors group can expect to earn $149,000 more during their lifetime than clerical workers and $93,000 more than sales workers (see table). The managers, officials, and proprietors occupational group can even look forward to earnings several thousands dollars higher than earnings of workers in the professional and technical group—where schooling averages more than 16 years.

Do these figures negate the basic education-income relationship? On the contrary, the table shows that, within each occupational group, income rises as education advances. What is revealed is that some types of jobs pay more than others, and education is not the only determinant of this pay. Many of the attributes that are marketable in the world of work can be learned in school, some are best learned on the job, and some are innate. For example, the salesman may be in a better position to cash in on his outgoing personality than the clerical worker, while the manager or proprietor may receive a premium for his ability to handle people or perhaps for his financial investment in a firm.

Estimated Lifetime Earnings for Males Ages 18 to 64, by Occupational Group and Education (In Thousands of 1959 Dollars)

Occupational Group	All Educational Levels	8 Years of Elementary School	4 Years of High School	4 or More Years of College
All occupations	$229	$184	$247	$418
Professional, technical, and kindred workers	355	227	288	418
Farmers and farm managers	140	126	167	266
Managers, officials, and proprietors, excluding farm	362	267	347	551
Clerical and kindred workers	213	189	218	262
Sales workers	269	206	265	387
Craftsmen, foremen, and kindred workers	222	207	242	323
Operatives and kindred workers	187	185	209	229
Service workers, including private household	156	146	180	198
Farm laborers and foremen	80	90	128	--
Laborers, excluding farm and mine	143	150	173	189

Source: Technical Paper 16, *Present Value of Estimated Lifetime Earnings*, U.S Department of Commerce, Bureau of the Census, table 1.

THE COST OF EDUCATION

Although absolute lifetime income may continue to rise with education, in some instances, the sacrifice cost of obtaining this schooling may not financially warrant the investment. Suppose a family were prepared to support a member until he received his college or graduate degree. But instead, the youth chose to work immediately after high school graduation and bank his earnings as well as the tuition and other costs that would have been incurred had he gone to college. Assuming this money earned five percent interest in the bank, how would his lifetime earnings compare with that of a college graudate?

Intrigued by this question, Arthur Carol and Samuel Parry[1] devised a model that would reflect a ranking of lifetime occupational earnings for men based upon the sacrifice cost of obtaining the income. Their computation differs from the Census Bureau's estimate of lifetime earnings in that it accounts for the costs of going to college, including tuition and living expenses. Their ranking of the 26 highest net life earnings follows:

Dentists
Managers, officials, proprietors—manufacturing*
Electrical engineers
Mechanical engineers
Physicians and surgeons
Managers, officials, proprietors—finance, insurance, real estate*
Toolmakers, diemakers, and setters
Personnel and labor relations workers
Civil engineers
Stationary engineers
Designers and draftsmen
Lawyers and judges
Electricians
Electrical and electronic technicians
Plumbers and pipefitters
Linemen and servicemen—telegraph, telephone, and power
Pharmacists
Metalworkers
Managers, officials, proprietors—wholesale and retail trade*
Cranemen, derrickmen, and hoistmen
Machinists and job setters
Accountants

---

[1] Arthur Carol and Samuel Parry, "Economic Rationale of Occupational Choice," *Industrial Labor Relations Review* 21 (January 1968): 188-189.
*Salaried positions only.

Insurance agents, brokers, and underwriters
Engineering and other technicians
Chemists
Airplane mechanics and repairmen

The ranking shows that, despite the cost of a college education and its sacrifice of several income producing years, greater education still generally pays off in higher lifetime income. Eighteen of the top 26 positions and nine of the top 10 are professional and managerial. There were some important exceptions, however. For instance, accountants and chemists would have been as well off financially as plumbers or electricians; lawyers' and judges' incomes are overshadowed by the earnings of toolmakers, diemakers, and setters.

Why would a man choose to be a chemist when, if he considered all of the costs involved, he could average higher lifetime earnings as a plumber? One reason, of course, is that people often do not figure all the costs involved. Furthermore, many young people do not consider themselves average. They know that top chemists earn far more than master plumbers; and who, after all, enters college with visions of becoming a mediocre chemist?

Finally, money is not the only allocator of manpower. For example, although earnings may be higher in some skilled blue-collar occupations, many people would prefer to attend college for four years or more and become teachers. For them, the cultural advantages of education, the challenge of a teaching career, as well as the prestige, security, and attractive working conditions often associated with this career more than compensate for lower lifetime earnings.

Although this article has dealt primarily with the material rewards associated with education, this should not be taken to imply that the more subtle cultural and social satisfactions often associated with higher education are not important. The only justification for focusing exclusively on the economic aspects of an education is that, at present, they are the only ones capable of even approximate measurement.

In general, these measurements indicate that education is an excellent financial investment. However, important as it is, education is only one ingredient in financial success. Top executives are rare not so much because of their education but because of unique combinations of education *and* intelligence *and* personality *and* willingness to work 10 hours or more each day.

OUR GRAVEST MILITARY PROBLEM IS MANPOWER

Juan Cameron

Three years ago, as candidate for President, Richard Nixon committed himself to end the draft and establish an all-volunteer military force. In January of this year, however, President Nixon called for a two-year extension of the draft. "Nobody knows precisely when we can end conscription," he told Congress. And he might well have added *or if we can.* For military manpower problems have become so severe and vast in scope that the nation's armed services are in an extremely perilous situation. Even with 650,000 men entering the services every year—most of them draftees or volunteers who are induced to enlist by the threat of conscription—dangerous shortages of men prevail in every branch of service, seriously impairing combat capability. Some low-priority units, like the 172nd Infantry Brigade in Alaska, are at only half of "foxhole," or combat, strength. Even high-priority forces are seriously undermanned. The Seventh Army is charged with the defense of Europe and, according to Nixon, stands next to Vietnam forces in its claim on men and equipment. But last winter the Seventh Army was 20,000 men short of its authorized strength (190,000 men).

Nor is the crisis one simply of numbers. The real pinch comes from the failure of the armed services to retain officers and men with the experience and skills needed to operate and maintain the complex weapon systems of modern warfare. The U.S. Army's crack Berlin Brigade has to rely on German civilians to maintain its tanks and other armor because there aren't enough trained technicians in the service. The Navy has reported a "critical" to "serious" shortage of skilled ratings in half of its air squadrons and a third of its ships. And the Air Force is finding it increasingly difficult to retain experienced pilots.

From *Fortune*, April 1971, pp. 60 ff. Copyright 1971. Reprinted by permission.

Discontent is rampant among servicemen of all ranks and ages—not just the raw recruit reluctantly putting in his draft time, but the tough Sheridan tank commander on patrol along the East German border, the operations officer aboard a destroyer escort in the Mediterranean Fleet, the missile-silo commander in North Dakota, and the infantry noncom just returned from a second tour in Vietnam. Low morale contributes to the high turnover in personnel, costing billions each year in wasted defense dollars and ruling out the possibility of any quick move toward all-volunteer services.

White House policy still aims at ending the draft in 1973, and the Administration has taken a number of steps to make military life more attractive. Secretary of Defense Melvin Laird has proposed a pay package, involving $1.5 billion a year, to mitigate some glaring inequities in the lower ranks of the services. "Mickey Mouse" rules regulating hair length, beards, and off-duty dress have been relaxed. Go-go girls do their thing in enlisted men's clubs, beer is available in mess halls, and a few barracks have been painted in psychedelic fashion. But as treatment for what ails the armed services, these measures are like treating a cancer with a Band-Aid.

Discontent in the armed services flows from many sources. The Indochina war has been an important irritant, of course, particularly because of controversial personnel decisions dictated by the political assessments of the Johnson Administration. When American troops are finally withdrawn from Vietnam, some of the wasteful and enervating policies that have contributed to what the services call "personnel turbulence" will be lessened.

But not even an end to the Vietnam war will cure ills that derive from decades of neglect. The brightest and most ambitious military commanders have never regarded personnel administration as the way to advance professionally. "These things have been snowballing for years and pose a pretty big problem now," says Roger Kelley, Assistant Secretary of Defense for Manpower and Reserve Affairs. On top of everything else, there has been a growth of antimilitary feeling among the young people whom the services must draw upon for manpower. Higher pay scales will help, but the Nixon proposals call for, at best, only about half the amount of money recommended last year by a presidential commission headed by Thomas S. Gates Jr., a former Defense Secretary who is now chairman of the executive committee of Morgan Guaranty Trust Co.

A HEMORRHAGE OF TALENT

The magnitude of discontent among military men shows up dramatically in the low percentage of officers and enlisted men who elect to remain in the service after their first tour of duty. Perhaps it is not surprising that only about one percent of draftees, who were inducted involuntarily, stay in after their two years' hitch is completed. But the services are falling far short of their goal in getting volunteers to sign up for additional tours after their first three to six years of duty. They would like to get 30 to 35 percent of these men to re-enlist, but the Army is retaining only about one out of nine of its enlistees at the end of their first hitch. The retention rate for Navy enlisted men is 12 percent; for the Air Force, about 11 percent. The Marines, for all the carefully nurtured pride in "the Corps," have the lowest re-enlistment rate of all—six out of every hundred enlisted men.

The Pentagon is quick to point out that re-enlistment rates can be misleading—especially at a time when the overall size of the military establishment is being reduced—because the services have different methods of computing the rates. Moreover, the Defense Department's manpower experts tend to denigrate the relevance of these figures with the argument that more than half of the "volunteers" were induced to sign up by the threat of being drafted for Army combat units in Vietnam. This is especially true, they argue, for many of today's young officers, who were not career-minded in the first place. There is some truth in that argument, but the trends of retention are down even among those who seemed intent on military careers. For example, in 1961 the Army was able to retain about one-third of the lieutenants and captains who had entered by way of Reserve Officers Training Corps. Today the Army's retention rate for these officers is down to about 11 percent. In 1966 the Navy retained 25 percent of the officers assigned to surface ships. The retention rate today is 16 percent.

As recently as 1966, the Navy could count on having nearly two-thirds of its pilots—each of whom takes up to two years to qualify for carrier duty at a training cost that may total $250,000—elect to stay in the service after the first obligatory service was finished. Today three out of four pilots are leaving at the end of their first six years. The situation, says one Navy personnel officer, is "getting to the point where we have no experience in the fleet." The elite nuclear-submarine force has had similar trouble keeping its officers. They are offered bonuses of up to $15,000 to remain in the submarine service, but the retention rate is only 36 percent, or slightly more than half of what it was several years ago. And in the noncommissioned ranks, men with six to eight years of service have been leaving the Navy in such numbers that the fleet is short of petty officers with critical skills—technicians who can handle sonar, missile, electronic, aviation, and data systems. Even boiler tenders are scarce.

In the Air Force, which in the past retained nearly half of its younger officers, the situation is also deteriorating. More than 13,000 officers who had previously indicated an intention of making a career in the Air Force have requested separation at the end of their current tours. Lieutenant General Robert Dixon, the deputy chief of staff for personnel, has estimated that it will cost $1 billion to train their replacements.

LIKE JUMPING ON A MOVING SURFBOARD

Few, if any, business executives ever witness the kind of turnover in manpower that the armed forces take for granted today. The military services turn

221

over 60 percent of their *total* personnel every two years. It is not uncommon for units in Vietnam and elsewhere to roll over personnel two to three times a year. Says the Army's Vice Chief of Staff, General Bruce Palmer Jr., "When your force is turning over at the rate of 100 percent a year, you have a tough job of training to start with. The training base required to cope with this is huge. And then as fast as you get the men up to any level of proficiency you lose them. When the rate is over 100 percent, it's a hopeless situation." It's expensive, too—about $5.3 billion annually to train new men, one study shows.

The 4th Infantry Division (Mechanized), stationed at Fort Carson, Colorado, is an example of Palmer's "hopeless situation." The 4th Infantry is one of four high-priority reserve forces supposedly able to move on short notice to bolster U.S. troops in a trouble zone. On paper, that is; for today the 4th is in a decidedly parlous state. Since most of its men are Vietnam veterans with only a few months of service remaining, the division sees 6,000 of its 15,000 men depart every three months, while men just returned from Southeast Asia stream in to take their places. Lieutenant Colonel Fred Bartlett Jr., today the division's personnel officer, says that the 15 months he spent as a battalion commander with the 4th Infantry seemed like five years. "In that short time I have had 3,700 men assigned to an 800-man battalion. With that kind of turnover, how do you get a man feeling he belongs to a unit? It gives you sort of a transitory feeling, like jumping on a moving surfboard." The game of musical chairs obviously affects the division's morale and sense of cohesiveness. In addition, the constant retraining required to integrate the newcomers into the division materially reduces the unit's combat capability.

This high rate of turnover also affects individual decisions about staying in the service. Navy Lieutenant John J. Costello, a 26-year-old Harvard graduate who is operations officer aboard the destroyer escort *Hammerberg,* has been in the service for four and a half years. His ship, based in Naples, is engaged in classified underwater detection operations. Now he says he is sick of trying to run a department (four officers and 51 enlisted men) whose personnel is replaced every few months. "This job is like shoveling sand against the tide. I'm constantly working to train officers who hardly know their jobs here before they're transferred to another position or ship. It's the same with my men. I've made known that we lack enough technicians to maintain the ship's electronics, but nothing happens. As soon as we get a man broken in, off he goes. The whole job has become a pain in the neck. Who wants to stay in and work like this?" Costello has sent in his resignation, along with a blistering critique of Navy personnel management and leadership

The situation that the Lieutenant Costellos and Colonel Bartletts have had to face is caused in large part by two decisions made early in the Vietnam war. The first one, made by President Johnson and Secretary of Defense Robert McNamara, was to rely on the draft instead of calling up the reserves when they found it necessary to expand the Army by 50 percent in 1965. The second decision, recommended by the service chiefs, was to limit the tour in Vietnam to 12 months. In retrospect, a number of Defense Department

222

officials, civilian and military, call these the two worst decisions of the war. They were based on a variety of political and morale factors—and on the expectation that the war would last merely months, instead of the more than five years it has lasted to date.

BUILDING IN SMALL INCREMENTS

During the Korean war, and again during the Berlin crisis in 1961, the reserves—on which the nation now spends about $3 billion a year—were partially mobilized. For Korea, over 800,000 out of a total force of 3,700,000 came from the call-up of reserves; for the Berlin crisis, 150,000 reservists were called up by President Kennedy. But only about 37,000 reservists were ever called up for Vietnam, after the *Pueblo* incident in 1968.

Because of the sharp public outcry over the 1961 call-up and the low state of readiness of the reserves, McNamara told his military commanders not to count on calling up the reserves again except for a major shooting war. In August, 1965, he affirmed this policy in a confrontation with the Joint Chiefs of Staff. His rationale was that the gradual buildup called for in Vietnam could best be met by drafting small increments of men as they were needed. This would have the advantage of leaving the reserve forces in being in case they were needed in another theatre. The policy also suited presidential politics. Lyndon Johnson was anxious to play down the U.S. involvement in Southeast Asia. He would have had to go to Congress for authority to call and hold the reserves, which would have meant a noisy debate. Using the draft instead of the reserves avoided this distasteful prospect.

Reliance on two-year draftees instead of reservists, who could have been held in service for the duration of the emergency, meant that a heavy inflow of replacements was needed as the war continued and the armed forces grew (to a peak of 3,500,000 men in 1968). The flow of new men into the services has ranged between 600,000 and one million annually over the past five years. Over five million men—half of all eligible American males between the ages of 19 and 26—have been in military service during the Vietnam war (and over 40 percent of them actually went to Southeast Asia). Because the Marines had to rely on the draft instead of volunteers, more men—about 700,000—have worn the Corps' green uniforms in this war than in all of World War II.

The decision to limit each man's tour in Vietnam to 12 months added greatly to the heavy turnover in the largely draftee Army. The aim of this policy was to spread the risks of war, as well as the hardships of family separation, over as many men as possible. However, to maintain the short tours has required rotating 25,000 to 45,000 troops a month—or up to 500,000 men a year—out of Southeast Asia and replacing them with a like number of troops from the U.S. or other theatres. The effects have been felt in military commands throughout the world. Career servicemen, particularly in the Army, have been continually shifted from post to post to fill recurring shortages caused by the rotation. It is not uncommon for officers to have been moved

223

five times in less than three years. The constant upheaval has disrupted family life for millions of military people and intensified their discontent with the services.

The drastic cutbacks in military manpower since 1969 have also taken a toll. Nixon and Defense Secretary Laird will have sliced one million men off military payrolls by June, 1972. The very swiftness of this manpower reduction is unsettling; a reduction of comparable size at the end of the Korean war was spread over six years. As ships are decommissioned, bases closed, and divisions demobilized, men must move to other commands, thus aggravating the turbulence. The services have tried to schedule these cutbacks in an orderly manner but when a war is being waged the schedules go awry. And sometimes the consequences are serious, as the predicament of the 82nd Airborne Division illustrated last autumn.

Like the 4th Division, the 82nd Airborne, stationed at Fort Bragg, North Carolina, is supposed to be ready to deploy anywhere in the world on a few hours' notice. But when the division was alerted last September to prepare for a move to Jordan in case U.S. citizens were endangered by the fighting there, its commander told the Joint Chiefs of Staff that only one of its three brigades was fully combat ready. The squeeze arose because the Army had cut the number of draft inductions, in the expectation that it would be reducing the size of its Vietnam force by 10,000 to 12,000 men a month. But when Nixon withdrew Marines instead of Army troops from Vietnam, he upset the Army's calculations of its manpower needs. To fill the gap, troops were levied from commands in Germany and Korea, and from U.S. outfits like the 82nd Airborne, for dispatch to Vietnam. When the Jordan emergency came, the 82nd was nearly 2,000 men short. Since then this shocking situation has been remedied for the 82nd, but not for other commands.

ICING ON THE CAKE

In a well-publicized campaign, the Pentagon has moved to show that it *does* care about its "grunts." The Chief of Naval Operations has issued "Z-grams" to abolish many restrictive regulations, and similar orders have come from the Army and Air Force Chiefs of Staff. To date there has been an encouraging pickup in re-enlistment rates due to these efforts. More important, a start has been made on a dialogue between officers and men on what's wrong with the services.

The old guard—particularly retired officers—have thundered against these reforms as steps that will turn the services into country clubs. But many enlisted men and officers regard them as inadequate, though welcome. To thirty-nine-year-old Odiss Sweet, a black first sergeant with the Seventh Army, the changes that have been made are "just cold icing on a hot cake." A career man who has put in 20 years' service, Sweet says: "When the cake is hot inside, the icing is going to melt. They're going all the way for the young trooper who's not going to stay anyway. But they haven't begun to touch the problems that bother the old soldiers. Until they do, they might get men to come into the Army but they won't stay."

In analyzing their manpower problems, senior officers often tend to blame society as a whole for the waning attraction of military life. A standard lecture for visitors to military bases dwells on the fact that much of today's discontent with the services stems from the children of a permissive society and the profoundly antimilitary temper of the times. Certainly the attitude toward the Vietnam war has had a sharp impact on servicemen's morale. Says Major General John Bennett, commander of the 4th Infantry at Fort Carson: "The Vietnam soldier has seen more combat than the man who fought from Normandy to Berlin in World War II. He's been through the real meat grinder. Yet when he comes home, there's no flag in the window, no free drink at his neighborhood bar. Only silence and neglect."

Harold Wool, a Department of Labor official who until recently was the Pentagon's career civilian expert on the draft and manpower, notes that there are still deeper reasons for the alienation of young people. Recruits must be drawn today from an increasingly white-collar urban society that tends to look down on the military professions. "Quite aside from pay," Wool says, "the services have a status problem." The young see most service work as a predominantly menial, blue-collar occupation. Furthermore, he finds, life in a disciplined career bureaucracy doesn't appeal to servicemen, whose median age is 23.

WHITEWALLS FROM BASE BARBERS

For centuries armies have been a haven for the unemployed. The Duke of Wellington once said that his conquering British Army was composed of "the mere scum of the earth ... all enlisted for drink." Until the 1940s the U.S. Army could find all the recruits it needed by offering food, shelter, and $22 a month. But today the military forces do not find much of a manpower pool among the unemployed, even in recession years such as this one.

Some critics have argued that an all-volunteer army would be an army made up of blacks and other minority groups with a low-income background. In fact, though, experience has shown that black servicemen like military life only slightly more than other young Americans. Their complaints, however, are sometimes different. They don't like the "whitewalls"—a trim above the natural hairline around the ears and back of the head—that base barbers mete out. They complain about the lack of combs and shampoos for Afros in PX's, and of magazines dealing with racial issues. Blacks charge they are discriminated against in promotions; and that military justice is applied in unfair ways, resulting in an unduly high percentage of their brothers' being put in the stockades.

The services have been moving to meet these complaints, as well as the overt or subtle discrimination practiced by bar owners and landlords here and in Europe. In the meantime, however, there is a serious disciplinary problem in many commands. On some U.S. bases, junior officers have been attacked when venturing at night into barrack areas where there is a heavy concentration of black troops. There have been instances in Germany of senior officers being struck in public by blacks. And in the rear areas of Vietnam there have been an ominous number of "fragging" incidents—the throwing of gas or fragmentation grenades at officers.

A few officers, like Major General Raymond Shoemaker, commanding general of the 32nd Army Air Defense Command in Kaiserslautern, West Germany, look inward to find the causes of discontent. A trim, white-haired man who began his career as an enlisted man in the 1930s, Shoemaker comments: "Personnel procedures have been our greatest weakness. We have tended to think of soldiers as great masses of numbers instead of individuals."

What attention has been paid to manpower has been mainly in terms of promotion and pay among the career force. There has been a comfortable feeling that men to fill the lower ranks could always be obtained, thanks to the draft, at cheap prices. When the choice has been between better housing and pay for the lower ranks and new weapons, the military chiefs have invariably opted for hardware.

50,000 MEN ON WELFARE

Today's military pay scales are badly skewed in favor of the upper enlisted and officer ranks. In its exhaustive study of military pay, the Gates Commission pointed out that there has been a long "history of discrimination" against the lower enlisted and officer grades. The commission found that between 1948 and 1965 the average basic pay of officers with two or more years of military service increased 45 percent, while the pay of officers with less than two years of service increased by only 13 percent. Pay for enlisted men with more than two years' service also increased by 45 percent in this 17-year period, but men with less than two years got an increase of only four percent, or less than one-tenth as much.

Partly as a result, it is estimated that at least 50,000 married enlisted men are actually on welfare or qualify for food-stamp programs, or both. Major General James Hollingsworth, Army commander in Alaska, has found that his married enlisted men in the four lower ranks (E-1 through E-4) go into the red by an average of $60.18 a month. By contrast, one of Hollingsworth's first sergeants with 22 years' service, Clarence Burdett, says he and his working wife saved $10,000 last year on their combined gross income of $20,000.

The pay and rank structure has been further distorted in recent years by a ragtag package of accelerated promotions and bonuses geared to spur re-enlistment rates. Enlisted men with skills that are in short supply can receive up to $10,000 in bonus pay by re-enlisting for a six-year tour; certain categories of officers also get bonuses to extend their service. The practice creates some inequities. For example, the skipper of the nuclear-attack submarine *Spadefish*, Commander George Henson, a Naval Academy graduate with 17

226

years' service, is the third-highest-paid man on his ship; some of his junior officers have received bonuses amounting to $15,000 for staying in the Navy.

The military pay system is both discriminatory and grossly inefficient in retaining men. For one thing, the pay structure is such a complex maze that most military men have little idea of what their actual compensation is. For instance, a married E-5 with 10 years' service perceives his pay to be $7,300. Actually, if quarters and subsistence allowances and medical care, which are tax free, are taken into account, his compensation may be equivalent to $10,400. Since servicemen fail to realize just how generous their total benefits are—they tend to exaggerate the gap between their wages and those of civilians—the Gates Commission recommended translating the various elements of pay and noncash benefits into a single lump sum. That would make the full value of military wages easily visible.

Although Congress and the Budget Bureau have turned a deaf ear to the fact, across-the-board pay increases, which make the rich richer and the poor relatively poorer, are also inefficient. An across-the-board increase means more for the $33,000 general than the $9,400-a-year captain, although it is the captain who leaves the Army because of low pay. Stephen Herbits, a member of the Gates Commission, points out that selective pay hikes would redress a system that continues to raise the total compensation of senior officers above parity with the civilian sector, while junior servicemen fall further behind.

Even the military retirement system works against the services' needs to retain more men in their middle years. Because the system provides benefits only after 20 years of duty, future retirement pay gives little incentive to remain in until a man has at least 10 to 12 years' service. The result is a surplus of men with over 19 years' service and a shortage of those with four to eight years' service. Again the services and Congress have long ignored suggestions to encourage midlength careers by letting men build some equity in retirement before they have served 20 years.

WHITEWASHING AND BRASS POLISHING

The availability of cheap labor in the lower ranks has encouraged the military to use its men to haul garbage and trash, wash dishes and peel potatoes, and perform such standard—and meaningless—tasks as chipping paint, polishing the base's traditional brass cannon, and whitewashing the stones lining the general's driveway. Many of these tasks could be mechanized to a greater degree, farmed out to civilians, or abolished altogether. For years the Air Force, which has a large training investment in its relatively small, highly specialized enlisted force, has contracted out its K.P. and much of its ground maintenance to civilian labor. Lieutenant General Dixon explains: "We felt it makes no economic sense to take a man capable of working on equipment worth millions of dollars and have him doing kitchen work."

The Air Force also provides its highly trained enlisted men with living quarters that are palatial in comparison to those provided by other services.

To be sure, some modern barracks are to be found on Navy, Army, and Marine bases. And recently a crash program has been undertaken to provide a minimum of habitability in older quarters. A little bit of paint, a few patches of carpeting, and wall lockers rearranged to serve as partitions are being breathlessly hailed in the news media as part of the mod Navy and modern Army. Nearer to the reality of what the majority of enlisted men have are the 30-year-old Henderson barracks, which house the Marines' headquarters force. Here, in the shadow of the Pentagon, the Marines live in cheerless open bays, stifling in Washington's summers; each bay accommodates 50 men. The bathroom facilities consist of open shower rooms and toilet stalls without doors.

Many younger men find drudgery and boredom to be the hallmarks of military life. Assistant Secretary of Defense Roger Kelley says that only among men aboard ship or among the pacification and combat units in Vietnam has he found a feeling of achievement in young officers and enlisted men. "People are either not being used at all, or are being used in jobs that aren't relevant to their mission. There just aren't the ordinary challenges in the life that are needed to sustain men."

The problem is one similar to that of a fire department, wonderfully equipped, that never has a fire to put out. A visitor to military bases is struck with the lack of activity that has any real importance. A tank crew in the U.S. is apt to spend the morning checking the oil and gas of its vehicle, starting the engine, tightening rattles and loose fittings. The rest of the day will be spent in repetitive lectures, physical training, and personal chores—or, for officers, in fighting a paper war with an endless stream of pointless correspondence and record keeping. A tank outfit not in combat might go out for training every two or three months and engage in a full firing exercise once a year. An infantry soldier might fire his M-16 once every six months. It makes for a boring life. David Gyongyos, 26, a sergeant in an engineering battalion with the 4th Infantry Division, says of life at Fort Carson: "There is an old Army concept that to be an enlisted man you must be dumb. You're just a serial number assigned to meaningless work."

Many Air Force officers and men likewise find little of the wild blue yonder in their jobs. For many officers of the 91st Strategic Missile Wing stationed at Minot, North Dakota, life in an ICBM silo is as dull as or duller than that for the tank trooper. One of them, a 25-year-old captain, comments that "it's hard to get much satisfaction out of 'flying' a capsule. You may work 30 minutes an hour. But for the next 30 minutes you twiddle your thumbs. After a while your mind goes stagnant."

In some instances, the feeling of frustration among military careerists is intensified by shortages of the parts and equipment that they need to do their jobs. Sergeant John Bushell, 27, has been a soldier for eight years and commands a Sheridan tank in the 1st Squadron of the 2nd Armored Cavalry. His unit, which spends one month out of three patrolling along the border between West and East Germany, has been plagued by a shortage of parts, which makes an already demanding assignment needlessly more difficult. "You're working half the night sometimes to rig these things up," Bushell says.

MEN FOR FANCY SYSTEMS

The deepseated manpower problems of the military must be overcome before the nation can hope to rely on an all-volunteer force. The gap between the number of men the services need and the number who volunteer is enormous—for the Army alone it is over 160,000 a year. If the day of a "zero draft" is ever to come, with U.S. forces still deployed around the world, the reform of military life will have to go far beyond anything so far proposed. It is plain what some of the needed changes are. For example, the continuous wholesale movement of men must be done away with. It will also be necessary to reform the entire pay and promotion—and retirement—system if the services are to achieve a stable career force; the Administration's proposals, and even the recommendations of the Gates Commission, are only a feeble first step in this direction.

Most vital of all, military life will have to be made more interesting and challenging. Just how this is to be done is not clear yet, nor is it clear that the Defense Department is gearing itself adequately for the job. But among some high-ranking officers a sense of urgency is appearing at last. Says the Army's General Shoemaker: "You can have all the fancy weapons systems you want. But they won't do you any good if you can't keep the men needed to run them."

PROBLEMS IN CENTRAL CITIES

National Advisory Commission
on Civil Disorders

THE FORMATION OF THE RACIAL GHETTO

Throughout the twentieth century, and particularly in the last three decades, the Negro population of the United States has been steadily moving— from rural areas to urban, from South to North and West.

In 1910, 2.7 million Negroes lived in American cities—28 percent of the nation's Negro population of 9.8 million. Today, about 15 million Negro Americans live in metropolitan areas, or 69 percent of the Negro population of 21.5 million. In 1910, 885,000 Negroes—nine percent—lived outside the South. Now, almost 10 million, about 45 percent, live in the North or West.

These shifts in population have resulted from three basic trends:

1. A rapid increase in the size of the Negro population.

2. A continuous flow of Negroes from Southern rural areas, partly to large cities in the South, but primarily to large cities in the North and West.

3. An increasing concentration of Negroes in large metropolitan areas within racially segregated neighborhoods.

Taken together, these trends have produced large and constantly growing concentrations of Negro population within big cities in all parts of the nation. . . .

The Concentration of Negro Population in Large Cities

Where Negro Urbanization Has Occurred

Statistically, the Negro population in America has become more urbanized, and more metropolitan, than the white population. According to Census

From *Report of the National Advisory Commission on Civil Disorders* (Washington, D.C., March 1968), pp. 115, 118-120, 123-127, 143-145, 230-231.

Bureau estimates, almost 70 percent of all Negroes in 1966 lived in metropolitan areas, compared to 64 percent of all whites. In the South, more than half the Negro population now lives in cities. Rural Negroes outnumber urban Negroes in only four states: Arkansas, Mississippi, North Carolina, and South Carolina.

Basic data concerning Negro urbanization trends . . . indicate that:

1. Almost all Negro population growth is occurring within metropolitan areas, primarily within central cities. From 1950 to 1966, the U.S. Negro population rose 6.5 million. Over 98 percent of that increase took place in metropolitan areas—86 percent within central cities, 12 percent in the urban fringe.

2. The vast majority of white population growth is occurring in suburban portions of metropolitan areas. From 1950 to 1966, 77.8 percent of the white population increase of 35.6 million took place in the suburbs. Central cities received only 2.5 percent of this total white increase. Since 1960, white central-city population has actually declined by 1.3 million.

3. As a result, central cities are steadily becoming more heavily Negro, while the urban fringes around them remain almost entirely white. The proportion of Negroes in all central cities rose steadily from 12 percent in 1950, to 17 percent in 1960, to 20 percent in 1966. Meanwhile, metropolitan areas outside of central cities remained 95 percent white from 1950 to 1960 and became 96 percent white by 1966.

4. The Negro population is growing faster, both absolutely and relatively, in the larger metropolitan areas than in the smaller ones. From 1950 to 1966, the proportion of nonwhites in the central cities of metropolitan areas with one million or more persons doubled, reaching 26 percent, as compared with 20 percent in the central cities of metropolitan areas containing from 250,000 to one million persons and 12 percent in the central cities of metropolitan areas containing under 250,000 persons.

5. The 12 largest central cities—New York, Chicago, Los Angeles, Philadelphia, Detroit, Baltimore, Houston, Cleveland, Washington, D.C., St. Louis, Milwaukee, and San Francisco—now contain over two-thirds of the Negro population outside the South and almost one-third of the total in the United States. All these cities have experienced rapid increases in Negro population since 1950. In six—Chicago, Detroit, Cleveland, St. Louis, Milwaukee, and San Francisco—the proportion of Negroes at least doubled. In two others—New York and Los Angeles—it probably doubled. In 1968, seven of these cities are over 30 percent Negro, and one, Washington, D.C., is two-thirds Negro.

Factors Causing Residential Segregation in Metropolitan Areas

The early pattern of Negro settlement within each metropolitan area followed that of immigrant groups. Migrants converged on the older sections of the central city because the lowest cost housing was located there, friends and relatives were likely to be living there, and the older neighborhoods then often had good public transportation.

231

But the later phases of Negro settlement and expansion in metropolitan areas diverge sharply from those typical of white immigrants. As the whites were absorbed by the larger society, many left their predominantly ethnic neighborhoods and moved to outlying areas to obtain newer housing and better schools. Some scattered randomly over the suburban area. Others established new ethnic clusters in the suburbs, but even these rarely contained solely members of a single ethnic group. As a result, most middle-class neighborhoods—both in the suburbs and within central cities—have no distinctive ethnic character, except that they are white.

Nowhere has the expansion of America's urban Negro population followed this pattern of dispersal. Thousands of Negro families have attained incomes, living standards, and cultural levels matching or surpassing those of whites who have "upgraded" themselves from distinctly ethnic neighborhoods. Yet most Negro families have remained within predominantly Negro neighborhoods, primarily because they have been effectively excluded from white residential areas. . . .

The Extent of Residential Segregation

The rapid expansion of all-Negro residential areas and large-scale white withdrawal have continued a pattern of residential segregation that has existed in American cities for decades. A recent study[1] reveals that this pattern is present to a high degree in every large city in America. The authors devised an index to measure the degree of residential segregation. The index indicates for each city the percentage of Negroes who would have to move from the blocks where they now live to other blocks in order to provide a perfectly proportional, unsegregated distribution of population.

According to their findings, the average segregation index for 207 of the largest U.S. cities was 86.2 in 1960. This means that an average of over 86 percent of all Negroes would have had to change blocks to create an unsegregated population distribution. Southern cities had a higher average index (90.9) than cities in the Northeast (79.2), the North Central (87.7), or the West (79.3). Only eight cities had index values below 70, whereas over 50 had values above 91.7.

The degree of residential segregation for all 207 cities has been relatively stable, averaging 85.2 in 1940, 87.3 in 1950, and 86.2 in 1960. Variations within individual regions were only slightly larger. However, a recent Census Bureau study shows that in most of the 12 large cities where special censuses were taken in the mid-1960s, the proportions of Negroes living in neighborhoods of greatest Negro concentration had increased since 1960.

Residential segregation is generally more prevalent with respect to Negroes than for any other minority group, including Puerto Ricans, Orientals, and

---

[1]*Negroes in Cities,* Karl and Alma Taeuber, (Aldine Publishing Co., Chicago, 1965).

Mexican-Americans. Moreover, it varies little between central city and suburb. This nearly universal pattern cannot be explained in terms of economic discrimination against all low-income groups. Analysis of 15 representative cities indicates that white upper and middle-income households are far more segregated from Negro upper and middle-income households than from white lower income households.

In summary, the concentration of Negroes in central cities results from a combination of forces. Some of these forces, such as migration and initial settlement patterns in older neighborhoods, are similar to those which affected previous ethnic minorities. Others—particularly discrimination in employment and segregation in housing and schools—are a result of white attitudes based on race and color. These forces continue to shape the future of the central city. . . .

Recent Economic Trends

The Negro population in our country is as diverse in income, occupation, family composition, and other variables as the white community. Nevertheless, for purposes of analysis, three major Negro economic groups can be identified.

The first and smallest group consists of middle and upper income individuals and households whose educational, occupational, and cultural characteristics are similar to those of middle and upper income white groups.

The second and largest group contains Negroes whose incomes are above the "poverty level" but who have not attained the educational, occupational, or income status typical of middle-class Americans.

The third group has very low educational, occupational, and income attainments and lives below the "poverty level."

A recent compilation of data on American Negroes by the Departments of Labor and Commerce shows that although incomes of both Negroes and whites have been rising rapidly,

1. Negro incomes still remain far below those of whites. Negro median family income was only 58 percent of the white median in 1966.

2. Negro family income is not keeping pace with white family income growth. In constant 1965 dollars, median nonwhite income in 1947 was $2,174 lower than median white income. By 1966, the gap had grown to $3,036.

3. The Negro upper income group is expanding rapidly and achieving sizeable income gains. In 1966, 28 percent of all Negro families received incomes of $7,000 or more, compared with 55 percent of white families. This was 1.6 times the proportion of Negroes receiving comparable incomes in 1960, and four times greater than the proportion receiving such incomes in 1947. Moreover, the proportion of Negroes employed in high-skill, high-status, and well-paying jobs rose faster than comparable proportions among whites from 1960 to 1966.

CONTEMPORARY ISSUES

4. As Negro incomes have risen, the size of the lowest income group has grown smaller, and the middle and upper groups have grown larger—both relatively and absolutely.

Group	Percentage of Negro Families			Percentage of White Families
	1947	1960	1966	1966
$7,000 and over	7	17	28	55
$3,000 to $6,999	29	40	41	33
Under $3,000	65	44	32	13

5. About two-thirds of the lowest income group—or 20 percent of all Negro families—are making no significant economic gains despite continued general prosperity. Half of these hard-core disadvantaged—more than two million persons—live in central-city neighborhoods. Recent special censuses in Los Angeles and Cleveland indicate that the incomes of persons living in the worst slum areas have not risen at all during this period, unemployment rates have declined only slightly, the proportion of families with female heads has increased, and housing conditions have worsened even though rents have risen.

Thus, between 2.0 and 2.5 million poor Negroes are living in disadvantaged neighborhoods of central cities in the United States. These persons comprise only slightly more than one percent of the Nation's total population, but they make up about 16 to 20 percent of the total Negro population of all central cities, and a much higher proportion in certain cities.

Unemployment and Underemployment

The Critical Significance of Employment

The capacity to obtain and hold a "good job" is the traditional test of participation in American society. Steady employment with adequate compensation provides both purchasing power and social status. It develops the capabilities, confidence, and self-esteem an individual needs to be a responsible citizen, and provides a basis for a stable family life. As Daniel P. Moynihan has written:*

The principal measure of progress toward equality will be that of employment. It is the primary source of individual or group identity. In America what you do is what you are: to do nothing is to be nothing; to do little is to be little. The equations are implacable and blunt, and ruthlessly public.

For the Negro American it is already, and will continue to be, the master problem. It is the measure of white bona fides. It is the measure of Negro

*Editor's note: Source not cited.

234

HUMAN RESOURCES

competence, and also of the competence of American society. Most importantly, the linkage between problems of employment and the range of social pathology that affects the Negro community is unmistakable. Employment not only controls the present for the Negro American but, in a most profound way, it is creating the future as well.

For residents of disadvantaged Negro neighborhoods, obtaining good jobs is vastly more difficult than for most workers in society. For decades, social, economic, and psychological disadvantages surrounding the urban Negro poor have impaired their work capacities and opportunities. The result is a cycle of failure—the employment disabilities of one generation breed those of the next.

Negro Unemployment

Unemployment rates among Negroes have declined from a post-Korean War high of 12.6 percent in 1958 to 8.2 percent in 1967. Among married Negro men, the unemployment rate for 1967 was down to 3.2 percent.[2]

Notwithstanding this decline, unemployment rates for Negroes are still double those for whites in every category, including married men, as they have been throughout the postwar period. Moreover, since 1954, even during the current unprecedented period of sustained economic growth, unemployment among Negroes has been continuously above the six percent "recession" level widely regarded as a sign of serious economic weakness when prevalent for the entire work force.

While the Negro unemployment rate remains high in relation to the white rate, the number of additional jobs needed to lower this to the level of white unemployment is surprisingly small. In 1967, approximately three million persons were unemployed during an average week, of whom about 638,000 or 21 percent, were nonwhites. When corrected for undercounting, total nonwhite unemployment was approximately 712,000 or eight percent of the nonwhite labor force. To reduce the unemployment rate to 3.4 percent, the rate prevalent among whites, jobs must be found for 57.5 percent of these unemployed persons. This amounts to nearly 409,000 jobs, or about 27 percent of the net number of new jobs added to the economy in the year 1967 alone and only slightly more than one-half of one percent of all jobs in the United States in 1967.

The Low-Status and Low-Paying Nature of Many Negro Jobs

Even more important perhaps than unemployment is the related problem of the undesirable nature of many jobs open to Negroes. Negro workers are

---

[2] Adjusted for Census Bureau undercounting.

235

concentrated in the lowest skilled and lowest paying occupations. These jobs often involve substandard wages, great instability and uncertainty of tenure, extremely low status in the eyes of both employer and employee, little or no chance for meaningful advancement, and unpleasant or exhausting duties. Negro men in particular are more than three times as likely as whites to be in unskilled or service jobs which pay far less than most:

Type of Occupation	Percentage of Male Workers in Each Type of Occupation, 1966		Median Earnings of All Male Civilians in Each Occupation, 1965
	White	Nonwhite	
Professional, technical, and managerial	27	9	$7,603*
Clerical and sales	14	9	5,532*
Craftsmen and foremen	20	12	6,270
Operatives	20	27	5,046
Service workers	6	16	3,436
Nonfarm laborers	6	20	2,410
Farmers and farm workers	7	8	1,669*

*Average of two categories from normal Census Bureau categories as combined in data presented in The Social and Economic Conditions of Negroes in the United States (BLS No. 332).

This concentration in the least desirable jobs can be viewed another way by calculating the changes which would occur if Negro men were employed in various occupations in the same proportions as the male labor force as a whole (not solely the white labor force).

Type of Occupation	Number of Male Nonwhite Workers, 1966			
	As Actually Distributed*	If Distributed the Same as All Male Workers	Difference	
			Number	Percent
Professional, technical, and managerial	415,000	1,173,000	+758,000	+183
Clerical and sales	415,000	628,000	+213,000	+51
Craftsmen and foremen	553,000	894,000	+341,000	+62
Operatives	1,244,000	964,000	−280,000	−23
Service workers	737,000	326,000	−411,000	−56
Nonfarm laborers	922,000	340,000	−582,000	−63
Farmers and farm workers	369,000	330,000	−39,000	−11

*Estimates based upon percentages set forth in BLS No. 332, p. 41.

Thus, upgrading the employment of Negro men to make their occupational distribution identical with that of the labor force as a whole would have an immense impact upon the nature of their occupations. About 1.3 million nonwhite men—or 28 percent of those employed in 1966—would move up the employment ladder into one of the higher status and higher paying categories.

The effect of such a shift upon the incomes of Negro men would be very great. Using the 1966 job distribution, the shift indicated above would produce about $4.8 billion more earned income for nonwhite men alone if they received the 1965 median income in each occupation. This would be a rise of approximately 30 percent in the earnings actually received by all non-white men in 1965 (not counting any sources of income other than wages and salaries).

Of course, the kind of "instant upgrading" visualized in these calculations does not represent a practical alternative for national policy. The economy cannot drastically reduce the total number of low-status jobs it now contains, or shift large numbers of people upward in occupation in any short period. Therefore, major upgrading in the employment status of Negro men must come through a faster relative expansion of higher level jobs than lower level jobs (which has been occurring for several decades), an improvement in the skills of nonwhite workers so they can obtain a high proportion of those added better jobs, and a drastic reduction of discriminatory hiring and promotion practices in all enterprises, both private and public.

Nevertheless, this hypothetical example clearly shows that the concentration of male Negro employment at the lowest end of the occupational scale is greatly depressing the incomes of U.S. Negroes is general. In fact this is the single most important source of poverty among Negroes. It is even more important than unemployment as can be shown by a second hypothetical calculation. In 1966, there were about 724,000 unemployed nonwhites in the United States on the average, including adults and teenagers, and allowing for the Census Bureau undercount of Negroes. If every one of these persons had been employed and had received the median amount earned by nonwhite males in 1966 ($3,864), this would have added a total of $2.8 billion to nonwhite income as a whole. If only enough of these persons had been employed at that wage to reduce nonwhite unemployment from 7.3 percent to 3.3 percent—the rate among whites in 1966—then the income gain for non-whites would have totaled about $1.5 billion. But if nonwhite unemployment remained at 7.3 percent, and nonwhite men were upgraded so that they had the same occupational distribution and incomes as all men in the labor force considered together, this would have produced about $4.8 billion in additional income, as noted above (using 1965 earnings for calculation). Thus the potential income gains from upgrading the male nonwhite labor force are much larger than those from reducing nonwhite unemployment.

This conclusion underlines the difficulty of improving the economic status of Negro men. It is far easier to create new jobs than either to create new jobs with relatively high status and earning power, or to upgrade existing employed or partly employed workers into such better quality employment. Yet only such upgrading will eliminate the fundamental basis of poverty and deprivation among Negro families.

Access to good-quality jobs clearly affects the willingness of Negro men actively to seek work. In riot cities surveyed by the Commission with the largest percentage of Negroes in skilled and semiskilled jobs, Negro men participated in the labor force to the same extent as, or greater than, white men. Conversely, where most Negro men were heavily concentrated in menial jobs, they participated less in the labor force than white men.

Even given similar employment, Negro workers with the same education as white workers are paid less. This disparity doubtless results to some extent from inferior training in segregated schools, and also from the fact that large numbers of Negroes are only now entering certain occupations for the first time. However, the differentials are so large and so universal at all educational levels that they clearly reflect the patterns of discrimination which characterize hiring and promotion practices in many segments of the economy. For example, in 1966, among persons who had completed high school, the median income of Negroes was only 73 percent that of whites. Even among persons with an eighth-grade education, Negro median income was only 80 percent of white median income.

At the same time, a higher proportion of Negro women than white women participates in the labor force at nearly all ages except 16 to 19. For instance in 1966, 55 percent of nonwhite women from 25 to 34 years of age were employed, compared to only 38 percent of white women in the same age group. The fact that almost half of all adult Negro women work reflects the fact that so many Negro males have unsteady and low-paying jobs. Yet even though Negro women are often better able to find work than Negro men, the unemployment rate among adult nonwhite women (20 years old and over) in 1967 was 7.1 percent, compared to the 4.3 percent rate among adult nonwhite men.

Unemployment rates are, of course, much higher among teenagers, both Negro and white, than among adults; in fact about one-third of all unemployed Negroes in 1967 were between 16 and 19 years old. During the first nine months of 1967, the unemployment rate among nonwhite teenagers was 26.5 percent; for whites, it was 10.6 percent. About 219,300 nonwhite teenagers were unemployed.[3] About 58,300 were still in school but were actively looking for jobs.

SUBEMPLOYMENT IN DISADVANTAGED NEGRO NEIGHBORHOODS

In disadvantaged areas, employment conditions for Negroes are in a chronic state of crisis. Surveys in low-income neighborhoods of nine large cities made by the Department of Labor late in 1966 revealed that the rate of unemployment there was 9.3 percent, compared to 7.3 percent for Negroes generally and 3.3 percent for whites. Moreover, a high proportion of the persons living in these areas were "underemployed," that is, they were either part-time workers looking for full-time employment, or full-time workers earning less than $3000 per year, or had dropped out of the labor force. The Department

---

[3] After adjusting for Census Bureau undercounting.

of Labor estimated that this underemployment is two and one-half times greater than the number of unemployed in these areas. Therefore, the "subemployment rates," including both the unemployed and the underemployed, was about 32.7 percent in the nine areas surveyed, or 8.8 times greater than the overall unemployment rate for all U.S. workers. Since underemployment also exists outside disadvantaged neighborhoods, comparing the full subemployment rate in these areas with the unemployment rate for the Nation as a whole is not entirely valid. However, it provides some measure of the enormous disparity between employment conditions in most of the Nation and those prevalent in disadvantaged Negro areas in our large cities. . . .

COMPARING THE IMMIGRANT AND NEGRO EXPERIENCE

. . . Here we address a fundamental question that many white Americans are asking today: Why has the Negro been unable to escape from poverty and the ghetto like the European immigrants?

The Maturing Economy

The changing nature of the American economy is one major reason. When the European immigrants were arriving in large numbers, America was becoming an urban-industrial society. To build its major cities and industries, America needed great pools of unskilled labor. The immigrants provided the labor, gained an economic foothold and thereby enabled their children and grandchildren to move up to skilled, white-collar and professional employment.

Since World War II especially, America's urban-industrial society has matured; unskilled labor is far less essential than before, and blue-collar jobs of all kinds are decreasing in number and importance as a source of new employment. The Negroes who migrated to the great urban centers lacked the skills essential to the new economy, and the schools of the ghetto have been unable to provide the education that can qualify them for decent jobs. The Negro migrant, unlike the immigrant, found little opportunity in the city; he had arrived too late, and the unskilled labor he had to offer was no longer needed.

The Disability of Race

Racial discrimination is undoubtedly the second major reason why the Negro has been unable to escape from poverty. The structure of discrimination has persistently narrowed his opportunities and restricted his prospects. Well before the high tide of immigration from overseas, Negroes were already relegated to the poorly paid, low status occupations. Had it not been for racial discrimination, the North might well have recruited southern Negroes after the Civil War to provide the labor for building the burgeoning urban-industrial economy. Instead, northern employers looked to Europe for their sources of unskilled labor. Upon the arrival of the immigrants, the Negroes were dislodged from the few urban occupations they had dominated. Not until World War II were Negroes generally hired for industrial jobs, and by that time the decline in the need for unskilled labor had already begun. European immigrants, too, suffered from discrimination, but never was it so pervasive. The prejudice against color in America has formed a bar to advancement unlike any other.

Entry into the Political System

Political opportunities also played an important role in enabling the European immigrants to escape from poverty. The immigrants settled for the most part in rapidly growing cities that had powerful and expanding political machines which gave them economic advantages in exchange for political support. The political machines were decentralized, and ward-level grievance machinery as well as personal representation enabled the immigrant to make his voice heard and his power felt. Since the local political organizations exercised considerable influence over public building in the cities, they provided employment in construction jobs for their immigrant voters. Ethnic groups often dominated one or more of the municipal services—police and fire protection, sanitation, and even public education.

By the time the Negroes arrived, the situation had altered dramatically. The great wave of public building had virtually come to an end; reform groups were beginning to attack the political machines; the machines were no longer so powerful or so well equipped to provide jobs and other favors.

Although the political machines retained their hold over the areas settled by Negroes, the scarcity of patronage jobs made them unwilling to share with Negroes the political positions they had created in these neighborhoods. For example, Harlem was dominated by white politicians for many years after it had become a Negro ghetto; even today, New York's Lower East Side, which is now predominantly Puerto Rican, is strongly influenced by politicians of the older immigrant groups.

This pattern exists in many other American cities. Negroes are still under-represented in city councils and in most city agencies.

Segregation played a role here too. The immigrants and their descendants, who felt threatened by the arrival of the Negro, prevented a Negro-immigrant coalition that might have saved the old political machines. Reform groups, nominally more liberal on the race issue, were often dominated by business-men and middle-class city residents who usually opposed coalition with any low-income group, white or black.

Cultural Factors

Cultural factors also made it easier for the immigrants to escape from poverty. They came to America from much poorer societies, with a low standard of living, and they came at a time when job aspirations were low. When most jobs in the American economy were unskilled, they sensed little deprivation in being forced to take the dirty and poorly paid jobs. Moreover, their families were large, and many breadwinners, some of whom never married, contributed to the total family income. As a result, family units managed to live even from the lowest paid jobs and still put some money aside for savings or investment, for example, to purchase a house or tenement or to open a store or factory. Since the immigrants spoke little English and had their own ethnic culture, they needed stores to supply them with ethnic foods and other services. Since their family structures were patriarchal, men found satisfactions in family life that helped compensate for the bad jobs they had to take and the hard work they had to endure.

Negroes came to the city under quite different circumstances. Generally relegated to jobs that others would not take, they were paid too little to be able to put money in savings for new enterprises. In addition, Negroes lacked the extended family characteristic of certain European groups; each household usually had only one or two breadwinners. Moreover, Negro men had fewer cultural incentives to work in a dirty job for the sake of the family. As a result of slavery and of long periods of male unemployment afterwards, the Negro family structure had become matriarchal; the man played a secondary and marginal role in his family. For many Negro men, then, there were few of the cultural and psychological rewards of family life; they often abandoned their homes because they felt themselves useless to their families.

Although Negro men worked as hard as the immigrants to support their families, their rewards were less. The jobs did not pay enough to enable them to support their families, for prices and living standards had risen since the immigrants had come, and the entrepreneurial opportunities that had allowed some immigrants to become independent, even rich, had vanished. Above all, Negroes suffered from segregation, which denied them access to the good jobs and the right unions and which deprived them of the opportunity to buy real estate or obtain business loans or move out of the ghetto and bring up their children in middle-class neighborhoods. Immigrants were able to leave their ghettos as soon as they had the money; segregation has denied Negroes the opportunity to live elsewhere.

The Vital Element of Time

Finally, nostalgia makes it easy to exaggerate the ease of escape of the white immigrants from the ghettos. When the immigrants were immersed in

241

poverty, they, too, lived in slums, and these neighborhoods exhibited fearfully high rates of alcoholism, desertion, illegitimacy, and the other pathologies associated with poverty. Just as some Negro men desert their families when they are unemployed and their wives can get jobs, so did the men of other ethnic groups, even though time and affluence has clouded white memories of the past.

Today, whites tend to contrast their experience with poverty-stricken Negroes. The fact is, among the southern and eastern Europeans who came to America in the last great wave of immigration, those who came already urbanized were the first to escape from poverty. The others who came to America from rural background, as Negroes did, are only now, after three generations, in the final stages of escaping from poverty. Until the last 10 years or so, most of these were employed in blue-collar jobs, and only a small proportion of their children were able or willing to attend college. In other words, only the third, and in many cases only the fourth, generation has been able to achieve the kind of middle-class income and status that allows it to send its children to college. Because of favorable economic and political conditions, these ethnic groups were able to escape from lower class status to working class and lower middle-class status, but it has taken them three generations.

Negroes have been concentrated in the city for only two generations, and they have been there under much less favorable conditions. Moreover, their escape from poverty has been blocked in part by the resistance of the European ethnic groups; they have been unable to enter some unions and to move into some neighborhoods outside the ghetto because descendants of the European immigrants who control these unions and neighborhoods have not yet abandoned them for middle-class occupations and areas.

Even so, some Negroes have escaped poverty, and they have done so in only two generations; their success is less visible than that of the immigrants in many cases, for residential segregation has forced them to remain in the ghetto. Still, the proportion of nonwhites employed in white-collar, technical and professional jobs has risen from 10.2 percent in 1950 to 20.8 percent in 1966 and the proportion attending college has risen an equal amount. Indeed, the development of a small but steadily increasing Negro middle class while a great part of the Negro population is stagnating economically is creating a growing gap between Negro haves and have-nots.

The awareness of this gap by those left behind undoubtedly adds to the feelings of desperation and anger which breed civil disorders. Low-income Negroes realize that segregation and lack of job opportunities have made it possible for only a small proportion of all Negroes to escape poverty, and the summer disorders are at least in part a protest against being left behind and left out.

The immigrant who labored long hours at hard and often menial work had the hope of a better future, if not for himself then for his children. This was the promise of the "American dream"—the society offered to all a future that was open-ended; with hard work and perseverance, a man and his family could in time achieve not only material well-being but "position" and status.

242

For the Negro family in the urban ghetto, there is a different vision—the future seems to lead only to a dead end.

What the American economy of the late nineteenth and early twentieth century was able to do to help the European immigrants escape from poverty is now largely impossible. New methods of escape must be found for the majority of today's poor.

... The Commission's Recommendations

We do not claim competence to chart the details of programs within such complex and interrelated fields as employment, welfare, education, and housing. We do believe it is essential to set forth goals and to recommend strategies to reach these goals.

That is the aim of the pages that follow. They contain our sense of the critical priorities. We discuss and recommend programs, not to commit each of us to specific parts of such programs, but to illustrate the type and dimension of action needed.

Much has been accomplished in recent years to formulate new directions for national policy and new channels for national energy. Resources devoted to social programs have been greatly increased in many areas. Hence, few of our program suggestions are entirely novel. In some form, many are already in effect.

All this serves to underscore our basic conclusion: the need is not so much for the government to design new programs as it is for the nation to generate new will. Private enterprise, labor unions, the churches, the foundations, the universities—all our urban institutions—must deepen their involvement in the life of the city and their commitment to its revival and welfare.

Objectives for National Action

Just as Lincoln, a century ago, put preservation of the Union above all else, so should we put creation of a true union—a single society and a single American identity—as our major goal. Toward that goal, we propose the following objectives for national action:

Opening up all opportunities to those who are restricted by racial segregation and discrimination, and eliminating all barriers to their choice of jobs, education, and housing.

Removing the frustration of powerlessness among the disadvantaged by providing the means to deal with problems that affect their own lives and by increasing the capacity of our public and private institutions to respond to those problems.

Increasing communication across racial lines to destroy stereotypes, halt polarization, end distrust and hostility, and create common ground for efforts toward common goals of public order and social justice.

243

There are those who oppose these aims as "rewarding the rioters." They are wrong. A great nation is not so easily intimidated. We propose these aims to fulfill our pledge of equality and to meet the fundamental needs of a democratic and civilized society—domestic peace, social justice, and urban centers that are citadels of the human spirit.

There are others who say that violence is necessary—that fear alone can prod the nation to act decisively on behalf of racial minorities. They too are wrong. Violence and disorder compound injustice; they must be ended and they will be ended.

Our strategy is neither blind repression nor capitulation to lawlessness. Rather it is the affirmation of common possibilities, for all, within a single society. . . .*

---

*Editor's note: Following this general statement of objectives, the Advisory Commission discusses its policy recommendations in the areas of employment, education, welfare, and housing. See pp. 231-263 of the Commission's *Report* for this discussion.

B.

Nonhuman Resources

THE ECONOMICS OF POLLUTION

Edwin L. Dale, Jr.

Now that environment has become a national concern, it might be well to clean up some of the economic rubbish associated with the subject. There are, alas, a few "iron laws" that cannot be escaped in the effort to reduce the pollution of our air and water, in disposing of solid waste and the like. The laws do not necessarily prevent a clean environment, but there is no hope of obtaining one unless they are understood.

We have all become vaguely aware that there will be a cost—perhaps higher monthly electric bills, perhaps higher taxes, perhaps a few cents or a few dollars more on anything made from steel—if there is a successful and massive effort to have a better environment. But that is only a beginning. There are other problems.

From *The New York Times Magazine,* April 19, 1970. © 1970 by The New York Times Company. Reprinted by permission.

This article will describe the three iron laws that matter. There is no point in hiding that all three are very depressing. The only purpose in adding more depressing information to a world already surfeited with it is a small one: to avoid useless effort based on false premises. A classic example has already arisen in wistful Congressional inquiries into whether we might think of a future with somewhat less electric power, or at least less growth in electric power.

In shorthand, the three laws are:

1. The law of economic growth.
2. The law of compound interest.
3. The law of the mix between public and private spending.

THE LAW OF ECONOMIC GROWTH

Whether we like it or not, and assuming no unusual increase in mass murders or epidemics, the American labor force for the next 20 years is already born and intends to work. It is hard for any of us—myself included—to imagine a deliberate policy to keep a large portion of it unemployed. But that simple fact has enormous consequences.

For more than a century, the average output of each worker for each hour worked has risen between two and three percent a year, thanks mainly to new machines, but also to better managerial methods and a more skilled labor force. This increase in what is called *productivity* is by far the most important cause of our gradually rising standard of living—which, pollution aside, nearly all of us have wanted. In simplest terms, each worker can be paid more because he produces more and he consumes more because he earns more. Inflation only increases the numbers and does not change the facts. Machines increase the productivity of an auto worker more than a barber, but both rightly share, through the general rise in real income, the expansion of productivity in the economy as a whole.

It is difficult to conceive of our society or any other wanting to halt the rise in productivity, or efficiency, which has made real incomes higher for all of us. But even if "we" wanted to, in our kind of society and economy "we" couldn't. The profit motive will almost always propel individual, daily decisions in the direction of higher productivity. A business will always buy a new machine if it will cut costs and increase efficiency—and thank goodness! That is what has made our standard of living—and we do enjoy it—rise.

It is not a matter of enjoying it, however. By any fair test, we are not really affluent; half of our households earn less than $8,500 a year. Apart from redistributing income, which has very real limits, the only way the society can continue to improve the well-being of those who are not affluent—really the majority—is through a continued increase in productivity. Anyone who wants us to go back to the ax, the wooden plow, the horse carriage and the water wheel is not only living a wholly impossible dream, he is asking for a return to a society in which nearly everybody was poor. We are not talking here about philosophical ideas of happiness, but of what people have proved they want in the way of material things. The society is not about to give up productivity growth. But every increase in productivity adds to output. Now consider the next step:

We can count on the output of the average worker to continue to rise in the years ahead, as it has in the past. Nearly all current forecasts put this rise in productivity much closer to three percent than to two, and three percent has been about our average in the years since World War II. So without any change in the labor force at all, our natonal output will go on rising by some three percent a year.

What does output mean?

It means electric power produced—and smoke produced.

It means cans and bottles produced.

It means steel produced—and, unless something is done about it, water and air polluted.

It means paper produced—with the same result as for steel.

And so on and on.

But that is not the end, for there will not be a static labor force. As noted, the force for the next 20 years is already born and it is going to grow year by year (with a caveat, to be described below).

Obviously, we want to offer these people employment opportunity. So, in addition to a three percent productivity growth, there will be an added growth of at least one percent a year in the number of workers. The result is that we are almost "condemned" to a rise in our total output of four percent a year. The only escape, it seems, would be a national decision either to have high unemployment or to try to be less efficient. Both are absurd on their face.

The law of economic growth says, then, that we already know that the national output in 1980 will be, and almost must be, some 50 percent higher than it is now. President Nixon said so publicly, and he is right. That is the result of an annual rate of real growth of about four percent, compounded. It is terrifying. If an economy of $900-billion in 1969 produces the pollution and clutter we are all familiar with, what will an economy half again as large produce?

Is there no escape from this law? The answer, essentially, is no. But there is one possible way to mitigate the awesome results. We might reduce the labor input (but, we hope, not the productivity input), without creating mass unemployment.

Each working person has a workday, workweek, workyear and worklife. Any one of them could be reduced by law or otherwise. We could reduce the legal workweek from the present 40 hours. We could add more holidays or lengthen vacations to reduce the workyear. We are already shortening the worklife, without planning it that way: increased participation in higher education has meant later entry into the labor force for many, and retirement plans, including Social Security, have brought about earlier retirement than in the past for others.

If, by chance or by law, the annual man-hours of employment are reduced in the years ahead, our output will grow a little less rapidly. This is the only way to cut our economic growth, short of deliberate unemployment or deliberate inefficiency.

There is a cost. It is most easily seen in a union-bargained settlement providing for longer vacations without any cut in annual wages, or a legal reduction in the workweek from 40 to 35 hours, with compulsory overtime payments after that. In each case, more workers must be hired to produce the same output, and if the employer—because of market demand—goes on producing at the same level, wage costs for each unit of output are higher than they otherwise would have been. Prices will therefore be higher. This is widely recognized. Maybe we would be willing to pay them.

But we cannot guarantee less output. Only if employers produce less—because of the extra cost—would that happen. And in that larger sense, the cost of a reduction of our annual labor input is simply less production per capita because the labor force is idle more of the time.

But less production was the objective of the exercise—the antipollution exercise. If we start with the proposition that the growth of production is the underlying cause of pollution, which has merit as a starting point, the only way we can get less growth in production, if we want it, is to have more of our labor force idle more of the time. In that case, we will have more leisure without mass unemployment, as we usually think of the term. Our national output, and our standard of living, will rise less rapidly.

That last idea we may learn to take, if we can cope with the leisure. But under any foreseeable circumstances, our output will still go on rising. With the most optimistic assumptions about a gradual reduction of the workday, workweek, workyear and worklife, we shall undoubtedly have a much higher output in 1980 than we have in 1970. To a man concerned about the environment, it might seem a blessing if our economic growth in the next 10 years could be two percent a year instead of four percent; he cannot hope for zero growth.

The law of economic growth, then, tells us a simple truth: "we" cannot choose to reduce production simply because we have found it to be the cause of a fouled environment. And if we want to reduce the rate of growth of production, the place to look is in our man-hours of work.

THE LAW OF COMPOUND INTEREST

It is a fair question to ask: Why weren't we bothered about pollution 12 or 15 years ago? In October, 1957, to pick a date, the Soviet Union sent the first earth satellite into orbit. The American economy had just begun a recession that was to send unemployment to seven percent of the labor force. The late George Magoffin Humphrey, who had just resigned as Secretary of the

Treasury, was warning of what he saw as vast Government spending, at that time $77-billion, and saying it would bring "a depression that would curl your hair." There were plenty of things to think about.

But nobody was worried about pollution. Conservation groups were properly bothered about parts of the wilderness (the Hell's Canyon Dam in Idaho, for example), but that was an entirely different thing. That was an issue of esthetics, not health. Nobody seemed to mention air pollution or waste that might overwhelm the space in which to put it. In a peculiarly sad irony, the late Adlai E. Stevenson had fought and lost an election against Dwight D. Eisenhower in 1956 partially on a "pollution" issue—radiation in the atmosphere from the explosion of atomic weapons.

The question, to repeat: Why didn't we worry about pollution then? The answer is that, relatively speaking, there *was* no pollution. Yes, there were electric power plants then, too. Yes, there were paper mills polluting streams. Yes, there were tin cans and paper and bottles. Some snowflakes, though we didn't know it, were already a bit black, and Pittsburgh got national attention because it tried to do some cleaning up.

But here we come to the law of compound interest. In 1957—*only 13 years ago*—our gross national product was $453-billion. In 1969, in constant dollars, it was $728-billion. That is an increase of nearly $300-billion in tin cans, electric power, automobiles, paper, chemicals, and all the rest. It is an increase of 60 percent.

So what? That was not the result of an unnaturally rapid growth rate, though a bit more rapid than in some periods of our past. The *so what* is this: in the preceding 13 years the growth had been *only $100-billion*. We were the same nation, with the same energy, in those preceding 13 years. We invested and we had a rise both in productivity and in our labor force. But in the first 13 years of this example our output rose $100-billion, and in the second 13 it rose $300-billion.

In the next 13 it will rise more than $500-billion.

That is the law of compound interest. These are not numbers; they are tin cans and smoke and auto exhaust. There is no visible escape from it. Applying the same percentage growth to a larger base every year, we have reached the point where our growth in one year is half the total output of Canada, fully adjusting for inflation. Another dizzying and rather horrifying way of putting it is that the real output of goods and services in the United States has grown as much since 1950 as it grew in the entire period from the landing of the Pilgrims in 1620 up to 1950.

Most investors know the law of compound interest. There is a magic rule, for example, known as the Rule of 72. It says, with mathematical certainty, that money invested at a 7.2 percent rate of interest, compounded each year, doubles in 10 years. Our GNP, happily, does not compound at 7.2 percent. But it compounds at between four and five percent, and it has been compounding. The result is that the same, routine, full-employment, desirable, nationally wanted, almost unavoidable percentage increase in our national output in 1970 means precisely twice as many extra tin cans, twice as much additional electric power, and so on, as the same rate of growth in 1950. And that is only 20 years ago! We are not doing anything different, or anything awful. We are the same people. Granting approximately the same amount of human carelessness and selfishness, we are the victims solely of the law of compound interest.

THE LAW OF THE MIX BETWEEN
PUBLIC AND PRIVATE SPENDING

Robert S. McNamara, the eternally energetic and constructive former Secretary of Defense and now president of the World Bank, gave a speech in February about the plight of the poor countries. In the speech he understandably criticized the United States for reducing its foreign aid effort. But in supporting his point he adopted, almost inadvertently, a piece of partly fallacious conventional wisdom:

Which is ultimately more in the nation's interest: to funnel national resources into an endlessly spiraling consumer economy—in effect, a pursuit of consumer gadgetry with all its senseless by-products of waste and pollution—or to dedicate a more reasonable share of those same resources to improving the fundamental quality of life both at home and abroad?

Fair enough. It means tax increases, of course, though Mr. McNamara did not say so. That is what the "mix" between public and private spending is all about. But for our purposes the point is different. Let us look more closely at the phrase: "... a pursuit of consumer gadgetry with all its senseless by-products of waste and pollution. . . ."

As it stands, it is true. Private consumption does create side effects like waste and pollution. But now, assume a Brave New World in which we are all happy to pay higher taxes and reduce our private consumption so that the government may have more money with which to solve our problems—ranging from poor education to poverty, from crime to inadequate health services. We shall not examine here the issue of whether more government money solves problems. It is obviously more effective in some areas than in others. But anyway, in our assumption, we are willing to give the government more money to solve problems, including pollution.

Now let us see what happens

The government spends the money to reduce pollution. Sewage plants are built. They need steel. They need electric power. They need paperwork. They need workers. The workers get paid, and they consume.

The government spends the money on education. New schools are built, which need steel, lumber, and electric power. Teachers are hired. They get paid, and they consume. They throw away tin cans.

The government spends the money on a better welfare system that treats all poor people alike, whether they work or not. Incomes among the poor rise by some amount between $4-billion and $20-billion, and these people consume. Electric power production rises and appliance and steel production rises, and so on and on.

The point is obvious by now. A shifting in our national income or production between "public goods" and "private goods" hardly changes the environment problem at all because it does not reduce total spending or output, in the economy.

Lest a careful economist raise a valid objection, a slightly technical point must be conceded here. Government spending is done in three categories:

Purchase of goods (tanks, typewriters, sanitation trucks, and school buildings).

Transfer payments to people outside government (Social Security, veterans' benefits, welfare).

Purchase of services, meaning the services of the people it employs (teachers, policemen, park rangers, tax collectors).

To the extent that a shift to more public spending, through higher taxes and a resulting reduction of private consumption, involves the first two of these categories, the point stands as made: there will be just as much production of steel, tin cans, electric power and toasters as before. To the extent that the higher public spending goes to the third category, employment of more teachers, policemen and the like, there will be slightly less production of goods even though these people spend their paychecks like everyone else. Essentially what happens in this case is that the society has chosen, through higher taxes, to have more services and fewer goods. If we assume that goods production brings pollution, a society with fewer auto- or steelworkers and more cops will crank out less pollution.

But this remains a relatively minor matter. Hardly anyone who proposes a solution to our problems thinks in terms of vast armies of government workers. Reforming welfare through the President's new family-assistance plan is the perfect example; this will be a simple expansion of transfer payments. And, for that matter, building more sewage plants will be a purchase of goods. The overriding fact is that we can spend 30 percent of our GNP for public purposes, as we do now, or 50 percent, and the GNP will still be there. The law of compound interest will apply, forcing the GNP upward. To the extent that the environment problem is caused by ever-expanding output, the third law says that it will not be essentially changed by altering the mix between private and public spending.

CONCLUSION

Three nice, depressing laws. They give us a starting point for any rational discussion of the environment problem. Our output is going to go on growing and growing under any conceivable set of choices we make.

But the starting point does not mean despair. It simply means that trying to solve the problem by reducing output, or the growth of output, is waste of time and energy. It won't and can't work.

How is the problem solved then? The purpose here is not, and has not been, to solve any problems. It has been to try to head off useless solutions. But a few things can be said:

There is, first, technology itself. The very energy and inventiveness that gave us this rising output—and got us to the moon—can do things about pollution. A fascinating case is the sulphur dioxide put into the air by coal-burning electric power plants. A very strong argument can be made that under any foreseeable circumstances we will have to burn more and more coal to produce the needed growth of electric power. And the ground does not yield much low-sulphur coal. Thus, somebody is going to have to have the incentive to develop a way to get the sulphur out before it leaves the smokestack; and if this costs the utilities money, the regulatory commissions are going to have to allow that cost to be passed along in electric bills.

Next, there is the related idea—being increasingly explored by economists, regulators and some legislators—of making antipollution part of the price-profit-incentive system. In simplest terms, this would involve charging a fee for every unit of pollutant discharged, with meters used to determine the amount. There would be an economic incentive to stop or reduce pollution, possibly backed up with the threat to close down the plant if the meter readings go above a specified level. The company—say a paper company—would be faced with both a carrot and a stick.

There is also the simple use of the police power, as with poisonous drugs or, lately, DDT. It is the "thou shalt not" power: automobiles can emit no more than such-and-such an amount of this or that chemical through the exhaust pipe. Once again, if the engineers cannot find a way out, the car simply cannot legally be sold. There will be, and should be, all sorts of debate "at the margin"—whether the higher cost of the different or improved engine is worth the extra reduction of pollution. The argument exists now over DDT; there are clearly costs, as well as benefits, in stopping its use. But the "thou shall not" power exists.

Finally, there are many possibilities for using a part of our public spending for environmental purposes. Sewage plants are the obvious case. President Nixon has proposed a big expansion of the current level of spending for these plants, though not as much as many interested in clean water—including Senator Edmund Muskie—would like to see.

In this case, and only in this case, a greater effort at curing pollution must be at the expense of some other government program unless we pay higher taxes. It is proper to point out here the subtle dimensions of the issue. There are all sorts of possible gimmicks like tax rebates for antipollution devices for industry and federally guaranteed state and local bonds. One way or another, spending more for pollution abatement will mean spending that much less for something else, and the something else could mean housing or medical services. Every local sewage plant bond sold means that much less investment money available for mortgages, for example.

A final reflection is perhaps in order, though it is almost banal. Our rising GNP gives us the "resources" to do the antipollution job. These resources include rising government receipts. Our technology, which has given us the rising GNP, might find the way out of one pollution problem after another—and they are all different.

But, in the end, we cannot be sure that the job will be done. Growth of total output per capita will continue. The longterm relief is perfectly obvious: *fewer "capita."* That sort of "solution" might help, in our country, by about 1990. If we survive until then, the law of compound interest will be much less horrifying if the population is 220 million instead of 250 million.

ECONOMICS AND ECOSYSTEMS

Jon Breslaw

The American economy can be best represented by the concept of a competitive market. If one regards the market as a black box, then there are two processes which do not come within the market's sphere of influence—inputs and outputs. The inputs are raw materials, or resources, used in the economy—air, water, metals, minerals, and wood. The outputs are the residuals—sewage, trash, carbon dioxide and other gases released to the atmosphere, radioactive waste, and so on. We shall consider the residuals first.

The environment has a certain limited capability to absorb wastes without harmful effects. Once the ambient residuals rise above a certain level, however, they become unwanted inputs to other production processes or to final consumers. The size of this residual, in fact, is massive. In an economy which is closed, the weight of residuals ejected into the environment is about equal to the weight of input materials, plus oxygen taken from the atmosphere. This result, while obvious upon reflection, leads to the surprising and even shocking corollary that the disposal of residuals is as large an operation, in sheer tonnage, as basic materials production. This incredible volume has to be disposed of. It is at this stage that the market process breaks down.

If the functioning of the economy gave rise to incentives, such as prices, which fully reflected the costs of disposing of residuals, such incentives would be very much in point. This would be especially true if the incentives fully reflected costs to the overall society associated with the discharge of the residuals to the environment. But it is clear that, whatever other normative properties the functioning of a market economy may have, it does not reflect these costs adequately.

Market economies are effective instruments for organizing production and allocating resources, insofar as the utility functions are associated with

---

two-party transactions. But in connection with waste disposal, the utility functions involve third parties, and the automatic market exchange process fails.

Thus the need to see man's activities as part of an ecosystem becomes clear. The outputs from the black box go through other black boxes and become inputs again. If our black box is putting out too much and overloading the system, one can only expect trouble—and that is what one gets.

If we look at a particular production process, we find that there is a flow of goods or services that consumers or businesses get whether they want it or not. An upstream river may be polluted by an industry, and the downstream user cannot usually control the quality of the water that he gets. If the polluted water wipes out a fishing industry, then there is some cost (the profit that used to be made by the fishing industry) that does not appear on the balance sheet of the upstream user. Similarly, there may be benefits involved—the upstream user may use the stream for cooling, and the hot water may support an oyster farm downstream.

The activities of an economic unit thus generate real effects that are external to it. These are called externalities. A society that relies completely on a decentralized decision-making system in which significant externalities occur, as they do in any society which contains significant concentrations of population and industrial activities, will find that certain resources are not used optimally.

The tool used by economists, and others, in determining a course of action in making social decisions is the technique of cost-benefit analysis. The basis is to list all the consequences arising from a course of action, such as building a new freeway, and to make estimates of the benefits or costs to the community of all these consequences. This is done in terms of money values and a balance is drawn up, which is compared with similar estimates of the consequences of alternative decisions, such as building a rapid transit network or doing nothing. The sensible decision is to go ahead with those projects where the benefits come out best, relative to the costs. The art of cost-benefit analysis lies in using the scanty information available to assign money values to these costs and benefits. Differences in house prices are a way of getting at noise valuation. Time is obviously worth money: how much can be estimated by looking at what people do when they have a choice between a faster and more expensive way of going from A to B and a slower but cheaper way?

Going back to our slaughtered fish, if the cost of reducing pollution by 50 percent were less than the profit that could be realized from fishing at this level of pollution, then it makes sense to spend that amount. In fact, the level of pollution should be reduced until the marginal cost of reducing pollution (the cost of reducing pollution by a very small amount) is just equal to the marginal revenue from fishing (the extra revenue that is received as a result of that amount less pollution). The question is, where there is no market, how does one get to this state of affairs?

Method One is to internalize the problem so that a single economic unit will take account of all of the costs and benefits associated with the external effects. To do this, the size of the economic unit has to be increased. A good

255

example of this is where one has several fisheries for one limited species of fish, e.g., whales. If the fisheries operate separately, each concern takes as many as it can, regardless of the effect on the total catch. If the fisheries were to act in unison, then the maximum catch compatible with a stable population of whales would be taken, and no more—the externalities would have been internalized. Unfortunately, waste products are often so widely propagated in nature and affect so many diverse interests that the merger route is not feasible.

Method Two is the one mostly used at the moment: the use of regulations set up by the government and enforceable by law. There are many examples of these: minimum net hole size in fishing, parking regulations on busy streets, limited number of flights at airports during the night, zoning regulations as applied to land use, and certain water quality laws for industrial and municipal river users. Ideally, these regulations would take into account the different nature of the environmental difficulty, varying both over place and time, e.g., high and low flows in streams, windy days for smoke control, etc. There are two main objections to such regulations. In the first place, they are often difficult to enforce, especially if there are high monetary returns involved and the likelihood of being caught is small—flushing oil tanks in the English Channel. The other objection is more sophisticated: in a competitive market the imposition of regulations does not normally lead to the best use of resources. It is better to do this by means of pricing, since this method makes it possible to balance incremental costs and gains in a relatively precise manner. Also, regulations do not provide the funds for the construction and operation measures of regional scope, should these prove economical.

Method Three involves the legal system and the law of nuisance. Thus when there is an oil spill on your shore and you and your property get covered in goo, then in such an obvious and easy case one would expect prompt damages—but ask the residents of Santa Barbara what they think of courts and oil companies. Thus, though in theory the courts provide a solution, in practice, they are slow and inefficient.

Method Four involves the paying of some monetary rent in order to get the practice of pollution stopped. One way is to pay a producer to stop polluting. Although such payments would be received favorably by the industries involved, the sheer size of the total payments necessary as a means of preventing pollution would put an impossible strain on any budget, and such a solution is only feasible for "special case" industrial operations. Moreover, if a steel mill is discharging its waste into a river, without charge, it is producing steel that is artificially cheap. Paying the mill to stop pollution does nothing to get the steel price back to its rightful value (i.e., when all costs are met) in the short run. In the long run, this remains true only if the assumption of a competitive market is weakened.

Another way to implement Method Four would be to charge a polluter for the pollution that he causes. Examples of such charges or taxes would be a tax on sewage effluents which is related to the quality and quantity of the discharge; or a surcharge on the price of fuels with a high sulfur content which is meant to take account of the broader cost to society external to the fuel-using enterprise. This procedure is one usually favored by economists, since it uses economic incentives to allocate the resources (the waste assimilative capacity of the environment) similar to those generated where market mechanisms can balance costs and returns. The revenue from these charges can be used to finance other antipollution facilities.

The use of charges for the wasted assimilative capacity of the environment implies that you have to pay in order to put things out of the black box. Before the environment's waste assimilative capacity was overloaded, it was not used to its full capacity. A resource which is not fully utilized has a zero price; once it is utilized it receives a positive price—which is why charges now have to be imposed. From an ecological point of view this is very good, since now that one has to pay to get rid of a product, it means that this product has a value attached to it, albeit negative. The effect is to restructure industrial processes to take this into account. A society that allows waste dischargers to neglect the offsite costs of waste disposal will not only devote too few resources to the treatment of waste, but will also produce too much waste in view of the damage it causes. Or more simply, if you charge for waste disposal, industries will produce less waste, and the wastes produced will often find use in some other process—recycling. A paper-producing company using the sulphite method will find it advantageous to change to the sulphate method through increased effluent charges. In England, many firms have found profitable uses for waste products when forced to stop polluting. In a few instances, mostly in already depressed areas, plants may be capable of continuing operation only because they are able to shift all or most of that portion of production costs associated with waste disposal to other economic units. When this situation is coupled with one in which the plant is a major part of the employment base of a community, society may have an interest in assisting the plant to stay in business, while at the same time controlling the external costs it is imposing. However, these would be special cases which are used to help the adjustment to the new position of equilibrium rather than change the position of the new equilibrium.

Just such an operation has been used in the Ruhr Valley in Germany, starting in 1913. The political power of the Ruhrverband lies in the governing board made up of owners of business and other facilities in the Ruhrverband area, communities in the area, and representatives of the waterworks and other water facilities. It has built over 100 waste-treatment plants, oxidation lakes, and waterworks facilities. Capital came from the bond market, and operating expenses from a series of charges contingent on the amount and quality of the effluent discharged by the industries and municipalities in the region. This scheme is so successful that, though the Ruhr River flows through one of the most heavily industrialized regions of Germany, one can find ducks living on it. Shed tears for the Potomac.

The inputs to our black box consist of renewable resources, such as food and water, and nonrenewable ones such as minerals and land. In considering free resources, it was stated that in a decentralized competitive market economy such resources are not used optimally. In fact, they are overutilized —rivers are overutilized as disposal units, hence pollution; roads are utilized above their intended capacity with resultant traffic snarl-ups. The same holds true for nonrenewable resources: they are not used optimally.

Given a fixed technology, at any time in the past we would have run into a critical condition with respect to our supplies of minerals and metals. It is only changing technology, which makes for the profitable extraction of pretechnical-change unprofitable deposits, that has enabled us to manage without really bad shortages. Hence, the present rate of extraction is only justifiable in the belief of future technical progress. Yet this is just the assumption that is now undergoing examination. In the past, man's technical progress was a function of man's incentive and ingenuity; now, however, he has to take into account another factor—the ability of the environment to accept his ravages.

As any child will comment, on observing the empty beer cans and discarded packets lying on the roadside and around "beauty spots," this is wrong. It is wrong because we do not put sufficient value on the natural resource—the countryside—to keep it clean. It is wrong for the same reason a second time: we do not put sufficient value on the natural resources— aluminum, plastic, paper, or whatever—so that when we have used them for their original purposes, they are disposed of, as rapidly as possible. The conclusion is clear: both our renewable and nonrenewable resources are not being used optimally.

Take a specific example—oil. What are the factors that determine its price? As usual, demand is a decreasing function of price, and supply an increasing function. The point of intersection dictates the price and quantity sold. When the optimal use of oil is considered, there are two points of view that have to be taken into account. One is the value of the oil to future generations, and the other is the social cost of the use of the oil.

In considering future generations, optimal behavior will take place in a competitive economy (with private ownership) if the private rate of return is the same as the social rate of return. In noneconomic terms, all this means is that the rate at which the future is discounted by individuals is the same as the rate at which it is discounted by society. There is dispute on this point— that is, whether the two rates are equal or not. However, even if they are, because the individual companies seek to maximize their private benefit, like in the fisheries example, the total exploration of the resources is likely to not be optimal.

At this stage, government comes into the picture. On the conservation side, a scientifically determined MER—maximum efficient rate (of oil flow)—is determined for a particular site. The main effect of this is to stop large fluctuations in the price of oil. Since half the total revenue of oil companies goes into the discovery and development of new deposits, this produces a high overhead cost. In the U.S., the aim is to produce as large a growth in the GNP as possible, subject to constraints (inflation, full employment, balance of payments, etc.). Hence the tradition of allowing industries to write off the cost of capital equipment against tax, since new capital stimulates the economy (investment) and makes for more efficient production. The oil industry felt that the same principal should apply to its capital costs—the rent it pays on oil deposits. Hence the oil depletion allowance, which allows the costs of rents to be partially offset against profits. The effect of this is to move the supply curve to the right—which results in more oil being sold at a lower price. Thus it encourages oil companies to extract more oil and find new deposits. This is great from a military point of view, but disastrous when the effect of such exploitation of the environment is considered: oil spills at sea, the probably permanent scarring of the tundra in Alaska, and smog in our cities. Yet this is exactly what is meant by social costs, the externalities which do not get considered in the market price.

If the oil depletion allowances were removed or sharply reduced the oil producing industry could not continue to function at its accustomed level of operation and maintain its accustomed price structure. Similar considerations apply to minerals (mineral depletion allowance). Yet this is only the first step. Another method that would produce the same desired results would be to make the extractor pay for the quantity of mineral or metal that he mines, just as he should pay for the right to discard his waste. This solves a whole lot of problems—by making the original substance more expensive, the demand is reduced, be it for power-using dishwashers, oil-eating automobiles, or resource-demanding economies. Moreover, these products, being more expensive, will not be discarded, but recycled, thus solving in part a pollution problem, as well as a litter problem (if they can be separated). By recycling, there will be less demand for the minerals or metals from the mining companies, since there is this new source of these materials.

To a certain extent, this view of things is recognized. In England one of the proposals considered for solving the problem of scrapped cars around the countryside was to charge an extra 25 pounds on the price of each new car. This would be refundable when the vehicle was brought in for scrapping—a bit like returnable bottles. In the U.S., the use of natural gas as boiler fuel was recognized as an inferior use of an exhaustible resource. "One apparent method of preventing waste of gas is to limit the uses to which it may be put, uses for which another more abundant fuel may serve equally well" (Supreme Court, 1961). This same result could have been achieved by charging the gas producer for the quantity of gas that he took (as well as rent to the owner of the gas deposit for the right to extract gas from his property). The prices that should be charged, like the prices charged for sewage disposal, vary from location to location and depend upon the characteristics of the environment. The price should be high enough to make recycling, if physically possible, both a feasible and desirable process. If the use of the resources causes some social cost—like air pollution—then this should be reflected in the price. So too should the relative scarcity of the resource, compared to substitutable alternatives, be a consideration.

If the socioeconomic system fails to change quickly enough to meet changing conditions, then it is incumbent on the people to facilitate such change.

A prerequisite to any lasting solution to environmental pollution is a zero growth rate—the birth rate equaling the death rate. However, a stable population produces a difficult economic problem in an economy like that of the United States. To remain healthy (to stay the same size or grow), the economy needs a growing market, since only in a growing market can the capital goods sector remain efficient, given present technology. At first sight, then, the achievement of a stable population is linked to a recession. One might make the assumption that a growing market could still be achieved by allowing per capita consumption to increase at the same rate as the growth of the GNP. However, with restrictions on extraction industries, this will probably not provide a total solution. The slack is more likely to be made up by producing a different type of service—education at regular periods throughout one's life, the move from cities to smaller communities and the investment involved in such a move, the rebuilding (or destruction) of old cities compatible with their new uses. Put another way, the economic slack that will have to be taken up to avoid a depression gives us the opportunity to plan for the future, without worrying about providing for an expanding population.

The essential cause of environmental pollution is overpopulation, combined with an excessive population growth rate; other antipollution measures can be used temporarily, but so long as the central problem is not solved, one can expect no lasting success.

THE FARM PROBLEM IDENTIFIED

Wallace Barr

The people in the United States have the highest standard of living and among the best diets in the world. This has been made possible, partly at least, by a highly productive agriculture. Productivity in farming has freed labor to produce other goods and services for consumers.

Change is one of the more persistent forces in our society. Farming has always been involved in the process of adjusting to economic growth and changing conditions. So have other industries. Farmers have made many adjustments in recent years. These adjustments are still going on, but they have not been rapid enough to bring farming into balance with the rest of the economy. The resources of land, labor, management, and capital which are devoted to farming produce so much that incomes of farm people are below those of nonfarm people. We need to take a closer look at this situation.

THE NATURE OF THE IMBALANCE

The imbalance that currently exists in farming seems to have three main facets.

First, there is a lack of balance within farming. There are wide variations among farms in the earnings of labor and capital that cannot be accounted for by differences in the quality of nonhuman resources used. Most well-organized farms of today use much more capital, more land, and less labor than in previous periods. These farms have made excellent use of the resources and have kept pace with new production methods. However, they constitute a minority of farms. What was an efficient farm in 1950 may now be an

One of a series of reports prepared by the National Agricultural Policy Committee, representing the Cooperative Extension Services of the State Land Grant Colleges and Universities and the United States Department of Agriculture. The series is sponsored by the Farm Foundation and the Center for Agriculture and Economic Development (Columbus, Ohio, 1965).

CONTEMPORARY ISSUES

inefficient farm. A great many farmers have lagged behind in organization, use of resources, and use of new production methods on their farms. This area of imbalance, due to a lack of organization and management, needs to be fully and clearly understood.

Second, there is the impact of agricultural adjustment on social institutions. The social impacts of adjustment are found in two broad areas. One area includes the individuals remaining in farming and the rural community itself. The other includes those leaving farming and settling in an urban area. We need to consider such factors as individual and family satisfactions, participation in community activities, welfare problems, delinquency, and improvement in real income. Attention also should be given to the impact on schools, marketing institutions, farm suppliers, water and sewer services, police and fire protection, churches, and taxes in both the old and new social situations.

The third consideration and the one to be developed more fully is the imbalance between the level of total output and the demand for farm products. Because of this imbalance, many farmers cannot sell their products at a price which covers their costs and returns an income somewhat comparable with the income received for similar labor effort and management ability in other segments of the economy. Rising costs of production, excess supplies of farm commodities (CCC stocks), and low real incomes to many farmers indicate the acute nature of the problem.

The imbalance arises because the adjustment made in the use of resources in farming has lagged behind changing supply and demand conditions. Three main factors seem to contribute to the imbalance.

1. The rapid adoption of new production methods or technology has induced a high rate of growth in farm output.

2. The demand for farm products is inelastic, so per capita consumption increases only slightly in times of large increases in consumer purchasing power or low farm prices.

3. The inability of farmers to quickly adjust the supply of products downward in response to low prices.

Technological Developments

Improvements in production methods are one of the most dynamic forces in our economy. New methods are being adopted in farming at an accelerating rate. New field crop machinery, livestock feeding and handling equipment, and other improved mechanical methods have been introduced. Pesticides and fungicides now control many insect and disease problems. Selective weed killers control weeds we once lived with. New fertilizers and methods of application and improved varieties have increased crop yields. Antibiotics and other feed improvements plus improved livestock breeding have reduced the feed required to produce a unit of livestock product.

Most new technology has had the effect of increasing total output. Individual producers find it profitable to introduce new production methods when such methods either reduce per unit costs or lessen the degree of uncertainty.

The reduction in costs may come about in numerous ways. Total costs may remain unchanged while output increases. Output may remain stable while total costs decline. Both output and total cost may increase with output increasing more than total costs.

The accelerated adoption rate of technological progress is not a historic accident. Neither is it only a result of the working of the free enterprise system. For 100 years it has been the public policy of the United States to invest heavily in research and education to bring it about. This investment has been eminently successful. Adoption of technology has some unpleasant side effects on the income to resources employed in farming. So the argument is made that facilitating adjustment to this progress also is appropriately a matter of public policy.

The result of this progress is amazing. About 10 to 12 percent of our population produces the abundant supplies of food and fiber for the entire population. In Russia, 45 to 50 percent of the population is required to produce the food and fiber. In the United States, the people not required to produce farm products are employed to produce the other goods and services that contribute to our rising standard of living.

Nature of Demand

The demand for farm products is relatively inelastic. This means that consumption per person increases very little even when farm product prices drop a great deal. Also, the total consumption per person of farm products increases very little even when large increases in purchasing power occur and farm product prices are stable.

The more important factors affecting the demand for agricultural goods include domestic population growth, rising incomes per person, and the world demand for farm products. In recent years, about 10 percent of our production has been exported. The only substantial increase in domestic consumption is in about direct proportion to population growth. Increasing consumer income per person, however, does mean some increased demand for at least some foods.

Adjusting Supply

There are numerous reasons why farmers are slow to adjust output to effective demand. On the supply side, these reasons include: (1) The nature of competition in farming with its millions of farm units and their individual decisions; (2) the fact that the individual farmer finds it advantageous to continue producing because he can't individually influence total output; (3) the nature of the costs in farming where a high percent of total costs are fixed; (4) the risks and uncertainties of farming revolving around prices, new technology, yields, health of operator, and other considerations; (5) the few alternative uses for farm land; (6) a lack of knowledge of alternative opportunities within or outside of farming; (7) a lack of training for nonfarm employment resulting in relative immobility, and (8) an inertia or the resistance to change to new employment.

Government programs and social, family, or institutional influences also tend to slow up adjustments in the use of resources. As a result, farm output does not drop rapidly in response to lower prices. Even over long periods of time the movement or mobility of land and labor resources out of farming is not fast enough to offset the rapid adoption of technology.

The land-grant college system, federal agencies, farmers, and many others are becoming increasingly aware of the adjustment problem facing farmers. This series of publications is evidence of the awareness and represents an attempt to increase understanding of the general problem and of some of the choices in public policy.

U.S. farmers face a difficult problem. In the foreseeable future, they will not be able to balance total production to market demand at prices that will give returns comparable to nonfarm returns. With relatively slow growth in the demand for farm products accompanied by rapidly improving technology and the slowness of agriculture to adjust its use of resources, the stage is set for large production and relatively unfavorable returns to agriculture in the period ahead.

Its Magnitude

There are wide differences of opinion as to the size of the imbalance in total farm production. There are various means of measuring the size. One method is to estimate the excess total production based on some price level. Various estimates indicate that current output may be from six to eight percent too large under existing programs and conditions. This refers to the excess capacity to produce as measured by the stocks held by the Commodity Credit Corporation. The CCC does hold loans on billions of dollars worth of agricultural stocks. Many view the CCC holdings as the farm problem. This is only a symptom of the need for the adjustment in resource use necessary to improve returns in farming. A basic part of the farm problem is a persistent excess capacity to produce.

Price supports on wheat were reduced from $2.25 to $1.81 per bushel from 1952 to 1958. It was hoped that these changes might let supplies clear the market. In spite of lower price supports, 20 percent of all the wheat produced during that period has had to be disposed of outside commercial markets. The record 1958 crop of almost one and one-half billion bushels was raised on 56 million acres. This was 28 million acres less than the record acreage. Cotton growers experienced two years of record yields in 1958 and 1959. Feed grain use has increased each year from 1956 through 1959. Even so, stocks have risen each year.

Many people believe that we not only have excess capacity but that this excess capacity is growing because of the accelerated rate of adoption of new technology.

The excess capacity to produce is reflected in farm income. Since 1950, net income per farm has ranged between $2,300 and $3,000. It averaged nearly $2,500 in the 10-year period. This is low when compared to the average nonfarm family income.

Per capita income from all sources for farm people in the United States averaged below $1,000 for the last five years. Nonfarmers' income per person has exceeded $2,000 since 1956. In 1950, the per person income of farm people was 53 percent of nonfarmers. In 1959, it was only 43 percent of nonfarmers' income.

The growth in per capita income of nonfarm people has greatly exceeded the per capita income growth of farm people in the last 10 years. The per capita income of nonfarmers increased 39 percent from 1950 through 1959. During the same period, per capita income from all sources for farm people increased about 15 percent.

Gross National Product, which is the value of all goods and services produced, increased about 70 percent from 1950 to 1959. The total income of farm people from all sources has not improved during this period. Total income from farming has declined at the same time. From 1950-1959, the economic impact upon some farm families was partially offset by an increase in income from nonfarm sources. Nonfarm sources of income to farm families made up about one-third of the total income of farm people in 1959 as compared with one-fourth in 1950.

The total farm income, income per farm, and per capita income of farm people have been below the growth in the total economy and the growth in income of the nonfarm people in the 1950's. None of the measures of farm income is entirely satisfactory for comparing returns to resources employed in farming and off the farm. All the evidence, however, indicates that incomes in farming have either been declining or growing at a much slower rate than in the rest of the economy. There is little doubt that farmers have not been fully sharing in the fruits of economic progress.

NEEDED ADJUSTMENTS

Farmers have been making adjustment in the use of land, labor and capital. The average net annual migration from farming in recent years has been about 800,000 people. Since 1950, the number of farms has been declining by about 100,000 annually. Cropland harvested has declined some since 1950 and is now about the same as in 1910. Man hours worked have declined 2.3 percent per year since 1940. Capital investment in farming has been increasing about 1.5 percent per year since 1940 replacing some of the labor resources. In spite of these adjustments of labor and land out of farming, the new combination of resources is bringing forth an increased output that exceeds the population growth.

These adjustments in resources have made important contributions to economic growth and toward an improved farming. Considering the forces of imbalance, income per farm and per capita incomes of farm people would have been even lower than today if these adjustments had not been made or had been made at a slower rate.

There will continue to be a need for the adjustment of resources used in farming. It is generally felt that these adjustments should be encouraged along lines which are naturally developing. This means more capital relative to land and labor devoted to farm production.

The total land area of the United States is about 1,904 million acres. About 965 million acres are in permanent hay and pasture. Another 450 million acres are plowland. The remaining 489 million acres are in nonpasture forest land, waste, and nonagricultural uses. To bring agricultural production and demand into a more desirable balance by reducing land means shifting something like 60 to 80 million acres of the 450 million acres of plowland out of production. The 60 to 80 million acres equals 13 to 18 percent of the total plowland. Of course, doing it this way only affects about 15 percent of the total inputs.

There is need for a large overall reduction in labor to achieve a well-balanced farm industry. Birth rates are much more than sufficient considering the limited opportunities to become established in farming. It is likely that the number of farm workers will need to decline in all areas of the United States. The reduction will be much larger in some areas than in others. The adjustment in the Corn Belt and the Great Plains will be smaller than in the southeastern and the lake states. The total reduction in the farm labor force to achieve a well-balanced farm industry might run as much as 50 percent.

Capitalization per farm unit needs to be increased as farms increase in size. The direction of the adjustment in the use of total capital is not clear. Research is needed to determine the ratio of capital to labor and land in various farming areas.

USDA Figures on Changing Physical Requirements
of U.S. Agriculture, 1910-1959

Year	Estimated Number of Farms (mil.)	Crops Harvested (mil. acres)	Man Hours Index (1947-49)= 100)	Capital Inputs Index (1947-49= 100)	Output Index (1947-49= 100)	Population Index (1947-49= 100)
1910	6.4	325	135	–	66	63
1920	6.4	360	143	--	70	72
1930	6.3	369	137	–	72	84
1940	6.1	339	122	91	82	90
1950	5.6	345	90	105	101	104
1954	5.2	346	78	112	109	110
1958	4.7	328	66	115	124	119

OBJECTIVES OF FARM ADJUSTMENT

A broad general policy objective relating to farm adjustment is to find ways that farm people may earn returns on resources comparable to returns on similar resources used in other segments of the economy. Other objectives related to this general objective are to enable farmers to participate more fully in the benefits of the nation's economic growth and to bring about an increased contribution by farmers to economic growth.

Farmers, as well as other citizens, have varied opinions as to the specific objectives of farm programs. Some of the more commonly mentioned objectives for a national policy for agriculture include the following:

1. Obtain an aggregate production in farming which meets the needs of the country but does not encourage the production of excess commodities for storage. The needs of the country include domestic requirements, export requirements, and a possible national defense stockpile.

2. Stabilize farm prices and income. The extreme seasonal and cyclical variations of farm production cause the familiar "boom and bust" of farm income. Smoothing out these variations will aid the development of a more stable national economy.

3. Improve efficiency in producing and marketing farm products. A requirement for national economic growth is the attainment of greater efficiency in all sectors of our national economy.

4. Allow farmers freedom in operating their farms. Freedom is an elusive term but is being used here to mean a minimum amount of interference in the decisions regarding farm operation.

5. Encourage conservation of natural resources. The productivity and future use of our resources need to be sustained and ready for use.

6. Encourage adjustments and shifts in farm resource use. The adjustments and shifts between farms and regions should be in line with both the productivity of the farms and areas with the developing demand patterns for various farm commodities.

7. Encourage needed adjustments and changes in the structure of total agriculture and in the organization of individual farms. For example, agricultural policies and programs should not prevent specialization, diversification, or farm expansion from taking place on an individual farm.

8. Keep taxpayer cost commensurate with the benefits to the nation.

9. Be consistent with national policies in regard to international trade, defense, foreign policy, economic development of foreign countries, and other national considerations.

WHAT ARE THE CHOICES?

There are many possible choices that society might use to help solve the farm income problem. The choice or method favored by an individual, group, or organization is related to the objective or objectives that they value most highly. It is recognized that political programs may be a combination of the alternative choices. . . .

EVALUATING FARM POLICY CHOICES

A major obstacle to effective solution of the difficult farm problem facing the United States evolves from the failure to understand the problem and to achieve realistic agreement on national agricultural objectives. In the final analysis, the attainment or lack of attainment of national objectives is the basis for program evaluation.

Individual policy choices may be evaluated in terms of what they contribute to the solution of immediate or shortrun problems. More importantly, the evaluation of alternative choices should be directed toward achieving objectives for ourselves and future generations over a period of five to 10 years or more. . . .

C.

What the Future Will Bring

THE GROWING MENACE OF OBSOLESCENCE

Edward J. Mishan

I

The appearance in history of mercantile societies is associated in the popular mind with the growth of the arts, philosophy, and literature. Yet only with the advent of modern industrial societies does it become possible to offer all men those material and educational opportunities undreamed of in pre-industrial civilizations. The path of progress has not always been smooth, however, and modern history books are seldom at a loss for examples of benighted resistance to technological innovations by ordinary people apparently deficient in historical vision. Indeed, any number of economists can testify today to uphill struggles undergone to induce native populations in economically backward regions to forsake the methods of their forefathers

From Edward J. Mishan, *Technology and Growth: The Price We Pay* (New York: Prager Publishers), chapter 15. Reprinted by permission.

and to come to terms with the notion of efficiency. For one of the prerequisites for the so-phrased "take-off into self-sustained economic growth" is the collapse of traditional values and the growth of dissatisfaction with the *status quo.*

Insofar as the traditional mode of life was indeed deficient in variety and opportunity, dissatisfaction with it is not to be deprecated. What the modern world tends to forget, however, is that dissatisfaction with existing circumstances too easily becomes a habit of mind—a by-product of the commercial society that brought it into being and a condition for the advancement of that kind of society. Bernard Shaw put it succinctly in calling discontent the mainspring of progress. And if, as so many of us seem to believe, progress is to be regarded as *the* social priority then such costs as are incurred in its promotion are incidental and secondary in importance. Even if some of the unhappy consequences are all too evident their imponderable nature tells against them. After all, this is a scientific age, and what cannot be measured need not be reckoned with.

Notwithstanding such modern prejudice, let us fasten our attention on considerations, too easily brushed aside, that are closely connected with the phenomenon of unabating material progress. First, that it is hardly possible to move along this golden path of self-perpetuating economic growth without subjecting people to manifold pressures, pressures that appear to increase both with the stage of economic growth and with the rate of economic growth. While it is true that a great deal of anxiety about the morrow was prevalent in previous ages—and for many good reasons; fear of famine, of plague or of unemployment—it is less excusable in the wealthy societies of today in which (excepting the hard core of poverty) material well-being and medical attention are assured for the mass of the people. For all that, whether viewed as producer or consumer or social being, few men today can say that they live, in this age of accelerating change, without any awareness of anxiety.

The status, if not the earnings, of the professional man, the scientist or the university don, has never been higher. To all appearances, his position is comfortable and secure. Yet today he has to keep up with a quite unprecedented flow of highly technical literature in his field of endeavour. He may, especially if young and impressionable, react to this sort of strain by talking about the "exhilaration of modern life" or the "challenge of living in an age of continuous change," but unless he is outstandingly gifted he has no certainty from one year to the next of being able to cope with technical developments that come at him thick and fast. If the pace is not too gruelling this year, it may well be so next year, or the year after that. The penalty of slipping behind, or of falling out of the race, may be the forfeit of all that he has struggled to achieve and to hold on to in a competitive society—prestige, position, the recognition and companionship of colleagues; the things that buoy him up in an ocean of anonymity.

For the workman, skilled or otherwise, the pressure to keep abreast of technical developments may be slight in comparison but his anxiety is also provided for. Gone are the days when a man, qualified to be a master of his

270

craft, ceased his climbing, stepped on to the plateau, his place recognized and secure in the community he served. There were trials a'plenty in a man's life, but there was not the fear that any year might see him undone and the skills by which he lived, the source of his pride and satisfaction, fall into desuetude. With the trend, however, towards rapid changes of demand, and, more important, rapid industrial innovation, it needs more than the power of his union, more even than the power of the welfare state, to afford a workman any assurance about his future. Skills painstakingly acquired over many years may become obsolete in as many months. And it is not earnings alone that matter to a man. High unemployment pay and retraining opportunities do not suffice to compensate him for losing his position in the hierarchy of his chosen occupation, for seeing his hard-earned skill and experience thrown on the mounting scrapheap of obsolete tools.

Since change today is faster and more thorough than it was, say, a generation ago, and a generation hence will be faster yet, every one of us, manager, workman or scientist, lives closer to the brink of obsolescence. Each one of us that is adult and qualified feels menaced in some degree by the push of new developments which establish themselves only by discarding the methods and techniques and theories that he has learned to master.

The same influence operates on a person regarded as a member of the family. Today's young people, those under 30 say, being breathless in pursuit of life-experience and opportunities for status-training are not acutely aware of any hiatus in their lives left by the disintegration of communities, once centred about church and temple, through which people of all ages and circumstances organized their social activities and became familiar with one another. This lack of a social community will, however, be felt as they move into their later years. Inasmuch as experience counts for less and knowledge, up-to-date knowledge, for more in a world of recurring obsolescence, the status of older men falls relative to that of younger men. And within the family the same force is at work. There was a time, not long ago, when grandparents were, as a matter of course, part of the family circle, and not necessarily an impediment to its activities. Being full of years gave them the right to be heard in virtue of long experience of the ways of the world: the young of all ages might turn to them for counsel, sympathy, and affection. The rapidity of change in social conventions and moral attitudes, associated with the technological transformation in the mode of living, renders a person's experience of the world a generation ago largely irrelevant to the problems of the young today. Never was there such a time when grandparents felt quite so useless and unwanted.[1]

---

[1]In this pace-making technological civilization the practice is to shunt old people, like obsolete machines, out of the way of today's smaller and more mobile families. And though some of the old are fortunate enough not to have to depend upon their pensions for their material wants, they perforce must suffer emotional deprivation. The growth in separate provision of old people's homes, and old people's flats and villages (considerably furnished

Finally, as a consumer, a person's welfare can be adversely affected by continuous product innovation. To have to choose from an ever-swelling variety of products, made possible by intensive advertising, whose comparative qualities and performances are, for the most part, beyond our powers to appraise, can be a tiresome and worrying business. Current analyses of the relative importance of the informative, entertainment, and persuasive elements in any type of advertisement, or statistics of the average degree of success of advertising campaigns, are of little relevance here. It may well be true that few people are actually cajoled or frightened into buying things they do not want, though it may also be true that the very ubiquity and near unavoidability, of modern advertising, can jar and exasperate. Far more important, however, is its overall influence as an integral institution of the economies of the West. Living in a world saturated with advertisements may well make a man cynical enough to resist the most persuasive selling technique. But though he success-fully ignores the message of each and every advertisement, their cumulative effect over time in teasing his sense and tapping repeatedly at his greeds, his vanity, his lusts and ambitions, can hardly leave his character unaffected. Again, by drawing his attention daily to the mundane and material, by hinting continually that the big prizes in life are the things that only money can buy, the influences of advertising and popular journalism conspire to leave a man restless and discontented with his lot. These influences, moreover, are rapidly producing a society in which standards of taste and of decorum are in a continuous state of obsolescence, leaving fashion alone as the arbiter of moral behavior.

II

Once we take economic growth to encompass not merely the growth of material goods and services, but the growth also of all the social consequences entailed in rapid technological advance—both the proliferation of disamenities which, as argued, might be mitigated by saner institutions, and the less tan-gible though, perhaps, more potent effects that impair our capacity to enjoy life—there is little one can salvage from the exhilarating vision of sustained economic growth that is suggestive of net social advantage. It might seem reasonable to suppose that although so much expenditure of time and re-source goes to producing gadgetry, the small expenditure devoted to cultural subjects is not insignificant when measured in absolute terms. Yet in the atmosphere created by rapid economic growth, an atmosphere in which the

---

with gadgets enabling the infirm to keep house without the help of the young and able), which promotes their isolation from the rest of society—where they are entertained from time to time by social workers and, somehow, jollied along to the grave—may well be the most efficient way of disposing of them. The least that can be said of this form of social vivisection is that it adds to the anxieties of growing old.

"new" and the "different" appear as the ultimate criteria, even statistics of cultural advance are suspect.

We are told, for example, that out of the 85 million records sold in Britain in 1964, 12 million were of classical music. These figures will almost certainly rise in the near future, but one would be hardpressed to elicit them as evidence of a cultural renaissance. Any multiplication of this number is obviously consistent with a general picture of a society of determined "pace-setters." What surely is relevant are the dominant motives of the record-collectors. And here one cannot lightly dismiss the notion that classical records are for many people tokens of taste and objects of display. It is possible that collectors play their records frequently but with an enjoyment somewhat alloyed by a concern with current vogues in music and sometimes marred by too determined a desire to acquire a musical vocabulary.

Sustained economic growth, at least in the richer communities, depends heavily on an atmosphere of being "with it," and though not all "with it" ambitions are unworthy, the more secondary is the purely aesthetic motivation the less intrinsically rewarding is the cultural pursuit in question, whether it be listening to music, visiting art galleries or attending operas. True, one does not have to wait the arrival of the twentieth century to find people attending cultural functions purely for reasons of fashion or in order to diversify their repertoire. Novelists throughout the centuries have made merry with stock characters. But this is neither here nor there in so far as the interpretation of current statistics is at issue. One may safely conjecture that along with the present confused interest in adult education, "culture," in small packages at least, happens to be currently in fashion. And the swelling sales figures of publishers and record companies are less plausibly interpreted as a mass renaissance and more plausibly interpreted as yet another manifestation of the growing affluence of young "status-seekers."

III

The effects of the postwar spread of television is relevant in this connection. Though occasionally it is agreed that television has destroyed much of the intimacy of family life by funnelling into the privacy of the home the raucous distractions and paraphernalia of other worlds, real and imaginary, it is held, at best, to be potentially an educative force of immense efficacy. The topics discussed by panels of speakers cover morals, politics, science, crime, economics, sex, history, art, music, and bringing-up-the-children, so enabling the alert public to appreciate all sides of a question. If people do not acquire encyclopedic knowledge—and most of them have forgotten by Thursday what they thought they had learned on the Wednesday—they at least acquire an increasing measure of tolerance. Such tolerance, however, is borne less of enlightenment as of uncertainty and bewilderment. The repeated re-examinations, for instance, of fundamental questions about religion, ethics, crime, etcetera, with their unavoidable inconclusiveness, serve further to weaken the moral props of an already disintegrating society and to destroy a belief in divinity that once gave hope and comfort to many. The distinctions between good and bad, between right and wrong, between virtue and vice, once held to be self-evident by our forebears, are blurred and reblurred. In consequence, the confidence of ordinary men and women both in their opinions and in their judgements is gradually being eroded, and along with it their self-respect and essential dignity.

What is more, this rapid extension of specialized opinion to every aspect of knowledge and daily living acts to inhibit the spontaneity of a man's thought and expression. Where a century or two ago the ordinary civilized man would speculate boldly on any subject and converse joyfully on all manner of topics, his spirit today is muted in dismal deference to the cumulative discoveries of science and the qualified pronouncements of the experts. His personality shrivels. He has no convictions to sustain him. His discourse perforce becomes restricted to jest, trivial observations, and personal reminiscence.[2] . . .

---

[2] Once one accepts the fact of an advanced technological society, in which television is the popular medium of entertainment and information, any recommendation that certain programs be discontinued invites the charge of being an enemy of "The Open Society." But if one is condemned, one need not remain silent. In so far as liberty is deemed extended as a larger number of people hear a greater variety of views, the only conclusion that follows from the above remarks is that, if true, there can be circumstances in which considerations of social welfare and of liberty pull in opposite directions.

THE FUTURE OF
THE INDUSTRIAL SYSTEM

John Kenneth Galbraith

I

In the latter part of the last century and the early decades of this, no subject was more discussed than the future of capitalism. Economists, men of unspecific wisdom, Chautauqua lecturers, editorial writers, knowledgeable ecclesiastics, and socialists contributed their personal revelation. It was taken for granted that the economic system was in a state of development and in time would transform itself into something hopefully better but certainly different. Socialists drew strength from the belief that theirs was the plausible next stage in a natural process of changes.

The future of the industrial system, by contrast, is not discussed. The prospect for agriculture is subject to debate—it is assumed to be in course of change. So are the chances for survival for the small entrepreneur or the private medical practitioner. But General Motors, General Electric and U.S. Steel are viewed as an ultimate achievement. One does not wonder where one is going if one is already there.

Yet to suppose that the industrial system is a terminal phenomenon is, *per se*, implausible. It is itself the product, in the last 60 years, of a vast and autonomous transformation. During this time the scale of the individual corporation has grown enormously. The entrepreneurial corporation has declined. The technostructure has developed, removed itself from control by the stockholders and acquired its own internal sources of capital. There has been a large change in its relations with the workers and yet a larger one in its relations with the state. It would be strange were such a manifestation of social dynamics to be now at an end. So to suggest is to deny one of the philosophical tenets of the system itself, one that is solemnly articulated on

From John Kenneth Galbraith, *The New Industrial State* (Boston: Houghton Mifflin Co., 1967), pp. 388-399. Reprinted by permission.

275

all occasions of business ritual—conventions, stockholders' meetings, board meetings, executive committee meetings, management development conferences, budget conferences, product review meetings, senior officer retreats, and dealer relations workshops. It is that change is the law of economic life.

The future of the industrial system is not discussed partly because of the power it exercises over belief. It has succeeded, tacitly, in excluding the notion that it is a transitory, which would be to say that it is a somehow imperfect, phenomenon. More important, perhaps, to consider the future would be to fix attention on where it has already arrived. Among the least enchanting words in the business lexicon are planning, government control, state support, and socialism. To consider the likelihood of these in the future would be to bring home the appalling extent to which they are already a fact. And it would not be ignored that these grievous things have arrived, at a minimum with the acquiescence and, at a maximum, on the demand, of the system itself.

II

Such reflection on the future would also emphasize the convergent tendencies of industrial societies, however different their popular or ideological billing; the convergence being to a roughly similar design for organization and planning. A word in review may be worthwhile. Convergence begins with modern large-scale production, with heavy requirements of capital, sophisticated technology and, as a prime consequence, elaborate organization. These require control of prices and, so far as possible, of what is bought at those prices. That is to say that planning must replace the market. In the Soviet-type economies, the control of prices is a function of the state. The management of demand (eased by the knowledge that their people will mostly want what Americans and Western Europeans already have) is partly by according preference to the alert and early-rising who are first to the store; partly, as in the case of houseroom, by direct allocation to the recipient; and partly, as in the case of automobiles, by making patience (as well as political position or need) a test of eligibility. With us this management is accomplished less formally by the corporations, their advertising agencies, salesmen, dealers, and retailers. But these, obviously, are differences in method rather than purpose. Large-scale industrialism requires, in both cases, that the market and consumer sovereignty be extensively superseded.

Large-scale organization also requires autonomy. The intrusion of an external and uninformed will is damaging. In the non-Soviet systems this means excluding the capitalist from effective power. But the same imperative operates in the socialist economy. There the business firm seeks to minimize or exclude control by the bureaucracy. To gain autonomy for the enterprise is what, in substantial measure, the modern Communist theoretician calls reform. Nothing in our time is more interesting than that the erstwhile capitalist corporation and the erstwhile Communist firm should, under the imperatives of organization, come together as oligarchies of their own members. Ideology is not the relevant force. Large and complex organizations can use diverse knowledge and talent and thus function effectively only if under their own authority. This, it must be stressed once more, is not autonomy that subordinates a firm to the market. It is autonomy that allows the firm authority over its planning.

The industrial system has no inherent capacity for regulating total demand —for insuring a supply of purchasing power sufficient to acquire what it produces. So it relies on the state for this. At full employment there is no mechanism for holding prices and wages stable. This stabilization too is a function of the state. The Soviet-type systems also make a careful calculation of the income that is being provided in relation to the value of the goods available for purchase. Stabilization of wages and prices in general is, of course, a natural consequence of fixing individual prices and wage rates.

Finally, the industrial system must rely on the state for trained and educated manpower, now the decisive factor of production. So it also is under socialist industrialism. A decade ago, following the flight of the first Sputnik, there was great and fashionable concern in the United States for scientific and technical education. Many argued that the Soviet system, with its higher priority for state functions, among which education is prominent, had a natural advantage in this regard.

Thus convergence between the two ostensibly different industrial systems occurs at all fundamental points. This is an exceedingly fortunate thing. In time, and perhaps in less time than may be imagined, it will dispose of the notion of inevitable conflict based on irreconcilable difference. This will not be soon agreed. Marx did not foresee the convergence and he is accorded, with suitable interpretation, the remarkable, even supernatural, power of foreseeing all. Those who speak for the unbridgeable gulf that divides the free world from the Communist world and free enterprise from Communism are protected by an equally ecclesiastical faith that whatever the evolution of free enterprise may be, it cannot conceivably come to resemble socialism. But these positions can survive the evidence only for a time. Only the most committed ideologist or the most fervent propagandist can stand firm against the feeling that an increasing number of people regard him as obsolete. Vanity is a great force for intellectual modernization.

To recognize that industrial systems are convergent in their development will, one imagines, help toward agreement on the common dangers in the weapons competition, on ending it or shifting it to more benign areas. Perhaps nothing casts more light on the future of the industrial system than this, for it implies, in contrast with the present images, that it could have a future.

III

Given the deep dependence of the industrial system on the state and the nature of its motivational relationship to the state, i.e., its identification with public goals and the adaptation of these to its needs, the industrial system will not long be regarded as something apart from government. Rather it will increasingly be seen as part of a much larger complex which embraces both the industrial system and the state. Private enterprise was anciently so characterized because it was subordinate to the market and those in command derived their power from ownership of private property. The modern corporation is no longer subordinate to the market; those who run in no longer depend on property ownership for their authority. They must have autonomy within a framework of goals. But this fully allows them to work in association with the bureaucracy and, indeed, to perform for the bureaucracy tasks that it cannot do, or cannot do as well, for itself. In consequence, so we have seen, for tasks of technical sophistication, there is a close fusion of the industrial system with the state. Members of the technostructure work closely with their public counterparts not only in the development and manufacture of products but in advising them of their needs. Were it not so celebrated in ideology, it would long since have been agreed that the line that now divides the public from so-called private organization in military procurement, space exploration, and atomic energy is so indistinct as to be nearly imperceptible. Men move easily across the line. On retirement, admirals and generals, as well as high civil servants, go more or less automatically to the more closely associated industries. One experienced observer has already called these firms the "semi-nationalized" branch of the economy.[1] It has been noted, "the Market mechanism, [is replaced by] . . . the administrative mechanism. For the profit share of private entrepreneurs, it substitutes the fixed fee, a payment in lieu of profits foregone. And for the independent private business unit, it substitutes the integrated hierarchical structure of an organization composed of an agency . . . and its contractors."[2]

The foregoing refers to firms which sell most of their output to the government—to Boeing which (at this writing) sells 65 percent of its output to the government; General Dynamics which sells a like percentage; Raytheon which sells 70 percent; Lockheed which sells 81 percent; and Republic Aviation which sells 100 percent.[3] But firms which have a smaller proportion of sales to the government are more dependent on it for the regulation of aggregate demand and not much less so for the stabilization of wages and prices, the underwriting of especially expensive technology and the supply of trained and educated manpower.

---

[1]Murray L. Weidenbaum, "The Defense-Space Complex: Impact on Whom?" *Challenge. The Magazine of Economic Affairs*, April, 1956. Professor Weidenbaum is a former employee of Boeing.

[2]From a study by Richard Tybout, *Government Contracting in Atomic Energy* (Ann Arbor: University of Michigan Press, 1956), p. 175. Professor Tybout is referring especially to cost-plus-fixed-fee contracts.

[3]Data from Michael D. Reagan, *Politics, Economics and the General Welfare* (Chicago: Scott, Foresman and Company, 1965), p. 113.

So comprehensive a relationship cannot be denied or ignored indefinitely. Increasingly it will be recognized that the mature corporation, as it develops, becomes part of the larger administrative complex associated with the state. In time the line between the two will disappear. Men will look back in amusement at the pretense that once caused people to refer to General Dynamics and North American Aviation and A T & T as *private* business.

Though this recognition will not be universally welcomed, it will be healthy. There is always a presumption in social matters in favor of reality as opposed to myth. The autonomy of the technostructure is, to repeat yet again, a functional necessity of the industrial system. But the goals this autonomy serves allow some range of choice. If the mature corporation is recognized to be part of the penumbra of the state, it will be more strongly in the service of social goals. It cannot plead its inherently private character or its subordination to the market as cover for the pursuit of different goals of particular interest to itself. The public agency has an unquestioned tendency to pursue goals that reflect its own interest and convenience and to adapt social objectives thereto. But it cannot plead this as a superior right. There may well be danger in this association of public and economic power. But it is less if it is recognized.

Other changes can be imagined. As the public character of the mature corporation comes to be recognized, attention will doubtless focus on the position of the stockholder in this corporation. This is anomalous. He is a passive and functionless figure, remarkable only in his capacity to share, without effort or even without appreciable risk, in the gains from the growth by which the technostructure measures its success. No grant of feudal privilege has ever been equaled, for effortless return, that of the grandparent who bought and endowed his descendants with a thousand shares of General Motors or General Electric. The beneficiaries of this foresight have become and remain rich by no exercise of effort or intelligence beyond the decision to do nothing, embracing as it did the decision not to sell. But these matters need not be pursued here. Questions of equity and social justice as between the fortuitously rich have their own special expertise.

IV

Most of the individual developments which are leading, if the harshest term may be employed, to the socialization of the mature corporation will be conceded, even by men of the most conservative disposition. The control by the mature corporation over its prices, its influence on consumer behavior, the euthanasia of stockholder power, the regulation by the state of aggregate demand, the effort to stabilize prices and wages, the role of publicly supported research and development, the role of military, space and related procurement, the influence of the firm on these government activities, and the modern role of education are more or less accepted facts of life.

What is avoided is reflection on the consequences of putting them all together, of seeing them as a system. But it cannot be supposed that the principal beams and buttresses of the industrial system have all been changed and that the structure remains as before. If the parts have changed, so then has the whole. If this associates the mature corporation inextricably with the state, the fact cannot be exorcised by a simple refusal to add.

It will be urged, of course, that the industrial system is not the whole economy. Apart from the world of General Motors, Standard Oil, Ford, General Electric, U.S. Steel, Chrysler, Texaco, Gulf, Western Electric, and Du Pont is that of the independent retailer, the farmer, the shoe repairman, the bookmaker, narcotics peddler, pizza merchant, and that of the car and the dog laundry. Here prices are not controlled. Here the consumer is sovereign. Here pecuniary motivation is unimpaired. Here technology is simple and there is no research or development to make it otherwise. Here there are no government contracts; independence from the state is a reality. None of these entrepreneurs patrol the precincts of the Massachusetts Institute of Technology in search of talent. The existence of all this I concede. And this part of the economic system is not insignificant. It is not, however, the part of the economy with which this book has been concerned. It has been concerned with the world of the large corporation. This too is important; and it is more deeply characteristic of the modern industrial scene than the dog laundry or the small manufacturer with a large idea. One should always cherish his critics and protect them where possible from foolish error. The tendency of the mature corporation in the industrial system to become part of the administrative complex of the state ought not to be refuted by appeal to contrary tendencies outside the industrial system.

Some who dislike the notion that the industrial system merges into the state in its development will be tempted to assault not the tendency but those who adumbrate it. This, it must be urged, is not in keeping with contemporary ethics and manners. Once the bearers of bad tidings were hanged, disembowled, or made subject to some other equally sanguinary mistreatment. Now such reaction is regarded as lacking in delicacy. A doctor can inform even the most petulant client that he has terminal cancer without fear of adverse physical consequences. The aide who must advise a politician that a new poll shows him to be held in all but universal distate need exercise only decent tact. Those who find unappealing the present intelligence are urged to exercise similar restraint.

They should also be aware of the causes. It is part of the vanity of modern man that he can decide the character of his economic system. His area of decision is, in fact exceedingly small. He could, conceivably, decide whether or not he wishes to have a high level of industrialization. Thereafter the imperatives of organization, technology, and planning operate similarly, and we have seen to a broadly similar result, on all societies. Given the decision to have modern industry, much of what happens is inevitable and the same.

V

The two questions most asked about an economic system are whether it serves man's physical needs and whether it is consistent with his liberty. There is little doubt as to the ability of the industrial system to serve man's needs. As we have seen, it is able to manage them only because it serves them abundantly. It requires a mechanism for making men want what it provides. But this mechanism would not work—wants would not be subject to manipulation—had not these wants been dulled by sufficiency.[4]

The prospects for liberty involve far more interesting questions. It has always been imagined, especially by conservatives, that to associate all, or a large part, of economic activity with the state is to endanger freedom. The individual and his preferences, in one way or another, will be sacrificed to the needs and conveniences of the apparatus created ostensibly to serve him. As the industrial system evolves into a penumbra of the state, the question of its relation to liberty thus arises in urgent form. In recent years, in the Soviet-type economies, there has been an ill-concealed conflict between the state and the intellectuals. In essence, this has been a conflict between those for whom the needs of the government, including above all its needs as economic planner and producer of goods, are pre-eminent and those who assert the high but inconvenient claims of uninhibited intellectual and artistic expression. Is this a warning?

The instinct which warns of dangers in this association of economic and public power is sound. It comes close to being the subject of this book. But conservatives have looked in the wrong direction for the danger. They have feared that the state might reach out and destroy the vigorous, money-making entrepreneur. They have not noticed that, all the while, the successors to the entrepreneur were uniting themselves ever more closely with the state and rejoicing in the result. They were also, and with enthusiasm, accepting abridgement of their freedom. Part of this is implicit in the subordination of individual personality to the needs of organization. Some of it is in the exact pattern of the classical business expectation. The president of Republic Aviation is not much more likely in public to speak critically, or even candidly, of the Air Force than is the head of a Soviet *combinat* of the ministry to which he reports. No modern head of the Ford Motor Company will ever react with the same pristine vigor to the presumed foolishness of Washington as did its founder. No head of Montgomery Ward will ever again breathe defiance of a President as did Sewell Avery. Manners may be involved. But it would also be conceded that "too much is at stake."

The problem, however, is not the freedom of the businessman. Business orators have spoken much about freedom in the past. But it can be laid down

---

[4] As . . . I have urged at length on other occasions, it excludes the unqualified and the unfortunate from its beneficence.

as a rule that those who speak most of liberty are least inclined to use it. The high executive who speaks fulsomely of personal freedom carefully submits his speeches on the subject for review and elimination of controversial words, phrases and ideas, as befits a good organization man. The general who tells his troops, and the world, that they are in the forefront of the fight for freedom is a man who has always submitted happily to army discipline. The high State Department official, who adverts feelingly to the value of the free world extravagantly admires the orthodoxy of his own views.

The danger to liberty lies in the subordination of belief to the needs of the industrial system. In this the state and the industrial system will be partners. This threat has already been assessed, as also the means for minimizing it.

VI

If we continue to believe that the goals of the industrial system—the expansion of output, the companion increase in consumption, technological advance, the public images that sustain it—are coordinate with life, then all of our lives will be in the service of these goals. What is consistent with these ends we shall have or be allowed; all else will be off limits. Our wants will be managed in accordance with the needs of the industrial system; the policies of the state will be subject to similar influence; education will be adapted to industrial need; the disciplines required by the industrial system will be the conventional morality of the community. All other goals will be made to seem precious, unimportant or antisocial. We will be bound to the ends of the industrial system. The state will add its moral, and perhaps some of its legal, power to their enforcement. What will eventuate, on the whole, will be the benign servitude of the household retainer who is taught to love her mistress and see her interests as her own, and not the compelled servitude of the field hand. But it will not be freedom.

If, on the other hand, the industrial system is only a part, and relatively a diminishing part, of life, there is much less occasion for concern. Aesthetic goals will have pride of place; those who serve them will not be subject to the goals of the industrial system; the industrial system itself will be subordinate to the claims of these dimensions of life. Intellectual preparation will be for its own sake and not for the better service to the industrial system. Men will not be entrapped by the belief that apart from the goals of the industrial system—apart from the production of goods and income by progressively more advanced technical methods—there is nothing important in life.

The foregoing being so, we may, over time, come to see the industrial system in fitting light as an essentially technical arrangement for providing convenient goods and services in adequate volume. Those who rise through its bureaucracy will so see themselves. And the public consequences will be in keeping, for if economic goals are the only goals of the society it is natural that the industrial system should dominate the state and the state should serve its ends. If other goals are strongly asserted, the industrial system will fall into its place as a detached and autonomous arm of the state, but responsible to the larger purposes of the society.

We have seen wherein the chance for salvation lies. The industrial system, in contrast with its economic antecedents, is intellectually demanding. It brings into existence, to serve its intellectual and scientific needs, the community that, hopefully, will reject its monopoly of social purpose.

4471